Bonus Chapter on Shotgun Tactics

ADVANCED HANDGUN SURVIVAL TACTICS

Real-World Techniques That Work When It Counts

David H. Leflet
with Curtis L. Porter

Paladin Press • Boulder, Colorado

Advanced Handgun Survival Tactics:
Real-World Techniques That Work When It Counts
by David H. Leflet, with Curtis L. Porter

Copyright © 2013 by Extreme Tactics, LLC
This publication includes images from CorelDRAW® 9, which are protected by copyright laws of the U.S., Canada, and elsewhere. Used under license.

ISBN 13: 978-1-61004-873-6
Printed in the United States of America

Published by Paladin Press, a division of
Paladin Enterprises, Inc.
Gunbarrel Tech Center
7077 Winchester Circle
Boulder, Colorado 80301 USA, +1.303.443.7250

Direct inquiries and/or orders to the above address.

Visit our website at www.paladin-press.com

TABLE OF CONTENTS

This book, *Advanced Handgun Survival Tactics,* is right on target. After two tours in Vietnam with the Army's 5th Special Forces (Green Berets), I questioned the quality of the firearm training I received in the police academy when I was getting certified to become a Florida police officer. In Vietnam we learned that the best way to end an enemy threat was to use a head shot, which usually caused immediate incapacitation and was often the only part of the enemy you could target.

This book is well written with a lot of tactical information about how to avoid and how to survive deadly confrontations, and it emphasizes what most combat veterans already know: being a good target shooter does not make you a good tactical shooter.

—Herbert L. Brown, Colonel, USAF (retired)

Advanced Handgun Survival Tactics is an authoritative training guide for effectively developing and maintaining tactical readiness for law enforcement officers and others interested in combat shooting. As a veteran law enforcement officer and a certified police firearms instructor, I feel that conventional law-enforcement training is often more concerned about decreasing departmental liability or cost than improving officer survival skills. By refusing to explore ways to improve tactical shooting, police departments perpetuate ineffective techniques that fail to protect both police officers and innocent bystanders from avoidable injuries. Not only is the Porter method an excellent example of the way tactical firearms training should be taught, but this book also addresses the extremely important issue of when a person can use deadly force.

—Harry Hamilton, Major, Holmes County Sheriff's Office (retired)

Harry Hamilton is retired from the Holmes County Sheriff's Office in Florida, where he served for more than 22 years. During his law enforcement career, he served as a supervisor for over 17 years and was a major (chief deputy) for three and a half years. Hamilton holds a number of certifications, including helicopter and fixed-wing pilot, rescue scuba diver, and law enforcement firearms instructor. During his career at the Holmes County Sheriff's Office, he had the opportunity to train with several tactical instructors, including Paul Castle, Eddie Ingram, and Johnny Davis. He now owns a canine training business, Hamilton Canine Training Center, in Bonifay, Florida, where among other K-9-related services he trains police dogs for criminal apprehension and drug detection.

DEDICATION

This book is dedicated to the police officers killed in the line of duty who might be alive today if they had been properly trained. Most of the major failures in tactical handgun training relate to tactical skills or shooting skills, and, despite decades of dismal failures in these two areas, most police departments still use the same ineffective training methods that perpetuate these failures. Rather than use reality-based or evidence-based training, most police departments prefer tradition-based training, which is usually far less effective than the firearms training most federal law-enforcement agencies, such as the Federal Bureau of Investigation (FBI), provide their agents.

What makes most police firearms training especially reprehensible is that better training methods are available, but they are not being used. Reality-based and evidence-based training is used when training first responders, but similar standards are seldom applied to firearms training. Traditional training methods are not bad when they work, and the following quotes illustrate some training principles that are just as valid now as they were hundreds of years ago.

- *"The final weapon is the brain, all else is supplemental."* (Good tactics are essential.)

  —John Steinbeck

- *"The mind of the perfect man is like a mirror."* (Maintain situational awareness.)

  —Chuang Tzu

- *"In my strategy the footwork does not change. I always walk as I usually do in the street."* (Use natural movements.)

  —Miyamoto Musashi

- *"Hence, to fight and conquer in all our battles is not supreme excellence; supreme excellence consists in breaking the enemy's resistance without fighting."*
  (Avoid unnecessary violence.)

  —Sun Tzu

- *"A skillful warrior strikes a decisive blow and stops. He does not continue the attack to assert mastery. He will strike the blow, but be on guard against being vain or arrogant over his success."*
  (Do not relax too soon).

  —Lao Tzu

- *"Bad is the plan which is not susceptible to change."*
  (Adapt and overcome.)

  —Publilius Syrus

WARNING

Handguns can cause serious bodily injury or death, and the writers and publisher of *Advanced Handgun Survival Tactics* disclaim any liability because of injury or loss that results from the use or misuse of information contained herein. People who use this material are responsible for their own safety and for knowing when they need to seek medical, legal, or other professional advice. The writers and publisher strongly recommend that you speak to a doctor and follow the doctor's advice concerning physical or mental limitations.

This book is being sold without any warranties. The information about handgun safety presented provides some general guidelines, but this book was written for people who have already mastered the basic skills needed to use a gun safely and with reasonable proficiency. The information in this book is for *academic study only* and should not be used as a substitute for professional and competent range or classroom instruction.

The information is based on personal field experience, scientific and medical studies, statistical data, historical information, logic, facts, and common sense. Whenever possible the authors tried to justify their reasons for taking a certain position on an issue, but they also realize some of the positions are going to be controversial. Readers must weigh the evidence presented and draw their own conclusions as to whether the methods satisfy their needs.

Rather than say the information in this book *can save* your life, the authors prefer to say that it *has saved* lives. Knowledge is not power if you do not use it, and this takes more than just reading a book. Like most motor skills, after you learn a tactical skill, you cannot maintain or improve it without correct and regular practice. To be an effective tactical shooter, your skills need to become almost automatic, and this requires more than a few repetitions.

The authors cannot provide specific information relating to the kind of guns you might be using for self-defense. Readers are responsible for knowing the characteristics of their own guns and for being familiar with the information in the owners' manuals.

Almost without exception, you should not shoot without high-quality eye and ear protection. Even though there may be times when you need to use a handgun for self-defense and you do not have ear protection available, this should never be used as a reason for practicing without ear protection. Prescription glasses might be suitable eye protection, but this is something you should verify.

Lead poisoning can result from skin contact with bullets that contain lead and can have serious medical consequences. Please contact a health care professional for a list of precautions to help you avoid lead poisoning, such as always washing your hands after you have contact with ammunition that contains lead.

LEGAL DISCLAIMER

The authors are not attorneys, and this book does not give legal advice. If you need legal guidance, please contact someone who is qualified to give the kind of counsel required. The laws relating to self-defense are different in each state, and what's legal in one state might well be illegal in another.

Self-defense laws are constantly changing, they can be reinterpreted because of case law, many of the laws have exceptions to the exceptions, and the instructions that judges give juries can have a significant impact on how the laws are applied. Doing something that is tactically correct and saves your life might not be legally correct and may result in criminal charges or civil lawsuits. In some cases, public opinion affects jury decisions more than admissible evidence or laws.

ACKNOWLEDGMENTS

It's not surprising that many of the most significant advances in tactical shooting were made by people with military backgrounds, because these experts used their combat experience to validate their methods and theories. Since some of the books authored by these veterans do not mention their military credentials, we would like to acknowledge their military service by listing their names and ranks:

- Major General Julian S. Hatcher
- Captain William E. Fairbairn
- Captain E.A. Sykes

In their book *Shooting to Live*, Captains Fairbairn and Sykes echoed a view that was expressed by most of the combat veterans who were also champion target shooters: much of what has been learned from target shooting "is best unlearned if proficiency is desired in the use of the pistol under actual fighting conditions."

- Colonel Rex Applegate
- Colonel Jeff Cooper
- Colonel Charles Askins

We would also like to acknowledge Don Mann and Robert K. Taubert. Mann, a U.S. Navy SEAL and decorated combat veteran, wrote the book *The Modern Day Gunslinger*. According to Mann, point-shooting (target-focused shooting) is the method most often used in gunfights and should be practiced in training. Many weapons instructors do not teach target-focused shooting, but according to Mann, research shows that "there is little or no time for sighted techniques in most gunfights."

Even people who were trained to use a front-sight focus "revert to unsighted point-shooting in a gunfight." In *Rattenkrieg!* Taubert—a U.S. Marine Corps veteran, U.S. Army Ranger School graduate, and retired FBI agent—seems to agree with Fairbairn and Sykes: firearms competition is a game and "has little to do with reality."

The military has consistently done more to develop and promote tactical shooting than police departments, but at least one other organization that provides police training has made a notable contribution. Despite the poor-quality firearms training that most police officers receive, police departments have known the difference between target shooting and tactical shooting for many years. The International Association of Chiefs of Police (IACP) has provided excellent police training for decades, and in 1971 IACP published training key #173, titled *Combat Shooting*. Unfortunately, most police departments ignore the information in it:

- During a deadly confrontation, you must react automatically.
- In most combat situations, either you or your adversary will be moving.
- Breath control and a perfect stance are neither essential nor practical.
- You need to keep your eyes on the suspect, not on the front sight.

WHY THIS
BOOK WAS
WRITTEN

This book was written to help tactical shooters understand why most of what is being taught about tactical shooting is almost worthless. In a book titled *Violent Encounters*—which was written by Anthony J. Pinizzotto, Edward F. Davis, and Charles Miller III and published by the U.S. Department of Justice, Federal Bureau of Investigation—one paragraph in particular helps to explain why most tactical shooting is based more on fantasy than facts:

> "Many of the officers interviewed for the present study lacked knowledge of human anatomy. They thought that, if forced into a situation where they must protect themselves or a member of the community, they could disable an offender quickly, effectively, and efficiently with their department-issued handguns. After lengthy discussions, the officers related that the majority of their real-world experience about gunshot wounds came from watching television and movies."

What *Advanced Handgun Survival Tactics* will do is help tactical shooters prevent the kind of scenario that was described in an FBI *Law Enforcement Bulletin* (October 2004, Volume 73, Number 10). The article is titled "One-Shot Drops," and the authors are Anthony J. Pinizzotto, Harry A. Kern, and Edward F. Davis:

> "In the authors' ongoing study of violence against law enforcement officers, they have examined several cases where officers used large-caliber handguns with limited effect displayed by the offenders. In one case, the subject attacked the officer with a knife. The officer shot the individual four times in the chest; then, his weapon malfunc-

tioned. The offender continued to walk toward the officer. After the officer cleared his weapon, he fired again and struck the subject in the chest. Only then did the offender drop the knife. This individual was hit five times with 230-grain, .45-caliber hollowpoint ammunition and never fell to the ground. The offender later stated, 'The wounds felt like bee stings.' "

This book consolidates evidence-based information that shows most tactical firearms training is worthless and recommends tactical skills and shooting skills that will make it easier for tactical shooters to quickly and correctly evaluate and respond to deadly threats. There are no magic handguns or magic bullets that will automatically give you one-shot stops, but intelligent, reality-based training can reduce your risk of being killed during a deadly confrontation.

PREFACE

People who believe they are tactical shooters because they have learned some basic target-shooting skills and people who have earned a black belt in karate by doing traditional kicks or strikes often suffer from the same delusion: the belief that what they have learned will help them survive a deadly confrontation in the real world. This false and unfounded belief becomes painfully apparent when people from these two groups are faced with a deadly threat and find that none of the highly valued skills they worked hard to learn actually work in the real world.

Police officers often suffer this kind of delusion until they face someone with a gun or knife and try to use the skills they learned in the academy. Since the average hit rate for police officers is estimated to be about 20 percent, which means eight misses out of every 10 shots fired at a subject, you would think police departments would improve their training methods—but you would be wrong.

Except for a few departments that have changed their approach to firearms training by making the training more realistic, giving their officers more time to practice, and raising the qualification standards, most departments use the same ineffective training methods they have used for decades. Even when there is no correlation between qualification scores and performance on the street, most departments continue to ignore something that Albert Einstein said: "Insanity is doing the same thing over and over again and expecting different results."

The Porter method is a reality-based, evidence-based approach to tactical handgun shooting. Many of the shooting and tactical skills in this book are based on combat-shooting techniques that were used as far back as the late 1700s. These techniques have been repeatedly field-tested and proven during actual combat, and the people who have survived deadly encounters using these techniques are often the same people who write essays or books about them.

The Porter method was developed by examining tactical handgun techniques used over the past several hundred years, including the ones favored by Old West gunfighters, combat veterans, military instructors, and law enforcement officers. After carefully examining these techniques, our next step was looking for ways to make them more effective and easier to teach.

The techniques in this book might be controversial because we disagree with experts who claim that target-shooting and tactical-shooting skills are the same, but nothing we can say will discredit their beliefs more than the 20-percent hit rate that results from using their methods. The experts we do respect are people like W.E. Fairbairn, E.A. Sykes, Rex Applegate, Jeff Cooper, Charles Askins, Jim Cirillo, and Paul Castle. There are very few subjects relating to tactical shooting that these experts did not address in one way or another.

It is not uncommon for the beliefs and recommendations made by one expert to disagree with those made by other experts, and disagreements between handgun experts can make it hard for the average person to know the difference between fact and fiction. The Porter method was built on a simple premise: determining which techniques are the most effective based on facts, logic, and research is more important than following conventional wisdom or listening to popular experts.

As Bertrand Russell stated: "The fact that an opinion has been widely held is no evidence whatever that it is not utterly absurd; indeed in view of the silliness of the majority of mankind, a widespread belief is more likely to be foolish than sensible." In other words, if conventional wisdom was always right, the Earth would be flat and the sun would rotate around it.

People who have never used a gun to win a deadly confrontation often view tactical shooting differently from people who have used a gun for self-defense. Scientific research is a good source of information, but knowledge without practical experience is incomplete and often leads to the wrong conclusions. Techniques that have never been field-tested and proven are speculation, not fact.

When we created the Porter method, we did not use police firearms training as a model because that offered by most police departments is badly flawed and dangerous for the people who try to use it in the real world. "Fight like you train" does not work if what you were trained to do does not work. We disagree with many aspects of police firearms training but sometimes mention police training to highlight techniques that should be avoided. We have also incorporated some valuable lessons police departments have learned because of fatal mistakes.

We believe tactical shooting should be as natural and simple as possible. So instead of teaching a target-shooting stance, such as the isoceles stance, we teach people to use the best stance possible under the circumstances.

Ideally, a good stance should provide both stability and mobility, especially when you are shooting at targets that shoot back, but it's more important to make the fastest combat-effective shot possible than to have a perfect stance before you shoot. We also believe that making the center of mass your aim point and always practicing with stationary paper targets facing you are two things that get police officers killed.

This book is about principles more than about rules because no two deadly confrontations are exactly the same and sometimes you need to follow the U.S. Marine Corps mantra: *improvise, adapt, and overcome.* Bad luck can work against you in a gunfight, but good training can help you improve your luck.

We wrote *Advanced Handgun Survival Tactics* for people who have completed basic handgun training and would like to become tactical shooters. Unlike experts who say a gunfight is nothing but a shooting match, we believe a gunfight is a thinking match and factors such as speed and accuracy are often secondary. Using your brain can give you the tactical advantages you need to make your shooting skills combat effective.

INTRODUCTION

It would be nice if we could use the firearms training that police departments use as a model for tactical handgun training, but most of these programs are badly flawed and better for demonstrating what you should not do than what you should do. With the exception of the special units some departments have, which often receive training based on a military model instead of a police model, most of the firearms training police departments offer is not worth imitating.

Poor training partially explains why there is no correlation between being a top performer on a police target range and being combat effective on the street. If police firearms training were more effective, the national hit rate for police officers would be higher than 20 percent. As Don Mann, a decorated combat veteran and SEAL special operations technician, reported in *The Modern Day Gunslinger*, about 80 percent of the shots U.S. police officers fire are misses.

Some of the basic training flaws that make it difficult for police officers to defend themselves during a deadly confrontation include:

- Using the isosceles stance instead of a tactical stance.
- Using silhouette targets that do not count head shots.
- Using center-of-mass instead of center-of-chest targets.

Based on tactical anatomy, you should earn more points for a head or heart shot than for a center-of-mass shot.

- Using stationary paper targets that always face forward.
- Insufficient practice after graduating from the academy.
- Not teaching tactical skills when teaching shooting skills.
- Not emphasizing the importance of target-focused shooting.
- Ignoring the fact that most gunfights take place at less than 21 feet.

- Not teaching one-handed shooting with the nondominant hand.
- Requiring police officers to use substandard handguns or ammunition.
- Not teaching how to shoot in low-light or no-light environments.
- Writing use-of-force policies that are more restrictive than state laws.
- Writing departmental policies that put officers at a tactical disadvantage.
- Having unwritten, confusing, or inconsistent use-of-deadly-force policies.
- Not providing legal or psychological support when officers use deadly force.

Even though this book is about tactical shooting, it would be negligent not to mention that the use-of-force policies implemented by some police departments will cause dangerous hesitation during a deadly confrontation because the policies fail to make it clear exactly what kinds of behavior justify the use of deadly force.

Like poor firearms training, hesitation can get you killed during a gunfight. Most people do not need to worry about departmental rules or policies, but inappropriate hesitation can have the same deadly consequence for people who are not police officers. Three of the main reasons private citizens hesitate to shoot are failure to recognize a deadly threat, failure to understand their legal rights, and moral or ethical constraints relating to the use of deadly force for self-defense.

The danger signs discussed in this book will help you recognize hazardous situations *before* you become a victim. If retreat is not possible or safe, knowing you are entering a dangerous situation will give you a chance to plan and prepare. If the threat level increases from potential threat to real threat, you will be less likely to hesitate if you have a workable plan. Early recognition of a dangerous situation may also give you a chance to call for help. One of the fatal mistakes overconfident police officers often make is not calling for backup when backup is available. Back in the 1970s, this mistake was called *tombstone courage*.

Ignorance of the law is no excuse, and there is no justification for not finding out what the basic laws are that relate to self-defense. You do not need the knowledge it would take to defend yourself in court, but having a basic understanding of self-defense law can help you avoid making bad decisions that would make it hard for an attorney to get you acquitted if you are charged with a crime. Two things people who carry or use a gun for self-defense need to understand are (1) having a legal right to use deadly force when defending yourself does not give you the right to commit murder and (2) most states place limits on your right to use deadly force when protecting personal property.

If you do not believe you have an ethical or moral right to protect yourself against a deadly threat by using deadly force, it's doubtful you should plan on using a handgun for self-defense. Most people do not consider wasp spray or a loud whistle more effective than a handgun when fighting for one's life, but if you believe that just showing you have a gun will always protect you or if you don't know how to use a gun, wasp spray or a whistle might be a better option for you.

One common mistake people make is believing that a gunfight is nothing but a shooting match and that people who can punch holes in paper targets that do not shoot back have the skills they need to prevail. On the contrary, a gunfight is a thinking match, and factors such as speed and accuracy are just parts of the process. In the real world, your brain should be running at full speed before you draw your gun, and you must use your brain to get the tactical advantages needed to win the gunfight. In other words: *no brain, no gain.*

Another common mistake people make is believing what they see on television or in the movies. The quick-draw showdowns seen in Westerns seldom if ever occurred in the Old West, and actors are the only people who get knocked off their feet by one shot from a handgun. In the real world, handguns do run out of ammunition, and you cannot shoot them when the safety is on. In the Old West, ambushing, shooting people in the back, or using a shotgun or rifle against a handgun were more common than standing face-to-face and testing your quick-draw skills. More than a few gunfights were won because the bad guys were too drunk to be fast or accurate or their handguns malfunctioned. Professional gunfighters tried to avoid fair fights because they realized a fair fight could result in both shooters getting killed. Historically, the closest thing to a fair gunfight was a prearranged duel. If shooting someone in the hand or shooting a gun out of someone's hand occurred in the Old West, it was probably unintentional.

Most of the major breakthroughs that changed the nature of tactical shooting resulted from military training that was based on combat experience. If you are fighting a war and soldiers are getting killed because of poor training, you try to develop training programs that will help you defeat real enemies in the real world.

Tactical shooting made tremendous progress in the 1940s because of the work done by Colonel Rex Applegate when he was training World War II soldiers. When military leaders realized that traditional target-shooting techniques did not work under battlefield conditions, they brought in people, such as Colonel Applegate, who recognized that target shooting and tactical shooting had very little in common.

The main difficulty that occurs when you try to apply military training to nonmilitary situations is that you cannot use the same rules of engagement. What a military court might consider acceptable collateral damage, a nonmilitary court might deem the negligent killing of innocent bystanders. Whereas the military, in most cases, tries to provide its soldiers with weapons equal to or more effective than those used by the enemy, police departments have a long history of providing officers with weapons and ammunition that are less effective than what criminals are using. Law enforcement officers have been killed because they were outgunned by criminals with high-capacity handguns or high-powered rifles.

Despite all the good information Colonel Applegate and people such as W.E. Fairbairn and E.A Sykes (who supervised the Shanghai Municipal Police) offered police departments, most departments are more likely to take advice from target shooters than from tactical shooters, and most police officers are taught basic target shooting instead of tactical shooting. Specialized units are the exception, because these units often use military techniques. Colonel Applegate believed soldiers and police officers have similar problems and should receive similar training.

We use the term *tactical shooting* because *practical shooting* and *defensive shooting* refer to a target-shooting sport. Some of the techniques used in competition shooting are useful, but others are useless and can even get you killed during a gunfight. In tactical shooting, you do not have second-place winners—you have people who survive and people who die, and this book teaches shooting techniques that will help you survive. No book can instantly make you a tactical shooter, but this book can point you in the right direction.

NEW YORK CITY POLICE DEPARTMENT (NYPD)

The Firearms and Tactics Section of the NYPD released a report in 1981 called *SOP 9* that had a lot of valuable information about handgun survival tactics and handgun training, and much of this information is still relevant today. This is some of the information extracted from *SOP 9*:

- Distance: Most police officers are shot and killed at less than 21 feet.
- Lighting: Dim lighting and highly visible muzzle blast are common.

- Alignment of gun: A target focus was used in 70 percent or more of the cases.
- Quick draw: The gun was already drawn in about 65 percent of the cases.
- Cover: Using cover saved officers more than any other factor.
- Position: Most officers (84 percent) were in a standing or crouched position.
- One-hand shooting: Almost all the officers used their dominant hand.
- Warning shots: Firing a warning shot may encourage return fire.
- Running: Hits while running resulted from chance more than skill.
- Shots fired: Most officers did not fire more than three shots.
- Reload: Only 6 percent of the officers needed to reload.
- Ammunition: Shot placement was more important than the ammunition.
- Hit rate: There were about 25 hits for every 100 shots fired at assailants.

Disconnects between range training and the real world:

- Hitting a target at 150 feet does not help you hit the same target at 3 feet.
- There is no correlation between range score and tactical shooting skills.
- Training does not emphasize shooting targets at distances less than 21 feet.
- Point shooting (target-focused shooting) should be used at short distances.

A review of the NYPD's *Annual Firearms Discharge Report* in 2009 revealed a few new comments since the *SOP 9* report in 1981. The overwhelming majority of officers (90 percent) fired five or fewer shots, but most officers (60 percent) fired three or fewer shots, which is the same as in 1981. The number of police officers who used target-focused shooting was 1 percent less than in 1981 (69 percent), which is probably not statistically significant. Two-handed shooting was used 62 percent of the time, and one-handed shooting occurred 38 percent of the time.

The Porter method is based on observations that are similar to the ones made by the NYPD. Most deadly confrontations occur at distances less than 21 feet, the lighting is usually poor, using cover can be beneficial, and most of the time fewer than five shots are fired, which means fast tactical reloading is seldom required.

It is no surprise that target-focused shooting is used about 70 percent of the time and that about 30 percent of all shooting is done with one hand. We strongly agree that shot placement is usually more important than the ammunition being used, and we also agree that high levels of stress can make it difficult or impossible to use the fine motor skills that are needed to focus on the front sight and get a good sight picture. When your body is under stress because of a deadly confrontation, gross motor skills are easier to control than fine motor skills, and heavy breathing is more likely to occur than controlled breathing.

As for running and shooting at the same time, luck determines your level of accuracy more than skill. We recommend shoot and move (shoot and scoot) or move, stop, and shoot (scoot, stop, and shoot) whenever possible, but walking and shooting or moving sideways and shooting can be done with combat-effective accuracy if you have learned and practiced moving and shooting at the same time.

Where we differ from the NYPD is how we apply these observations. We agree shot placement is very important and that police officers should shoot to stop, not shoot to kill, but we do not believe that shooting at the center of mass, which the NYPD also calls the *center of gravity*, is a reliable way to stop a deadly threat.

The odds that a center-of-mass hit will cause immediate or timely incapacitation are not much better than the odds of hitting someone while you are running. *Immediate* implies that incapacitation is instantaneous, and *timely* implies that incapacitation occurs before your assailant causes serious bodily harm or death. If people who are pointing a gun at you or a hostage decide to pull the trigger, anything less than immediate incapacitation will not stop them from pulling the trigger. This belief is based on anatomy and physiology, not speculation, and any competent forensic pathologist can verify it.

It was reported that the NYPD had a 13-percent hit rate in 1999 and 18 percent between 1998 and 2006, and it's doubtful any of the hit rates after 2006 were much higher. This means the officers were missing more than four out of every five shots fired. Low hit rates, combined with the observation that there is no correlation between range score and tactical shooting skills, would seem to indicate a need for change. The national average hit rate for police is about 20 percent.

The Porter method was designed for individuals, but organizations are welcome to compare our techniques with the ones they are using if they would like to improve their hit rates. We also encourage people who would like to become tactical shooters to avoid using training methods that consistently produce poor results. Our goal is to give people the information they need to make intelligent choices about the skills they need to learn in order to become tactical shooters and to help them understand how to develop these skills. The Porter method uses natural body movements that are intuitive and easy to learn, but you will still need correct and regular practice to maintain these or any other motor skills.

SELF-DEFENSE

As discussed in the legal disclaimer in the warning, this book cannot give you legal advice, and you are strongly advised to consult an attorney if you have questions about the federal, state, or local ordinances that relate to deadly force or self-defense. These laws are very complex, they are often reinterpreted or changed because of case law, and the self-defense laws in one state are usually different from the ones in other states.

This book can tell you how to shoot and how to avoid or survive a deadly confrontation, but it cannot tell you when you have a legal right to shoot or if you will be charged with a crime or sued in civil court if you do shoot. People who are in possession of a handgun for the purpose of self-defense should make certain they understand their legal rights and duties regarding the use of deadly force.

Different states may have different opinions concerning the elements of self-defense, such as when you have a duty to retreat, but here are some elements that might be required to avoid prosecution by claiming that your use of deadly force was justified because of self-defense. Whether or how these elements are applied can depend on state laws, jurisdiction, case law, or jury instructions.

1. You did not start, perpetuate, escalate, or agree to engage in the conflict.
2. You had reasonable belief the threat was happening, immediate, or imminent.
3. You had reasonable belief the threat would cause serious bodily harm or death.
4. You used force that was reasonable and necessary—but not excessive.
5. You used force as last resort because retreat was no longer possible or safe.
6. You used deadly force to protect against an illegal threat of deadly force.

A force likely or intended to cause serious bodily injury or death is called *deadly force*, and the word *imminent* implies immediacy, which means it is likely to happen at any moment. For a threat to be reasonable or credible, your attacker must have the ability (i.e., means and opportunity) to carry out the threat. In most cases, your attacker will also have a motive. *Excessive* implies the force used was unreasonable or unnecessary or that force was used after the threat stopped. If you claim a threat was deadly or imminent, you may need to show your beliefs were reasonable, prudent, or actual. Some states do not demand retreat when attacked in your home (Castle doctrine) or other special places, but others might require retreat regardless of where you are. Some state laws make it hard to know exactly what is required.

Some states may allow you to stand your ground rather than retreat when you are in a special place, such as your business or vehicle, but you might not have the same right in other states. Even if you have a legal right to stand your ground and use deadly force, for tactical reasons you might be better off retreating if you can do so safely and avoiding deadly force. Making the enemy come to you so you can fight at a time and place of your choosing is often better than standing your ground and fighting from a position that gives your enemy the advantage. Having a legal right to use deadly force does not make using it mandatory or tactically superior to retreating.

Since we cannot know what jurisdiction you are going to be in or what laws are going to apply if you decide to use deadly force, you are responsible for knowing whether the tactics we present are likely to result in criminal or civil liability. It would be irresponsible for us not to acknowledge the fact that using deadly force can have unpleasant legal, social, or psychological consequences, and we have no way of knowing how these consequences might affect you.

We strongly believe that people have a right to bear arms and protect themselves against dangerous criminals, and we also believe the threat of serious bodily harm or death justifies a use of force that creates a significant risk of death. Even if you are trying to incapacitate and not kill, death will sometimes occur.

The following factors may increase your risk of being charged with a crime or sued in civil court if they are present before or during the use of deadly force:

1. Being under the influence of alcohol or illegal drugs, being engaged in some kind of criminal activity, or attempting to collect money.
2. Failure to call the police before or after the use of deadly force, not remaining on the scene until the police arrive, or obstructing the investigation.

3. Planting or tampering with evidence or tampering with witnesses.
4. Having a motive other than self-defense for using deadly force, such as anger, revenge, jealousy, hatred, punishment, property protection, or economic gain.
5. Shooting an unarmed assailant or an innocent bystander.

Some additional factors that might get you charged or sued because of their social or psychological impact include shooting a juvenile or female, shooting someone in the back, and shooting someone who appears to be reaching for a weapon before you actually see the gun, regardless of whether or not your attacker was armed. These are the kinds of cases that most people, including police officers, hope they never get involved in, and your ultimate fate may rest in the hands of a jury that has a hard time deciding if a reasonable and prudent person would have acted the same way under similar circumstances.

If a case involving any of these five factors goes to court, the best thing you can do is hire a very good attorney who knows how to present the evidence to a judge or jury, knows how to use the testimony from expert witnesses, and knows how to deal with political pressure and the news media. Cases of this nature often become even more controversial and more emotional if racial or ethnic issues are involved.

You might be acquitted after shooting a child or a woman, or an unarmed person in the back, but doing these things can make it much harder to prove your innocence. On the other hand, when fighting to protect yourself against a deadly threat, hesitating because of age or gender, not shooting until your adversary is facing you, or waiting until you can see the gun can get you killed. Even with good training, always making the right decision will not be easy.

Police officers have appeared in court more than a few times for shooting someone in the back, and they have been found innocent of all charges. Shooting someone in the back can be unavoidable if the person turns just after you start to pull the trigger or he is turning to shoot at you while moving away. In some cases, shooting someone in the back might be the only way you can save your life or someone else's life. Shooting someone in the back will likely have serious legal consequences when that person is no longer a threat, such as when he is unconscious or walking out the door with your television.

Many people believe shooting someone in the back is a sign of cowardice, and people with integrity will fight their adversaries face-to-face in a fair fight. In the real world, if a dangerous criminal is trying to kill you, shooting that person in the back is usually safer than waiting until he can turn around. If you are an innocent victim facing a ruthless criminal, you need to be more concerned about survival than fairness. One of the most important things you can do during a deadly confrontation is to look for a weakness you can exploit that will give you a tactical advantage and put your adversary at a tactical disadvantage.

If you believe exercising your right to make a citizen's arrest gives you the right to shoot a criminal who is trying to escape in the back, you might be wrong. Even in states where making a citizen's arrest is legal if you witness a felony, private citizens do not have the same legal protections as police officers and even police officers cannot use deadly force to apprehend most fleeing felons.

Another issue that may be raised in court is how close someone needs to be to pose an imminent deadly threat. If you shoot someone in the back who is armed with a handgun and 75 feet away, a prosecutor may argue the person was not close enough to be an imminent threat or that you had time to escape.

Shooting someone you thought was reaching for a gun will probably not be a major problem if a gun is found, but it can be a serious problem if the gun is never found and it appears you shot an unarmed person. Even if you believed the person was armed and you were defending yourself, you will probably be arrested.

Because the person who initiates an action, such as reaching for a gun, will usually have an advantage over the person who must first recognize the threat and then respond to it, you need to recognize threats quickly and respond immediately if you want to avoid getting shot. If juries understood the relationship between action and reaction, it might be easier for them to understand why a fraction of a second between not waiting long enough and waiting too long can make the difference between getting killed and killing an unarmed person.

Shooting someone who appears to be reaching for a gun is a tactical problem that can be affected by many different variables, such as tolerance for risk, quality of training, quality of equipment, or quality of your partner. It's hard to say how much time you have to decide to shoot someone who is holding a gun but not pointing it directly at you, but taking too long to decide can get you killed.

Shooting an innocent person by mistake is not something a normal person would do, but people who have never tried to defend themselves against a deadly threat are less likely to understand how chaotic a deadly confrontation can be than those who have repeatedly had to use deadly force to defend themselves. If someone is threatening you with a gun, it takes a lot more self-control than most people realize to think about where a bullet might go after it penetrates your adversary's body than to think about what might happen if your adversary's bullet penetrates your body. Most people do not have this much self-control.

Accidently shooting an innocent person because you failed to verify your target is almost always preventable. If you shoot through a closed door or a wall because you believe the person on the other side is a burglar, you are violating the safety rule that states you should always verify your target before you pull the trigger. If luck is on your side, the person you shot sight unseen might turn out to be someone who was trying to kill you and you will not be charged with a crime. If luck is not on your side, you might be arrested, charged with murder, and go to jail.

Guns are the most common weapon criminals use to cause serious bodily injury or death, but knives and other sharp objects have killed thousands of people in the United States over the past 10 years. Contrary to the belief that someone who is armed with a knife and standing 21 feet away cannot be an imminent threat, a person can travel 21 feet in 1.5 seconds and kill you within a matter of seconds by stabbing you in the heart, slashing your throat, or driving the knife into your brain stem. If a judge or jury believes someone armed with a knife is not an imminent threat from 21 feet, even having a good attorney and testimony from an expert witness might not be enough to change their minds and get you acquitted.

Of all the elements related to deadly force, the one that covers excessive force is often the most controversial. Any force that is used after someone is no longer an imminent threat is usually referred to as excessive. If someone who was threatening you with a gun drops the weapon and surrenders, using deadly force at that point would be excessive and completely unjustified unless the person tried to pick up the gun or threatened you with a different gun.

A circumstance in which excessive force might become the center of controversy is when you shoot someone three times and the judge or members of the jury believe one or two times would have been sufficient. It's reasonable to say you should stop shooting when someone is no longer a threat, but it's not reasonable to believe the average person has the ability to know exactly when this occurs. The fear that someone still holding a gun is faking unconsciousness is rational, and most people have no idea how many rounds they fired during a deadly confrontation. Some people do not even remember firing a gun or anything about the event.

Proving that excessive force was used can be difficult, but that does not mean excessive force is never used. If someone is incapacitated and appears to be dead, going out to your car and getting more ammunition so you can shoot the body several more times would be considered excessive. Having the right to stop a deadly threat by causing incapacitation does not give you the right to kill.

If the person you have just shot appears to be incapacitated or dead, you should retreat to a safe position and call 911. Even though the last thing you want to hear is that someone you shot might have lived if you had called for an ambulance immediately after the shooting, it is better to let the police request emergency personnel than request them yourself. If you let the police make the request, the medical units responding to the scene will normally not enter until they know the person is no longer a dangerous threat and the crime scene is relatively secure. If you do call them yourself, be certain to tell them that the person you are calling for was shot and that the person or the area could still be dangerous.

If you are no longer facing a dangerous threat, find a safe place to secure any weapons you might have before the police arrive. If possible, give the police a full description of what you look like and where they can find you. Do not give the police any reason to believe that you are a criminal or a dangerous threat.

Another thing that can complicate a use-of-deadly-force situation is not being in legal possession of the handgun at the time you used it. Permits to carry a concealed handgun are now available in a large number of states, and it has never been easier for the average law-abiding citizen to secure one. Even though you can normally get a permit without going through an attorney, it might be wise to speak with one about the appropriate laws in your area before deciding to carry a concealed handgun.

Never assume the state you live in will use the same terminology that we have used in this book, but understanding the basic terminology that relates to self-defense can help you understand the relationship between laws and tactics. Since each state has its own self-defense laws, you may need to modify your tactics to be more compatible with its laws. Even if a frontal attack saves your life, pressing a frontal attack could result in criminal charges if state law mandates retreat.

After you have used deadly force and the scene has been secured, call your attorney and wait until your attorney arrives before trying to explain or justify why you thought it was necessary to use deadly force. Even if you believe you do understand the state laws that apply to your situation, you are probably not familiar with case law, which is based on rulings or interpretations formed in previously adjudicated cases. Very few people other than attorneys have access to case law.

Even though most police officers have a good working knowledge of the law, unless they are also attorneys, they are not qualified to give legal advice. You need to remember that the laws relating to self-defense for police officers may be different than the ones for civilians.

Most police officers are more familiar with arresting people than defending people who are charged with a crime. It's nice to hear an officer tell you that you are not going to be arrested, but it's even better to hear your attorney tell you that you have not violated any laws. Even if the police decide not to arrest you on the scene, it's still possible you might be charged later by the state attorney's office, indicted by a grand jury, or charged with a federal civil-rights violation.

Most people have a difficult time remembering exactly what they did after a deadly confrontation is over, and some people never remember their actions. Even though it's important to cooperate and be honest with the police, you should speak to an attorney before you discuss any specific information that relates to using deadly force. This is the same kind of advice most police unions give their officers. Just being in fear for your life is not enough; you will need to show that your actions complied with local, state, and federal laws.

Even if what you did was reasonable under the circumstances, your attorney might be able to anticipate problems that need to be addressed before you give an official statement. Most attorneys will advise you not to discuss your case with anyone, especially police or the media, until you have legal representation. This principle should be applied to anything you post on the Internet or messages you email or text on your phone. Remember that anything you post on the Internet, text, say over a telephone, or tell a news reporter "off the record" can be used against you in court.

What you did might be completely legal, but political pressure or media exposure can sometimes turn a justifiable shooting into a witch hunt that results in unnecessary charges and enormous legal expenses. Activist groups that oppose the existing self-defense laws may try to make your case controversial at your expense.

LEGENDARY GUNFIGHTERS

If you are trying to develop a practical, evidence-based training program for tactical shooters, examining the way shooters in the past were able to survive gunfights is a good place to start. Handguns and ammunition have certainly improved over the past few hundred years, but the handgun skills and tactical skills gunfighters have used to stay alive are almost identical to those that will help a modern tactical shooter survive a gunfight. Because of the influence target shooters have had on tactical shooting, many of the tactical handgun skills being used today are less effective than the ones used by legendary gunfighters.

DUELS

Duelists who fought with single-shot pistols never received the recognition in books, movies, or on television shows that gunfighters who used six-shot revolvers have enjoyed, but dueling with pistols taught people many of the same lessons people learned in the Old West when shooting revolvers.

Single-shot, flintlock pistols used specifically for dueling appeared during the late 1700s. Misfires were very common, but a good-quality, smoothbore dueling pistol could shoot a 2-inch group at 15 feet using a .50- to .60-caliber ball.

In some duels, if a misfire occurred, the person whose pistol misfired was allowed to reload and start over if he was still physically capable of continuing. In other duels, a misfire might be counted as a shot, and cocking the hammer to see if the gun would fire the second time the trigger was pulled was considered a violation of the "code." Most Old West gunfighters were less concerned about honor and fairness than duelists.

If the rules required walking toward each other and stopping after a shot was fired, the first to fire would be shooting at a moving target while the second duelist would be shooting at a stationary target. Rules such as

This famous 1899 painting by Ilya Repin is titled *The Duel Between Onegin and Lenski*. It depicts the literary duel between Eugene Onegin and Vladimir Lenski described in *Onegin* by Alexander Pushkin. The original painting resides in the Pushkin Museum of Fine Art, Moscow, Russia.

The early dueling pistols were unsophisticated by modern standards, and many of them had no sights. The pistol pictured above was considered more reliable than a flintlock pistol because it used a percussion cap to ignite the main charge instead of a separate powder charge set off by a wedge of flint. If they functioned properly, dueling pistols that used a flintlock ignition system were just as deadly as the dueling pistols that used a percussion cap. According to the French, the minimum distance for a pistol duel was 15 yards, and the maximum distance was 25 yards.

"fire your shot and then stand where you are until your opponent has a chance to fire his shot" largely disappeared about the same time that dueling was outlawed.

Dueling pistols did not always have sights, and they were normally fired with one hand. To get a shot off quickly, a duelist normally fired as soon as the gun was raised to eye level. Too much speed could result in missing a shot, and not enough speed could result in being dead before you had a chance to take a shot. The minimum time needed to fire an accurate shot tended to increase as the distance between the two adversaries increased. History provides many examples that being a good target shooter did not make one a good duelist, and being able to control stress was often more important than being the best marksman.

Some dueling pistols were equipped with hair-triggers (set triggers), which often caused accidental discharges because of nervous tension or inexperience. People who were familiar with hair-triggers knew that hearing the report after your adversary shoots can be sufficient to cause an involuntary contraction that is strong enough to activate a hair-trigger. To avoid accidental discharges, they would keep their finger off the trigger until their gun was aligned and they were ready to shoot. This precaution was not used when dueling with pistols with a heavy trigger.

Some of the first reasons for using target-focused shooting were discussed in *Helps and Hints: How to Protect Life and Property,* written in 1835 by Lieutenant Colonel Baron de Berenger: "Self-defense requires rapid pistol shooting, and therefore precludes a deliberate aim along the barrel." Baron de Berenger recommended looking at a target when shooting in the same way that a swordsman watches his target when striking. He also noted the similarity between target-focused shooting and pointing your finger, which might be why the term *point shooting* is often associated with target-focused shooting. The unscientific belief that pointing your finger is a reflex action may help explain why target-focused shooting is also called *reflex shooting.*

One mistake people make about target-focused shooting is thinking it is not aimed. By definition, aiming is the process of pointing your gun at a target, and you can do this without focusing on the front sight to get a sight picture. It is also incorrect to say target-focused shooting is always unsighted. For example, you can look through the sights and also focus on your target, a method of aiming used by W.R. (Bat) Masterson and other Old-West gunfighters.

Many people believe Brian Enos and Rob Leatham are two of the best competition target shooters who ever lived, and they also believe Enos' book, *Practical Shooting: Beyond Fundamentals*, is one of the best guides ever written on competition handgun shooting. For people who are unfamiliar with the International Practical Shooting Confederation (IPSC), it's a shooting-sport organization, and Jeff Cooper served as its first president. In his book, Enos mentioned that target-focused shooting is not very popular with people who participate in shooting sports, and Leatham was probably the first IPSC shooter to admit that you can use a target-focus instead of a front-sight focus when shooting targets at close range. Leatham was faster than most other IPSC shooters when shooting at close range because using a target-focus allowed him to acquire his target faster than using a front-sight focus.

Another widely recognized handgun expert, Massad Ayoob, commented on target-focused shooting in his book *Combat Shooting with Massad Ayoob*. According to Ayoob, you can shoot through unfocused sights at fairly close range, but you will probably need to use a front-sight focus and a sharply focused sight picture to make an accurate shot at 75 feet.

In *Shooting from Within*, J. Michael Plaxco made it clear that he considers looking through sights as a type of target-focused shooting, and he recommended this method, which is also called *indirect attention*, when shooting high-speed courses.

We agree with all three of these experts—Enos, Ayoob, and Plaxco—that target-focused shooting is very effective when shooting at short distances, such as 21 feet or less, and in some situations at distances of more than 21 feet. We also agree with Ayoob that front-sight-focus shooting is normally required when shooting at 75 feet or more, although historians say James Butler "Wild Bill" Hickok raised his gun to eye level and used target-focused shooting even at distances much greater than 75 feet.

Since most gunfights take place at less than 21 feet, it seems obvious that most tactical shooting should be done with a target focus. What we do not understand is why more police officers are never properly trained to use target-focused shooting at close range. The need for target-focused shooting becomes even more important when your target is moving and you have low or inconsistent lighting. It appears that police departments have the same irrational bias against target-focus shooting that many competition target shooters seem to have.

Most tactical shooting will be target focused when you reach a distance that makes front-sight-focused shooting more effective. When using a target focus, advanced tactical shooters are combat effective at longer distances than entry-level tactical shooters. Even when shooting at short distances, a front-sight focus may be more effective than a target focus if the target is stationary and very small. Use the method of aiming that suits your immediate needs and skills.

People who always shoot with a front-sight focus will be at a disadvantage when dealing with the kind of deadly confrontations you are most likely to face in the real world. If two people are equally skilled, using a front-sight focus at close range is slower than using a target focus. Not only that, but you might not be able to use the front sight if dim lighting makes the outline of the front sight indistinct. It is also difficult to use a front-sight focus if your target is moving or you need to see if someone is still armed and dangerous before deciding whether to shoot.

OLD-TIME GUNFIGHTERS

A quote taken from an essay written in 1875 titled "The Pistol as a Weapon of Defense in the House and on the Road" is a good starting point for a discussion of gunfights. (The author of the original essay is unknown, but when Paladin published the essay as a book with the same title in 2004, Jeff Cooper penned the foreword.) J. Michael Plaxco might call this kind of aiming *looking through your sights* and Jeff Cooper might call it *using a flash sight picture*, which is aiming without focusing on the front sight, but regardless of what you call it, the unknown author is not using or recommending that you use a front-sight focus and standard sight picture.

> "Neither is it ever necessary to hit so small an object as a two-inch circle. He who can hit a four-inch circle at six paces will be master of the situation *provided he is quick enough*. But the aim, if aim it can be called, must be taken with the rapidity of thought; there must be no dallying to find the sights; no hesitation in the hope of bettering the aim. Delay, however occasioned, may cost us our life. Not that we would counsel hurry or want of coolness, for this will inevitably cause us to shoot wide of the mark. There is such a thing as being rapid, cool, and accurate, and this is what is needed."

The essay also stated that dry-fire practice can reduce flinching and using a good grip and cover are very important. People in 1875 realized a correctly placed head shot would be instantly fatal, a bullet entering the heart region of the chest (mediastinum) was not as instantly fatal as a head shot, and a chest shot is easier to make than a head shot. It's doubtful anyone in 1875 realized that hitting one of the major blood vessels next to the heart might cause death faster than hitting the heart.

One thing that becomes apparent when you study early gunfighters is the value of practice. It's hard to say how many of the early gunfighters used front-sight-focused shooting, but it's fairly clear that some of them used their sights when making shots at a long distance and they probably used the sights on their handguns the same way they used the sights on their rifles.

It appears that some professional gunfighters could draw, look through their sights, and shoot faster than most gunfighters could draw and shoot from the hip. Competition shooters who fire thousands of rounds per year are able to draw, use a front-sight focus, and shoot with incredible speed. Even though a target focus is usually faster than a front-sight focus if both shooters are equally skilled, a highly trained target shooter who uses a front-sight focus at close range will sometimes be faster than a poorly trained tactical shooter who uses a target focus at close range.

It's doubtful that any competent gunfighters focused on the front sight when shooting at a human target at close range. Unlike target shooters, who need to shoot a tight group at close range to be competitive, most gunfighters realized that speed and combat-effective accuracy are more important than shooting a very tight group. Most gunfighters also realized that when you are standing face-to-face, shooting too quickly can result in a missed shot, but also not shooting quickly enough can result in getting shot and not living long enough to return fire.

Most of what many people believe about the legendary gunfighters in the Old West is more fiction than fact, and many of their deadly confrontations involved whiskey, women, and gambling. Some of them worked as both lawmen and outlaws, and some of them were much better at shooting people in the back than winning gunfights because of their quick-draw skills. That being said, it's hard to deny that some lived longer than others because of their handgun skills.

According to Joseph G. Rosa, who wrote *The Gunfighters: Man or Myth?,* most gunfighters had their pistols in their hands if they expected trouble, and quick-draw confrontations were extremely rare. If two gunfighters were equally skilled, they generally killed each other, which is probably why very few of the gunfights that took place between professionals were fair fights.

Rosa noted in his book that the better target shooter was not always the winner in a gunfight and people with a killer instinct who didn't hesitate to shoot were more likely to win a gunfight than people with a less aggressive mindset. In a study that examined the characteristics of police officers who get killed in the line of duty, being less aggressive and using less force than other officers would use in a similar situation increases your risk of getting killed. Several lessons can be drawn from Rosa's observations: (1) if possible, have your handgun out and ready before you get into a gunfight,

(2) do not hesitate when you need to use deadly force, and (3) being aggressive can save your life.

Rosa also discussed the relationship between target shooting and tactical shooting. According to Walter Winans, who was a legendary target shooter in the late 1800s and one of the finest revolver shots of all time, shooting stationary targets, especially at long ranges, will not make you a better gunfighter. When a handgun is used for self-defense, most shooting is done within a few yards at a rapidly moving target and the gunfight will be over within a few seconds.

Many people, including the famous lawman Wyatt Earp, believed that Wild Bill Hickok was the deadliest gunfighter who ever lived. If that's true, Earp was not far behind. Both men were excellent marksmen and had nerves of steel, and neither believed fanning a gun or using fast and fancy hip shooting was the way to win a gunfight. In the authorized biography of Earp's life, *Wyatt Earp*, Stuart N. Lake, wrote about the way Earp approached a gunfight.

According to Lake, when Earp said take your time, he meant you need to be mentally deliberate, but your muscles need to move faster than thought. Do not rush a shot and miss, but do not take more than a split fraction of a second to get your gun properly aligned. Earp did not believe in using techniques like fanning a gun or hip shooting, but like most gunfighters, he probably used a target focus during close-quarter gunfights and held his gun in front of his body with his forearm about level and his bent elbow held at or slightly above the waist.

In *The Gunfighters,* Paul Trachtmart quoted Bat Masterson as saying that gunfighters practiced with guns the way cardsharps practiced with cards, and they practiced enough to make their movements smooth, lightning fast, and automatic. This kind of automatic behavior is also called *unconscious competence* because drawing and shooting can be performed with very little conscious thought.

Lessons to Be Learned from These Old-Timers

Many of the techniques used more than 150 years ago are still effective today, and one thing gunfighters and target shooters have made very clear for more than a century is that being a good target shooter does not make you a good gunfighter. For some strange reason, most police departments largely ignore the valuable tactics the early gunfighters used to stay alive and instead offer firearms training programs that use watered-down target-shooting techniques instead of time-honored tactical-shooting techniques. The incompetent use of handguns that results from poor training can lead to officers or innocent bystanders getting killed.

Useless handgun training not only increases the risk police officers face when they get involved in close-quarter combat, but it also makes it hard for police officers to protect the public when they cannot protect themselves. How can police departments that have a 20-percent hit rate continue to ignore the obvious fact that something is wrong with the kind of firearms training they are giving their officers?

Some departments believe high-quality firearms training is too expensive and not worth the effort. On the other hand, the lawsuits that often result when police officers kill someone in a no-shoot situation or accidentally shoot an innocent bystander or a fellow officer can be extremely expensive. Good training does not need to be expensive, but poor training is almost always expensive in one respect or another because of a loss of money or an unnecessary loss of life.

One thing many police departments do not realize, or want to realize, is that being able to shoot stationary paper targets on a police range and being able to survive a deadly confrontation on the street are two entirely different things. Competitive target shooting—regardless of whether you call it combat, practical, or defensive shooting—is a sport, and most of the top competitors who have competed in this challenging sport will acknowledge this fact.

The targets used in competition shooting are good for separating the first-place winner from everyone else, but they do not teach or test the tactical skills you normally need to win a gunfight. For example, shooting at stationary targets 75 to 150 feet away is fine for target shooters, but shooting at these distances has limited value for police officers. About 85 percent of the gunfights that kill police officers occur within less than 21 feet, and only about 6 percent occur at distances of more than 50 feet.

It should also be pointed out that top competition shooters might shoot more than 10,000 rounds per year, whereas most police officers shoot no more than 50 rounds per year. Rather than design a firearms-training program for police officers that fails to make them good at competition shooting or tactical shooting, the time wasted on ineffective training should be used for realistic training that will give the officers a better chance of being able to survive deadly confrontations. For most police departments, a 50-percent hit rate, which means the officers miss only half the shots they fire at subjects, would more than double their present hit rate.

People who understand that most police departments do not have a firearms training program that consistently produces well-trained tactical shooters will also understand why this book does not use conventional police training as a model for creating an effective tactical handgun training program. The poor-quality training most police officers get is more the result of departmental policy decisions than a lack of competent firearms instructors. Instructors who provide almost useless training to the average police officer often give excellent training to some of the tactical units that operate within the same department, such as special weapons and tactics teams (SWAT), hostage release teams (HRT), or special response teams (SRT). The hit rates for special units can be four times the national hit rate for police officers.

The high-quality training specialized units receive partially explains why their hit rates are higher than those for the average police officer and why the average officer is much more likely to get killed in a gunfight than members of a specialized unit. Most police officers do not need to have all the tactical skills that members of a tactical unit require, but they should be given enough training to make them combat effective in the kind of situations they are likely to face.

Most of this history section relates to shooting skills, but you can also learn a few things about such factors as attitude and advantage. Many of the lawmen who were recognized as good gunfighters, such as Wyatt Earp, had the ability to remain calm and focused during a deadly confrontation. This characteristic might not have applied to other parts of their personal life, but when they were confronted by a gunman, they managed to devote all their attention to the problem at hand.

Police officers who are well trained and have confidence in their shooting skills and their handguns are less likely to panic during a deadly confrontation than officers who do not. Officers who have never been trained to shoot a moving target may panic and start shooting even though they have no chance of hitting the person at whom they are shooting. Officers who try to focus on the front sight may panic and shoot an unarmed person because they cannot see if the person is still holding the gun when their eyes are focused on the front sight instead of the target.

Besides learning about shooting skills, you can learn a lot about tactical skills from some of these legendary gunfighters. When you see a right-handed police officer approaching a car during a vehicle stop with his flashlight in his right hand, do you really think a successful gunfighter from the Old West would have made the same kind of mistake? Shifting what you have in your right hand to your left hand so you can draw and shoot your gun, and then dropping what you have in your left hand so you can shoot with both hands, is not the best way to win a gunfight. Most successful Old West gunfighters realized they needed practical handgun skills combined with good tactical skills and the right mindset to win gunfights, but the firearms training most police departments offer today seldom teaches any of these things.

MODERN GUNFIGHTERS

Jeff Cooper recognized the difference between front-sight-focused shooting and target-focused shooting, and he divided target-focused shooting into two categories: type 3 and type 4. In type-3 shooting, the shooting arm is straight and the sights are just below eye level; in type-4 shooting, the shooting arm is bent and about level with the diaphragm. Cooper discussed type-3 and type-4 shooting in *The Complete Book of Modern Handgunning*. Cooper stated that type-3 shooting is used for hitting a human enemy with great speed at ranges where instinct is not accurate enough, but real precision is not necessary. He called type-4 shooting *instinct shooting*, but he acknowledged that you can see the handgun in your peripheral vision. Type-4 shooting is similar to the stance Old West gunfighters used and the stance Bill Jordon called the *gun throwing method* in his book *No Second Place Winner*.

Since bringing your gun just below eye level tends to be more accurate than shooting with your gun at diaphragm level, Colonel Cooper stated type-3 shooting is effective between 15 feet and 60 feet and type-4 shooting should be used at 21 feet or less. The maximum distance for the gun-throwing method was also 21 feet. For most police officers, the maximum distance for type-4 shooting is about 7 feet.

The imaginary straight line that connects your eye with your target is called the *line of sight,* and bringing the top of the gun into alignment with your line of sight tends to improve accuracy. If your target is at eye level, bringing your gun just below eye level will probably align the top of the gun with your line of sight.

In *No Second Place Winner*, Jordan made another statement that leads you to question why anyone with practical experience and who had used a handgun for self-defense would recommend using front-sight focus at close range. According to Jordan, most of the affrays between police officers and criminals take place at close distances and involve the element of surprise and poor lighting, conditions that make deliberate aimed fire not only inadvisable but also impossible.

Jim Cirillo, who was on the famous New York Stakeout Squad, was an expert on tactical shooting; being a target shooter as well did not stop him from realizing a target focus is better than a front-sight focus in most tactical situations. Unlike target shooting, tactical shooting teaches people to shoot from behind cover and rewards combat-effective accuracy instead of precision accuracy.

In *Jim Cirillo's Tale of the Stakeout Squad* by Paul Kirchner, Cirillo advised that if you are shooting at a great distance, you should use your sights, but if you are shooting toe-to-toe, you need to be looking at your target and not wasting time seeking out the sights. If you are focused on your sights, you can't see whether the poor guy in front of you is pulling out his wallet or a gun. Cirillo developed a method of target-focused shooting he called the *geometric nose point*.

In essence, you keep the gun parallel to the ground and perpendicular with your nose. He stated that this method takes a short time to learn and makes it easier to hit the spinal cord shot, which he considered a primary tactical target for shot placement. He also developed a method of target-focused shooting that uses the silhouette of your gun as a visual index for sight alignment, which he called a *weapon silhouette point*. Officer Cirillo reported that many of his students were able to achieve combat effectiveness even when their sights were covered with tape.

Another tactical technique Cirillo used was teaching people to shoot with a canted (tilted) grip when using the dominant (strong) hand or non-dominant (weak) hand. In 1976, Massad Ayoob called this grip the *Cirillo cant*. The famous marksman, Brian Enos, canted his hand inward when shooting with his nondominant hand, and Paul Castle used an inward cant when shooting with one or both hands and an outward cant when shooting with one hand from the hip.

Three other handgun experts who deserve to be mentioned here are W.E Fairbairn, E.A. Sykes, and Rex Applegate. These three men clearly showed that target-focused shooting is more practical than front-sight focused shooting in most tactical situations. Most of the techniques they used are explained in a book co-written by Colonel Rex Applegate and Michael D. Janich titled *Bullseyes Don't Shoot Back*. Some of the advice they gave includes shooting with both eyes open, employing a combat crouch, and using realistic targets, such as man-sized targets that charge, retreat, bob, traverse (move crosswise), or appear suddenly and unexpectedly.

In *Kill or Get Killed*, Colonel Applegate made the same observation that Captains Fairbairn and Sykes made: target shooting will not prepare you for combat. He also noted that many police departments spend too much time on target shooting and not enough time developing practical skills that will help the average officer survive a gunfight.

Many police officers believe political pressure keeps their departments from offering realistic firearms training or giving them the support they need if they shoot someone. This is not a new problem; Ed McGiverns noted the same problem back in 1938 in *Ed McGivern's Book on Fast and Fancy Revolver Shooting and Police Training*. According to McGivern, police officers who are forced to kill a criminal are often called on the carpet and severely reprimanded, criticized, penalized, or prosecuted. Cirillo maintained that the NYPD Stake Out Squad was disbanded and he was not promoted because of political pressure.

Economic considerations are probably part of the reason federal law enforcement agencies, such as the FBI, qualify four times per year and shoot 300 rounds per qualification, whereas most police officers qualify only once a year and shoot no more than 50 rounds per qualification. Unlike federal law enforcement officers, who normally receive additional training when they qualify, most police officers sign in, shoot the minimum required score, and leave.

Major General Julian Hatcher, who wrote *Textbook of Pistols and Revolvers*, believed a front-sight focus has a place in tactical shooting if time permits and the target is either a long distance away or very small, but a tactical shooter should know how to get fairly good results without using the sights. This means being able to point a gun the way you would point your finger at someone. After tactical shooters learn basic handgun marksmanship, they should concentrate on speed and accuracy when shooting without sights.

Hatcher—like many other experts—believed that basic target shooting provides a good foundation for learning tactical shooting, but being able to shoot without focusing on the front sight is essential for people who are going to be involved in deadly confrontations, such as military or police personnel. At best, the firearms training most police officers get will help them learn basic marksmanship.

Most of the legendary handgun experts seemed to have an obvious love for handguns, and many of them shot thousands of rounds per year in competition. But when it came to knowing the difference between competition target shooting and tactical shooting, they clearly realized a gunfight is more than a shooting match. Target shooting is a fascinating sport and some forms of competition target shooting more closely resemble a gunfight than others. However, being a champion competition shooter will not make you combat effective, and being a highly trained tactical shooter will not turn you into a champion target shooter. Trick shooters are closer to having the skills needed to win a gunfight than target shooters.

In *Colonel Askins on Pistols & Revolvers*, Charles Askins observed that good target shooters do not focus the aiming eye on the target at all, but rather on the front post, and a hunter should keep the eyes focused on the critter, not the sights. He also recommended moving the sights into line with the shooter's eye and the living target, which might be similar to looking through the sights. Since critters are more like human targets than stationary paper targets, it seems reasonable to believe that Colonel Askins switched to target-focused shooting when he used a handgun for self-defense.

Even though Colonel Askins was an avid competition shooter who reported having fired 334,000 rounds in 10 years and he often wrote about competition target shooting, he clearly knew that shooting at a moving target requires target-focused shooting. Photos in *Colonel Askins on Pistols & Revolvers* show him doing target-focused shooting with two hands, with the gun held below his line of sight.

In another of his books, *The Art of Handgun Shooting*, Colonel Askins made an even stronger statement about the difference between target shooting and tactical shooting. He clearly stated that if our hides are in jeopardy, target-focused shooting is clearly a better choice than front-sight focused shooting. A picture in this book shows Colonel Askins using a stance that resembles the kind used by Old West gunfighters, which Jeff Cooper might have referred to as a type-4 stance.

SUMMARY

It might be helpful to summarize some of the points on which famous gunfighters and famous handgun experts seem to agree:

- Most deadly confrontations occur at very close range.
- Target-focused shooting can be similar to pointing a finger.
- Tactical shooters can aim a gun with or without using the sights.
- Target-focused shooting is used in most tactical situations.
- A target focus is most effective when a target is close and moving.
- A target focus is faster than a front-sight focus at short distances.
- Front-sight-focused shooting is used for most target shooting.
- A front-sight focus is hard to use when lighting is poor or inconsistent.
- A front-sight focus is useful at 75 feet or more.
- A front-sight focus is useful when shooting at small or stationary targets.
- A tactical shooter should normally keep both eyes open when shooting.
- Being a good target shooter will not make you a good tactical shooter.
- After learning basic marksmanship, tactical shooters need realistic practice.
- Tactical shooters need to modify their techniques to match the situation.

Jeff Cooper might have been the first person to use the phrase *flash sight picture*. One explanation of what this phrase means can be found in Gregory Boyce Morrison's *The Modern Technique of the Pistol*, for which Cooper served as editorial advisor and contributed the foreword. According to *The Modern Technique of the Pistol*, a flash sight picture uses a glimpse of a sight picture to confirm alignment. This method is used because a target shooter's gaze at the front sight has proven "inappropriate" during a gunfight. With practice, achieving a flash sight picture becomes reflexive, effortless, and instantaneous.

Morrison wrote that point shooting is a "specialty technique" not suitable for a "general curriculum," which means the general public. For people who are not recreational or competitive shooters, target-focused shooting is a critical skill.

The word *reflexive* implies that, with practice, being able to achieve a flash sight picture will not require conscious thought and the movements will be almost automatic. Even though most people can learn to align a handgun without using the sights, Morrison seemed to imply that you should try to get a flash sight picture, which he called *training wheels*, to confirm your gun is aligned. Using a flash sight picture is not front-sight-focused shooting, but it does require at least a vague image of the sights, as well as aligning the sights with the shooter's line of sight, which is the imaginary straight line between your eye and the target.

SHOT PLACEMENT

If you are faced with a deadly threat, causing incapacitation means doing something that stops someone from threatening you with deadly force. A threat is considered deadly when it's capable of causing serious bodily harm or death. When faced with an illegal deadly threat, three deadly weapons that are often used to counteract it are a handgun, a rifle, and a shotgun. The handgun is the most portable and the weapon people are most likely to have available, but a military rifle or a tactical shotgun is usually more effective than a handgun.

Incapacitation can be immediate or timely. Immediate incapacitation stops a deadly threat instantly, while timely incapacitation stops a deadly threat before it causes serious bodily injury or death. A brain stem shot would cause immediate incapacitation, and a heart shot might cause timely incapacitation if the person who was shot becomes disabled before he can carry out the threat. A person can sometimes function for 10 to 15 seconds even after complete stoppage of the heart.

Incapacitation can also be permanent or temporary, and wounds that cause permanent incapacitation may or may not cause death. A bullet that penetrates the brain stem would cause permanent incapacitation and almost instant death, but a bullet that penetrates the thoracic spine may cause permanent incapacitation but not death. A bullet that hits the intestines may cause permanent incapacitation and death days after the gunshot wound because of inflammation from peritonitis.

Temporary incapacitation might be caused by a bullet that glances off the skull and causes temporary unconsciousness because of the blunt trauma. If you react properly, you might be able to take advantage of the situation and stop the person from continuing to pose a deadly threat. Do not assume that someone who falls down or appears to be unconscious after you shoot is no longer a threat. Some people will fall down even if they are not hit, and some people will pretend to be unconscious and hope you get careless. If you determine that your assailant is temporarily incapacitated, do not relax too soon and fail to protect yourself. Even if help is on the way, your best option is to retreat. If that is not possible, try to remove any weapons that might be used against you if you can do so without risking injury. If you cannot safely approach your assailant, try to find cover or concealment, reload if necessary, and be prepared to shoot.

When deadly force is used to stop a deadly threat, the objective is to cause immediate or timely incapacitation, not immediate or eventual death. After a person is no longer a threat, firing additional shots to make certain the person is dead can have serious legal consequences. Having the right to use deadly force to protect yourself from a deadly threat does not give you the right to commit murder.

HEAD SHOT: BRAIN STEM AND UPPER CERVICAL SPINE

To achieve combat effectiveness, the actions you take when facing a deadly threat need to neutralize the threat by causing immediate or timely incapacitation. A 4-inch group can be just as combat effective as a 2-inch group if you select the right aim point and your bullet penetrates far enough to reach the critical tissues.

If your aim point is the traditional center of mass, none of the shots that hit the aim point will cause immediate incapacitation, and most of them will not cause timely incapacitation because your chances of hitting critical tissue are very small. Center of mass is a good aim point if you are trying to qualify at the range, but it's not if you are trying to cause immediate or timely incapacitation.

The only two shots that reliably cause immediate incapacitation are those that penetrate the brain stem (midbrain, pons, and medulla oblongata) and the upper cervical spinal cord. The neck has seven cervical vertebrae, and the upper four—C1, C2, C3, and C4—are considered the upper cervical spine. C1 connects with an opening in the skull (occipital bone) called the *foramen magnum*. The upper cervical spine is the aim point, but the target is the upper cervical spinal cord.

The first cervical vertebra is just below the base of the skull when viewed from the back, and the last cervical vertebra (C7) is the bump you feel when you run your hand down the back of your neck. The third cervical vertebra is about level with the bottom of your chin when your head is level. The aim points for a head shot are the middle of the bridge of the nose, the ear canals (external auditory meatus), and the occipital protuberance (bump) above the foramen magnum.

When the ear canal is used as an aim point, any shot that misses and passes through facial bones, such as the jawbone (mandible), will not cause significant incapacitation. If a person is standing erect, a shot that goes slightly over the top of the ear will usually cause immediate or timely incapacitation. The aim point for a head shot is a 4-inch circle, but you have a margin of error because a bullet that is 1 or 2 inches high or low may still cause timely or immediate incapacitation.

To practice head shots, think of a 4-inch band going around the head that has an imaginary line dividing the top half from the bottom half. To position this band on the head, place the imaginary line over the middle of the bridge of the nose, over both ear canals, and over the occipital bump (protuberance), which is just above the juncture between the back of the skull and the neck. Regardless of where you are standing, the aim point is in the center of the part of the 4-inch band that is visible from your position. If you are standing in front of the head, the aim point would be the center of the bridge of the nose; if you are standing to the side, the aim point would be the ear canal; and if you are standing behind the head, the aim point would be the occipital bump. If you are standing at any other angle, the aim point would be somewhere between two of these standard aim points.

Bullets that penetrate the brain stem cause immediate incapacitation because of flaccid paralysis, which stops muscle contractions. Bullets that go just over the brain stem and hit the basal ganglia may cause immediate incapacitation because of a loss of consciousness and the inability to move. Even if they eventually cause incapacitation, bullets that hit higher parts of the brain might cause involuntary muscle contractions, as a result of reflex activity, that are strong enough to pull a trigger and kill a hostage. Besides causing quadriplegia (tetraplegia), a bullet that penetrates the upper spinal cord can cause death if damage to the phrenic nerve or paralysis of the intercostal muscles or diaphragm terminates normal breathing.

Bullets that sever the spinal cord below C4 may cause a loss of motor function below the level of the injury, and bullets that penetrate the carotid artery or jugular vein may cause death because of hemorrhage. Bullets that hit the windpipe (trachea) or cause profuse bleeding may obstruct breathing, but bullets that penetrate neck muscles might not cause any significant loss of function.

Because the brain is confined by the cranium, a sudden rise in intracranial pressure may cause immediate death, but high-velocity rifle bullets are more likely to have this effect than handgun bullets unless the end of the barrel is making solid contact with the head when the handgun is fired. Contact or near-contact wounds usually result from suicide or execution shootings.

The damage from a handgun bullet might be greater than expected if the bullet penetrates but fails to exit the skull and ricochets off the inner

Table 38

Law Enforcement Officers Feloniously Killed with Firearms

Location of Fatal Firearm Wound and Number of Victim Officers Wearing Body Armor, 2001–2010

Location of fatal firearm wound		Total	2001	2002	2003	2004	2005	2006	2007	2008
Number of victim officers killed with firearms	Total	**498**	**61**	**51**	**45**	**54**	**50**	**46**	**56**	**35**
	Front head	141	27	14	9	10	17	10	18	9
	Rear head	42	3	8	5	6	6	5	3	1
	Side head	62	4	7	7	7	2	5	7	8
	Neck/throat	45	3	3	5	3	5	7	2	5
	Front upper torso/chest	136	16	12	12	19	14	11	19	7
	Rear upper torso/back	21	3	1	3	0	2	3	5	7
	Front lower torso/stomach	31	5	3	3	4	3	2	1	1
	Rear lower torso/back	9	0	1	0	3	1	1	1	4
	Front below waist	5	0	1	1	0	0	2	0	0
	Rear below waist	4	0	1	0	2	0	0	0	0
	Arms/hands	0	0	0	0	0	0	0	0	0
	Fatal wound location not reported	2	0	0	0	0	0	0	0	0
Number of victim officers killed with firearms while wearing body armor	Total	**324**	**38**	**34**	**31**	**31**	**30**	**26**	**34**	**29**
	Front head	108	21	12	6	5	12	9	15	9
	Rear head	29	1	5	3	5	4	3	2	1
	Side head	47	2	4	5	3	2	3	7	6
	Neck/throat	36	3	3	4	3	3	4	1	4
	Front upper torso/chest	72	9	4	8	11	8	6	7	5
	Rear upper torso/back	7	1	0	1	0	0	1	1	1
	Front lower torso/stomach	15	1	3	3	1	1	0	0	3
	Rear lower torso/back	5	0	1	0	2	0	0	0	0
	Front below waist	2	0	1	1	0	0	0	1	0
	Rear below waist	3	0	0	0	1	0	0	0	0
	Arms/hands	0	0	0	0	0	0	0	0	0

surface (table) of the skull or glides along the inner surface. Bullets that hit but fail to penetrate the skull may cause fractures or concussions, and the severity of these injuries can range from minor damage to immediate incapacitation or death if the concussion affects the brain stem. Most handgun bullets will penetrate the skull if the angle of impact (incidence) is perpendicular or within 10 degrees of being perpendicular to the skull. If the angle of impact is parallel or within 10 degrees of being parallel to the skull, the bullet may cause only minor flesh damage and glance off.

Head shots are the only reliable way to cause immediate incapacitation, but most police departments do not teach them. Any police officer who can make a heart shot can make a head shot. Unlike the large-caliber lead balls used in flintlock pistols, modern defense ammunition will usually penetrate any part of the skull, including the frontal bone, if a bullet hits at or close to a 90-degree angle.

Rather than ignoring head shots, police departments should teach their officers how to make them. The aim point for a head shot and a heart shot are about the same size, and a lateral head shot is usually easier to make than a lateral heart shot. Knowing how to make head shots is a critical skill for tactical shooters. Criminals understand the value of head shots because about 40 percent of the people they kill with handguns are shot in the head, while only about 25 percent are shot in the heart.

As further proof that criminals have no problem making head shots, consider the FBI table on page 34. From 2001 to 2010, head shots accounted for about 49 percent of the law enforcement officers fatally wounded by criminals and about 57 percent of the officers wearing body armor who were fatally wounded by criminals.

Head shots might be mentioned as a possible defense against criminals who are wearing body armor, but most departments do not train officers to make head shots, often citing a lack of handgun skills as the reason. This argument is not entirely without merit, since, as we know, the average hit rate for police officers is only about 20 percent. What this argument does not explain is why the quality of police firearms training has not been improved.

One mistake most police departments make is training officers to hit frontal targets only, such as paper targets. In the real world, adversaries can be standing with their back or side facing you, instead of their front, or standing at angles somewhere between parallel and perpendicular. When your adversary is closer to being sideways than facing you, a head shot might be easier to make than a center-of-mass shot—which is a shot that is more likely to make your adversary angry or more aggressive than to cause immediate or timely incapacitation.

Another mistake police departments often make is not training officers to shoot adversaries who are using cover, such as a vehicle or a tree. When shooting from behind cover, people are more likely to expose their head than other parts of the body, and hitting the bridge of the nose or an ear canal is more likely to cause immediate incapacitation than hitting the upper part of the head or the lower jaw.

If you have one hand on your adversary's knife or gun and you are holding your gun in the other, it is safer to raise your gun and try to make a brain stem or upper-cervical-spine shot by shooting upward into the space under the chin than to use the bridge of your adversary's nose or an ear canal as your aim point. If someone is reaching for your gun, a pelvic or heart shot might be faster and easier.

By shooting upward, you can keep your elbow pointed down and use your forearm to protect your body while the other arm tries to control your adversary's weapon. If you cannot hit the space under the chin, try to hit the heart. If you are using a semiautomatic pistol, keep in mind that pressing the barrel against your adversary may push the slide back (out of battery) and prevent the gun from firing.

Head shots that are too high to hit the brain stem or basal ganglia can still damage critical tissues if they penetrate the cranium. The impact from a bullet hitting the outer surface of the cranium will be significant, and a bullet that hits the frontal bone at close to a perpendicular angle will probably penetrate the skull if the ammunition you are using can penetrate 10 percent ballistic gelatin at least 12 inches.

Bullets that hit the frontal bone have been known to glance off or stop before they penetrate the skull, but using ammunition that has good penetration will increase your chances of penetrating brain tissue and causing timely incapacitation. Bullets that tumble or ricochet within the skull will increase tissue damage.

Blunt trauma to the temporal area of the skull may cause unconsciousness or death if it fractures the temporal bone, ruptures a meningeal artery, and causes intracranial hemorrhage. A handgun bullet hits the body with about the same force as a fast-moving baseball, and just the impact from a bullet hitting the temple, which is weak and thin compared to other parts of the skull, can be fatal. The temporal region is not used as an aim point because a bullet that hits this area is less likely to cause immediate incapacitation than a bullet that hits the brain stem. Bullets that penetrate the temporal bone do not always cause death—in one case, a woman lived for three months after she shot herself in the temple.

HEART SHOT: HEART AND THORACIC SPINE

The heart shot aim point is a 4-inch circle near the center of the sternum and between a man's nipples. If you add the large blood vessels above the heart, such as the aorta (aortic arch), to the height of the heart, you can make the aim point a 5-inch-high by 4-inch-wide oval. Bullets that hit the aorta may cause more internal bleeding than bullets that hit the heart. Two-thirds of the heart is on the left side of the body, but shooting to the left reduces your chances of hitting the spinal cord.

Even if a bullet completely stops the heart, the body can remain functional for 10 to 15 seconds, which is more than enough time to return fire and cause a fatal gunshot wound. If the heart, aorta, or pulmonary arteries or veins are severely damaged, unconsciousness may occur in less than 30 seconds. Psychological factors or drug usage can affect how quickly a bullet that penetrates (enters) or perforates (enters and exits) your adversary's heart causes incapacitation.

Bullets that hit the heart do not always cause permanent incapacitation or death. Some people can stay conscious and functional for much longer than 15 seconds after a bullet penetrates the heart, and with immediate medical treatment, they might survive and fully recover. According to Doctors Stanley Wiener and John Barrett, who wrote *Trauma Management*, a high-velocity bullet (2,000 to 2,500 feet per second, or fps) that penetrates the heart may cause immediate incapacitation and death—but most handgun bullets will not have a similar effect. High-velocity rifle bullets are faster and produce much more kinetic energy than most handgun bullets, and rifle bullets have more of a tendency to travel sideways (yaw), tumble, or fragment than handgun bullets, which makes them more lethal.

When you are making a heart shot, the primary target is the heart, and the secondary target is the thoracic spine. If the target's shoulders are perpendicular to the path of your bullet, you will hit the heart before the spine if the target is facing you and the spine before the heart if you are standing behind him. A bullet that has shallow penetration might not penetrate the sternum, heart, and spine when the target is facing you or the vertebrae and heart when you are behind the target.

The anterior (front) aim point for the heart is the center of the sternum or the center of the chest, and the anterior (back) aim point is the center of the space between the scapulas. If the body is not covered by clothing, the spine can be used to establish the midline between the scapulas. The lateral aim point when the target is turned sideways is the lower border of the axilla (armpit).

The heart is below the middle of the sternum, and more is on the left side of the midline than on the right. A line drawn between the nipples on a male will cross near the bottom of the heart, but a method similar to the one first responders use to locate the heart when doing cardiopulmonary resuscitation can also be used, and this method applies to both males or females.

To use this method, locate the lower end of your sternum (xiphoid process) with the tip of the middle finger and touch the sternum with the index finger. If you are using the right hand, your palm will be facing inward, and the middle index finger will point left. The top edge of the right index finger will be near the bottom of the heart. The average heart is about 5 inches long, 3 inches wide, and 2.5 inches thick, and is tilted to the right, with two-thirds of the heart on the left side of the body.

It may improve combat effectiveness to move the aim point for a heart to your right when facing the target or to the left when standing behind the target because more of the heart is to the left than to the right, but firing two or three quick shots at the aim point is usually a better solution. It is easier to make small adjustments when punching holes in a stationary target than it is when shooting at a moving three-dimensional target during a gunfight.

If the front, back, or side of a body is not perpendicular to the path of your bullet, repositioning the aim points during a gunfight can be hard. One method is to visualize where a laser beam would need to enter the body to hit the tissues you are shooting at and make this your aim point. Most aim points have a small margin of error, and firing two or more shots at the same aim point will increase your combat effectiveness. Having an aim point in mind before you align your gun will be faster than pointing your gun at someone and then searching for an aim point.

Bullets that hit the sternum at an angle between 0 and 10 degrees may glance off or ricochet instead of penetrating the sternum. Bullets that hit the sternum at an angle between 80 and 90 degrees will usually penetrate the sternum and enter the chest. If your adversary is standing sideways, a head shot might be a better option than a heart shot regardless of which way the head is turned.

A heart shot is considered the primary target and the thoracic spine the secondary target because a bullet that severs the spinal cord seldom causes more than partial incapacitation but a bullet that completely stops the heart may cause total incapacitation in 10 to 15 seconds. Additional shots to the spine will not make a spinal shot more effective after the spine has been severed, but additional shots can make a heart shot more effective and reduce the time it takes for bleeding to reduce blood flow and cause shock or termination of brain functions.

Since a frontal heart-spine shot can be made when the gun is angled upward or downward, a bullet that penetrates the heart and spine while angled upward would hit the thoracic spine at a higher level and be more likely to disable the arms than a bullet that hits the heart and thoracic spine while angled downward.

If you are entering a dangerous situation that might result in serious injuries, try to arrange for immediate load-and-go transport to the nearest hospital before you get injured. Timely surgical intervention will improve your chances of being able to survive a gunshot wound to the heart. Reducing the time it takes to arrive at a hospital (scoop and run) is more important than being treated on the scene.

PELVIC SHOT: PELVIS AND LUMBAR SPINE

To make a pelvic shot more effective when using a handgun, this aim point does not extend below the upper edge of the sacrum. The pelvis—a basin-shaped bony structure formed by the innominate bones, sacrum, and coccyx—supports the spinal column. The hip joints, which are on the lateral sides of the pelvis, are the articulations between the pelvis and the head of the femurs. Unlike a bullet from a high-powered rifle, a handgun bullet that hits the pelvis is unlikely to shatter bone or cause instability, but it may cause death weeks after the injury.

Causing immobility with a handgun by fracturing the hip joint, which is the articulation between the acetabulum and the head of the femur, or the lateral pelvis, is possible but unlikely. The hip joint is hard to hit because it's small (about 2 inches in diameter) and hard to see even when it's not covered by clothing. Many people cannot find their own hip joints. Handgun bullets that strike the hip joint seldom cause significant instability unless they break the neck of the femur, and they would need to break the pelvis in two places to cause major pelvic instability.

When viewed from the front or back, the aim point for a pelvic shot is the juncture between the fourth and fifth lumbar vertebrae, which is located at about the same level as the top of the pelvis (iliac crests). You will not damage the 18-inch spinal cord because it ends at the lower border of the first lumbar vertebrae, but you may damage a collection of spinal nerve roots called the *cauda equina,* which descends from the bottom of the spinal cord. Damage to these nerves can affect leg or foot movements and may cause paraplegia. Handgun bullets are more likely to penetrate than fracture the pelvis, but a bullet that hits the lower lumbar spine or the top edge of the sacrum may cause instability between the spine and sacrum.

If a pelvic shot misses spinal nerves, it might rupture a major blood vessel, such as an iliac artery or the abdominal aorta. Severing the abdominal aorta may cause unconsciousness in less than 60 seconds. This aim point is close to where the aorta and the inferior vena cava split into two branches and descend into the legs.

Even if a large blood vessel is severely damaged, a bullet that severs large blood vessels or spinal nerves will not incapacitate the upper body or prevent people from shooting at you with a gun, although it may cause them to fall down, disturb their aim, or buy you some extra time to find cover or take some follow-up shots. A pelvic shot is more likely to be effective against a knife than a gun, and it might be useful against someone who is wearing a bullet-resistant (ballistic) vest.

A pelvic shot makes it easier to watch someone's hands than using a brain or heart shot because the barrel of your handgun will be pointed downward if both you and your adversary are standing. If you are drawing your gun, the pelvis will be the first aim point available as you lift your gun upward. If you miss the pelvic aim point, a high miss will usually be more effective than a low miss.

Calling a pelvic shot a belt buckle shot is almost meaningless because people do not always wear belt buckles in the same place. Highly renowned medical examiner Vincent J.M. Di Maio considered the pelvis a good target, but *Jim Cirillo's Tales of the Stakeout Squad* gives one example where belt-buckle shots were not very effective. One of the members of the New York Stakeout Squad, George Ballinger, was involved in a gunfight during which he shot a suspect (armed robber) five times in the vicinity of the belt buckle with a handgun and the suspect did not go down. Rather than fire more shots, Ballinger charged the suspect and knocked him down, which gave his partner a chance to get the suspect's gun. The book does not explain why these five shots, which were probably fired from a .38 Special revolver, did not cause incapacitation, but a plausible conclusion is that none of them caused serious neurologic damage or severe bleeding. The suspect died a couple of hours later.

The aim point for a pelvic-lumbar-spine shot is easier to find than the hip joint. When facing the front or back of your adversary, the aim point is where the midline of the body and a horizontal line drawn a few inches below the top of the hip bones (iliac crest) cross. If someone is sideways, using this aim point or hitting the hip joint will be harder and less effective than making a head or heart shot.

Depending on the difference between the height of your gun and the height of your target, a bullet angled downward should hit spinal nerves somewhere near L5 or S1. A shot made from behind the target might be easier to make than a shot made while in front of the target because the spinal column can help you locate the midline if the upper body is not covered by heavy clothing.

After you make a pelvic-lumbar spine shot, some people recommend making one follow-up shot to the heart and one to the head. If you have just drawn your gun, this sequence will be faster than a head-heart-pelvis sequence. Another option would be to fire additional shots at the pelvic-lumbar-spine aim point. If your adversary is wearing a bullet-resistant vest, a pelvic shot might be useful as preparation for a head shot if it causes your adversary to look down and pause.

Cirillo thought the pelvis was a good aim point, especially when using a high-velocity rifle or a shotgun and hitting the buttocks, but his personal preference was a head shot. According to *Jim Cirillo's Tales of the Stakeout Squad*, Cirillo's nickname was "the Brain Surgeon" because he made so many head shots. The nickname for an officer who liked pelvic shots was "Proctologist."

A pelvic shot might cause psychological incapacitation because of fear, pain, or the awareness of being shot, which might prompt someone to surrender. The ideal pelvic shot would sever nerves and cause a loss of motor control below the level of the wound, damage the lumbar spine or sacrum and cause spinal instability, or rupture the descending aorta just above the iliac arteries and cause severe bleeding. If the descending aorta is severed, unconsciousness might occur within 30 seconds.

TARGETING AIM POINTS

The effective aim points are harder to hit than shooting at center of mass when someone is facing you, but you can improve your chances of hitting them by shooting twice at the same aim point and by aiming at the body's midline.

If a shot is high or low, aiming at the midline of the body will increase your chances of hitting the brain stem, spinal cord, or heart if you are facing the front or back of your target. The upper cervical spine is used as an aim point, but hitting a vertebra and missing the spinal cord might not cause incapacitation. When your target is sideways, aiming for midline can help you hit the heart or the brain stem.

Visual aim points should be as precise as possible under the circumstances, but do not waste time trying to get a perfect sight picture. Trying to shoot with the accuracy you need to win a target-shooting competition can get you killed in a high-speed, high-stress, close-quarter, low-light, or no-light deadly confrontation.

Most police officers are not required to shoot targets that are standing sideways or with their back exposed, and most police departments do not mention that a target may be moving and you may need to lead the target a few inches. Using realistic aim points can help you become a better tactical shooter, but knowing how to use these aim points under a wide variety of circumstances is also important.

Anyone hoping to use the aim points listed in this chapter with a minimum level of competence should be able to put one shot in a 4-inch circle at 21 feet or less in 1.5 seconds or less when starting with the gun already in your hand. This will give you a good chance of hitting these aim points regardless of whether you are in front of, behind, or to the side of your target. Being able to hit a smaller circle at the same distance will improve your chances of surviving a gunfight.

Visualizing an aim point as a small spot instead of a larger circle may improve your accuracy (aim small, miss small). All the aim points have a small margin of error, which means even a near miss can be combat effective.

One-shot stops with a handgun are not completely a myth, but being able to make one requires good shot placement. The brain stem and upper cervical spinal cord are not easy targets to hit with a handgun during a deadly confrontation.

When people use a handgun to commit suicide, the muzzle is often pressed hard against the head, and the gunshot rapidly increases intracranial pressure. A contact head shot made with a high-velocity handgun bullet is more likely to cause massive tissue damage than one made with a low-velocity bullet. Most contact head shots are instantly fatal, but some people survive for months. Contact head shots from a shotgun or high-velocity rifle are almost always fatal. If the muzzle does not make contact with the head, the permanent wound cavity made by a .22 rimfire can look similar to one that is made by a .45 ACP. A .22 rimfire is seldom used for self-defense, but with good shot placement, most of them can be lethal.

Contact wounds are more likely to occur when handguns are used to commit suicide or carry out an execution than when they are used for self-defense, but the possibility does exist. If someone standing in front of you tries to grab your gun, your best option might be to block with your non-dominant hand, step back, and make a *near-contact* head shot. If you make a contact shot with a semiautomatic pistol, you may push the slide out of battery and prevent the gun from firing.

You could also use a near-contact head shot if you approach from behind someone who is pointing a gun at a hostage. Unlike heart shots, head shots cause immediate incapacitation and can stop someone from pulling a trigger. Heart shots can be useful when they are easier to make than head shots, and you can use them to slow someone down long enough to make head shots. A good sequence is two quick heart shots followed immediately by two quick head shots.

Head shots cause immediate incapacitation, but making them when facing multiple adversaries might be harder than making heart shots. If you cannot make head shots, use heart shots and hope your adversaries do not have time to return fire. To reduce the risks of getting shot, shoot the most immediate deadly threat first, learn how to make head shots, use cover, and avoid standing still.

UNEXPECTED INCAPACITATION

Reliable shot placement depends on disruption of the central nervous system because of trauma to the brain stem or spinal cord, disruption of the circulatory system because of trauma to the heart or large blood vessels, disruption of the respiratory system because of trauma to the central nervous system or the circulatory system, or a biomechanical disruption because of trauma to soft-tissue or bony structures. It is possible but not likely that a handgun bullet penetrating only one lung will cause enough tissue damage to stop normal breathing.

The relationship between bullet wounds and incapacitation becomes less predictable when incapacitation is unexpected or far more extensive than similar gunshot wounds would normally cause. Cases have been reported in which people with a minor wound or no wound have dropped to the ground shortly after a gunshot is fired. Some people do so because it makes them a smaller target or because they are frightened, but others drop because they faint (syncope).

Shock

Shock, which is a state of inadequate blood supply (perfusion) to the brain that affects the entire body, is one condition that might cause almost immediate incapacitation because of a minor wound or no wound. When caused by a bullet, shock is usually the result of bleeding and low blood volume (hypovolemic shock).

The four specific kinds of shock that may be caused by a gunshot wound are psychogenic, neurogenic, spinal, and hemorrhagic.

Psychogenic Shock

Fainting (syncope) is classified as psychogenic, not neurogenic, shock. Both conditions are caused by a generalized vascular dilation and a reduction of blood supply to the brain, but psychogenic shock is caused by psychological factors, such as severe pain or the sight of blood, and neurogenic shock is caused by factors such as cerebral or spinal-cord trauma. Strong emotions—including anger, rage, hate, or determination—might reduce the perception of pain and counteract psychogenic shock, but they are less likely to mitigate neurogenic shock. People who did not realize they were shot may not show symptoms of psychogenic shock until someone points out they have been shot or are bleeding.

Neurologic Shock

Neurologic shock can result from cerebral trauma or a spinal cord injury and cause a loss of blood pressure (hypotension), but spinal-cord injuries can also cause spinal shock, which disrupts the nerve supply below the level of the injury and causes an immediate but temporary loss of sensory and motor activity, which might last an hour or less. But such a temporary loss of reflex activity and paralysis might cause enough incapacitation to stop a knife or gun attack.

Hemorrhagic Shock

A gunshot that damages an organ, such as the liver or spleen, or ruptures a large blood vessel, such as the abdominal aorta, may cause hemorrhagic shock if blood loss (hemorrhage) causes a rapid reduction in blood flow to the brain. Shock results when about one-fifth to one-third of the blood volume is lost rapidly, and death results when about half the blood volume is lost rapidly (exsanguination).

Shooting for center of mass might result in causing enough blood loss to induce hemorrhagic shock, but this is unpredictable because you have no way of knowing what organs or blood vessels will be hit or how much blood loss will occur. Even if you hit the liver, which is a large organ on the upper right side of the abdominal cavity, you can't know if hemorrhagic shock will occur or how long it will take if it does occur. Multiple shots to the center of mass can miss the organs or large blood vessels that might cause profuse bleeding.

VOLUNTARY INCAPACITATION

Unlike immediate or timely incapacitation, during which force is used to end a threat, voluntary incapacitation occurs because the person threatening you with deadly force stops the attack or decides to surrender. The main problems with surrender are (1) people who surrender can change their mind, and (2) some people pretend to surrender to gain a tactical advantage.

Unexpected incapacitation can also result from unintended injuries. If a bullet enters a kidney or knee when you are aiming at the heart, the unintended wound may stop a deadly threat because of excruciating pain or a loss of mobility. A kidney wound may cause someone to drop a gun because of the pain, and a knee wound may stop a knife attack because of a decrease in mobility. Unintended wounds may cause incapacitation, but recommending that a difficult target, such as a kidney or knee, be used instead of a standard aim point would not be reasonable.

REASONABLE FORCE

Although it's reasonable to continue shooting until you believe that a deadly threat has ended, no one can tell you exactly where the line is between (1) shooting enough times to stop someone from being a threat and (2) using excessive force because you continued shooting after the threat was gone. A deadly criminal may continue to function normally for several minutes after being shot multiple times, and it takes only a fraction of a second to return fire and make one fatal shot. Even if numerous bullets hit a target, none may cause incapacitation.

People who have no comprehension of human physiology or who have their own personal agendas are often quick to claim that a person was shot more times than was necessary, even though they have no idea how many shots were needed to neutralize the threat. Even after an autopsy, medical examiners are not always certain which particular shot was the cause of death or whether it was the first or last one fired.

It is difficult to know if you have hit a major blood vessel, and some people with multiple gunshot wounds to the upper torso have managed to leave the scene because none of the shots caused serious damage to the heart or major blood vessels. Contrary to folklore, this can happen even after being hit multiple times with a .45 ACP because shot placement is usually more significant than caliber.

For most people in most situations, an upper-torso heart shot with the center of the sternum used as the aim point will be the best option, and a three-shot burst is more likely to be combat effective than a single shot. Based on crime scene reports and medical studies, it is hard to say how many shots are excessive or unreasonable, but claims that excessive force was used are seldom based on logic or science. If three shots at the heart do not produce visible effects, more shots at the same aim point or at a different aim point might be reasonable and necessary.

Firing two or three quick shots should be viewed as a tactical guideline, not a universal rule. The number of shots fired and the aim points used need to be compatible with your circumstances. If you shoot three times and the person continues to attack, keep shooting at the same or different aim points until the attack stops. If your attacker drops to the ground and surrenders after one shot, more shots will not be needed unless he renews the attack.

As a precaution, do not assume that someone who has surrendered is no longer a dangerous threat. If possible, stay behind cover, be prepared to shoot again if necessary, maintain situational awareness, and wait for backup. If for some reason you need to approach the person on the ground, do it with extreme caution, remove any visible weapons, try to find and remove any weapons that are not visible, and be prepared for the unexpected. Relaxing too soon is a fatal mistake that far too many police officers have made.

TACTICAL ANATOMY

Firearms training that ignores tactical anatomy and shot placement is more about target shooting than tactical shooting. At best, most police firearms training is mediocre, but few things make it look worse than the poor correlation between traditional center-of-mass targets and human anatomy.

If you are going to develop tactical skills that will help you survive deadly confrontations by using a handgun for self-defense, you need to know exactly what your targets are and what you can expect if you hit them. Even when using the best defense ammunition, without intelligent shot placement, a handgun might be less combat effective than a knife, broken bottle, baseball bat, or steel pipe.

For a handgun to be an effective self-defense weapon, you need high-quality ammunition, tactical shooting skills, and a good understanding of shot placement. Using a high-quality handgun is also essential, but compared to the days of the Old West, you have many options to choose from because a large number of companies make handguns that are functional, reliable, and designed for self-defense.

Tactical anatomy and physiology are not the only avenues that need to be explored when trying to improve the quality of firearms training, but they are clearly among the most important. Regardless of how accurate your shooting is, hitting the wrong aim point can get you killed just as quickly as missing the entire target. This is a proven fact that no competent tactical shooter can afford to ignore.

Three things that make police firearms training ineffective are using the isosceles stance, shooting nothing but stationary targets, and making the center of mass the only aim point. Silhouette targets that give you more points for hitting an X-ring that represents the center of mass than for hitting the head ignore the fact that hitting the brain stem or the upper cervical spinal cord is the only reliable way to cause immediate incapacitation. A bullet that stops the heart takes at least 10 to 15 seconds to cause incapacitation.

A reason that's often given for not teaching head shots is that head shots are impossible to make during a deadly confrontation, and this might be true if you are trying to focus on your front sight. Even if you ignore research that shows it's nearly impossible for people to focus on something close, such as the front sight, when something farther away or moving unexpectedly threatens your life, you need to consider Hick's law: *As the number of alternatives increases, the time it takes to respond also increases.* When using a front-sight focus, your mind is constantly trying to decide which is more important: focus on the front sight or focus on the target to see if you have a shoot-or-don't-shoot situation. Regrettably, the human eye cannot focus on the front sight and on your target at the same time. If you use a target focus, you can direct all your attention onto your target and avoid making unnecessary decisions that only increase your response time.

ANTERIOR AND POSTERIOR AIM POINTS

Aim point one: brain stem and the upper cervical spine. The size of the aim point is a 4-inch circle, which includes the brain stem and upper cervical spine, and the crosshairs represent the center of the circle. A bullet that goes slightly over the top of the brain stem may hit the basal ganglia, and one that goes below the head may hit the neck. Penetrating the brain stem or upper cervical spinal cord above C4 causes immediate incapacitation, penetrating the basal ganglia usually causes immediate incapacitation, and hitting the neck may cause timely incapacitation.

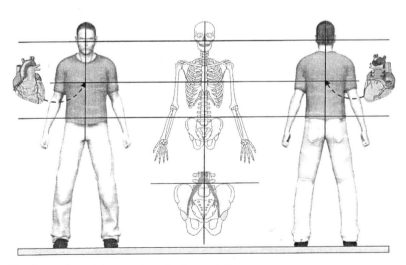

The three aim points are where the lines cross.

Aim point two: heart, major blood vessels near the heart (such as the aorta and vena cava), and the thoracic spine. The size of this aim point is a 4-inch circle, but you could also use an oval 5 inches high by 4 inches wide if you add the large blood vessels above the heart to the height of the heart. A bullet that hits the aorta may cause incapacitation faster than a bullet that penetrates the heart.

Aim point three: first sacral vertebrae, lumbar vertebrae, and blood vessels, such as the abdominal aorta or iliac artery. The size of the aim point is a 4-inch circle, and the center of the aim point is the juncture between the fourth and fifth lumbar vertebrae. This juncture and the top of the pelvis (iliac crests) are about the same level. The only part of the pelvis located within the aim point is the upper sacrum, and the lateral aim point is approximate and does not include the hip joint.

LATERAL AIM POINTS AND CENTER OF MASS

The three primary aim points are where the lines cross. The heart is harder to hit from the side than from the front or back because the width is slightly less and it might be covered by the arm. The lateral pelvic aim point does not include the hip joint, and the spine and large blood vessels are more vulnerable than the sacrum. A head shot is often easier to make than a lateral heart or pelvic shot.

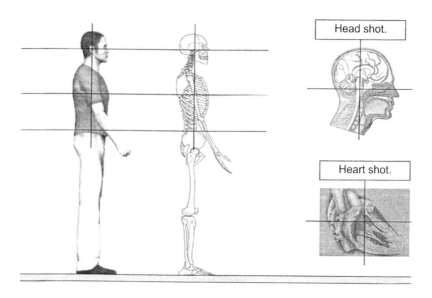

Head shot.

Heart shot.

The areas enclosed by ovals, (illustrated below, are often included as part of the center of mass. Multiple hits to these areas are unlikely to stop a deadly threat unless a bullet hits a large blood vessel or the spinal cord. If the torso is also part of the center of mass, a bullet that penetrates only one lung is unlikely to cause timely incapacitation.

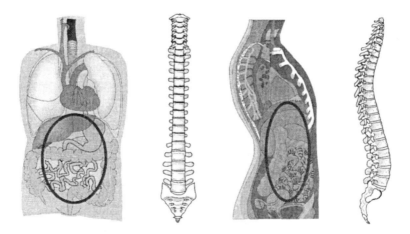

BRAIN STEM AND UPPER
CERVICAL SPINE AIM POINTS

The only way to cause immediate incapacitation with a handgun is to fire a bullet that penetrates the brain stem or upper cervical spine. Despite the belief that a head shot is not practical, the size of the aim point for a head shot is about the same as the size of the aim point for a heart shot. To be combat effective, you must be able to make head shots from different angles, and the illustrations on the following page show the brain stem and upper cervical spine aim points from different angles. Making a lateral head shot can be easier than making a lateral heart or pelvic shot.

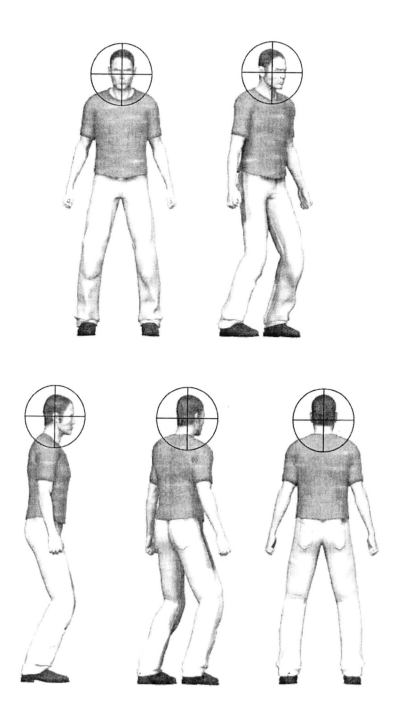

SUMMARY

If you are facing an imminent deadly threat and you want to use a handgun to cause physical incapacitation as soon as possible, the four essential elements are represented by the acronym ASAP:

A—Aim point: only a head shot will cause immediate incapacitation.

S—Speed: you must shoot before your adversary shoots (quick or dead).

A—Accuracy: you need to have combat-effective shot placement.

P—Penetration: the bullet must reach the brain stem or upper cervical spine.

A heart shot with a handgun is unlikely to cause immediate incapacitation because even if a bullet stops the heart, it usually takes at least 10 to 15 seconds before the shooting victim becomes dysfunctional. This 10 or more seconds of functionality explains why police officers have been shot to death by criminals after they shot the criminals through the heart. Furthermore, a handgun bullet is much less likely to stop the heart than a bullet from a high-velocity rifle.

Under ideal conditions, a pelvic shot might cause immobility, but it will not cause immediate incapacitation or prevent someone from shooting you with a gun. A pelvic shot is unlikely to be effective unless you are facing the front or back of your adversary because the lower lumbar spine, upper sacrum, and iliac arteries are protected by the pelvis when your adversary is sideways. Since knowing exactly where the hip joint is located when it's covered by clothing is almost impossible and hitting the hip joint with a handgun bullet does not always cause dysfunction, a lateral pelvic shot aimed at the hip joint might not decrease stability or mobility.

Most police departments teach their officers to shoot at center of mass even though numerous cases have occurred where multiple shots to the torso with large-caliber handgun bullets did not stop a criminal from killing a police officer. It's hard to say how many officers have been killed because no head shots were taken when criminals were close enough to easily make these shots—such as when a criminal is trying to take your partner's handgun—but almost every police officer who was killed after making multiple center-of-mass hits would not have been killed if just one of those multiple center-of-mass shots had been a head shot.

In the 2004 shootout between Los Angeles Police Department officers and two bank robbers, the officers fired about 650 rounds at the robbers, who were heavily armed and wearing body armor but no head protection. If the officers had tried to make head shots instead of center-of-mass shots, the situation might have ended in less than 44 minutes. Even if the robbers were wearing ballistic helmets, it's doubtful the helmets would have protected the bridge of the nose, and some ballistic helmets do not protect the ear canal or the upper cervical spine.

DEFENSE AMMUNITION

If shot placement is good, the most important characteristic that ammunition can have is adequate penetration. If a bullet does not penetrate deeply enough to reach critical tissues, the tissue damage that results might not be serious enough to cause incapacitation or keep your adversary from killing you. Compared to shot placement and penetration, any other properties a bullet might possess are less important. Even the relatively ineffective .22 short can kill someone if shot placement is good and the bullet has enough penetration to reach critical tissues.

That being said, you need every advantage you can get in a gunfight, and some ammunition gives you a slight advantage over other ammunition. We are not going to perpetuate the myth that good ammunition is more important than shot placement or that any handgun ammunition guarantees knock-down power or one-shot stops when you make a center-of-mass hit, but we will give you some realistic guidelines for selecting the best possible defense ammunition.

Determining what kind of ammunition you should not use is easier than determining what kind will be most effective. Exclude ammunition that has more recoil than a user can manage when trying to make quick and accurate follow-up shots. Other factors that can make ammunition unsuitable are unreliability or poor accuracy. Most modern defense ammunition is reliable and sufficiently accurate, but some handguns are more accurate and less prone to malfunction when using one type of ammunition as compared to another.

Seven basic principles that will make this chapter easier to understand:

1. Good ammunition will not compensate for poor shot placement.
2. Other than brain stem or upper spinal cord hits, one-shot stops seldom occur.
3. Gunshot wounds to the heart do not cause immediate incapacitation.

4. Single factors such as velocity or muzzle energy do not guarantee effectiveness.
5. No single bullet design will give optimal performance in every situation.
6. Jacketed hollowpoints (JHP) are usually the best choice for self-defense.
7. The most important factors in a gunfight are shot placement and penetration.

Flintlock pistols can be extremely effective with good shot placement, and modern pistols with the best defense ammunition can be ineffective without good shot placement. Unlike the military definition of incapacitation (killing the enemy or stopping him from functioning as a normal soldier), the civilian definition means using force—including deadly force—to stop someone from posing an immediate deadly threat and causing serious bodily harm or death.

Immediate incapacitation means the threat ends almost the instant a bullet penetrates critical tissues, and *timely incapacitation* means the threat ends before the person being threatened with deadly force can be harmed. Incapacitation does not always cause death, although death may occur almost instantly in some cases but not until minutes, hours, or weeks after incapacitation in other cases.

Since the reason for using defense ammunition is to cause incapacitation, the quality of the ammunition can be measured by using this criterion. If ammunition has adequate penetration, a large number of secondary factors (such as caliber or expansion) can give you a small but significant advantage in a gunfight, whereas some factors (such as excessive recoil or unreliability) can put you at a disadvantage. This chapter is not going to tell you exactly what kind of ammunition you should use, but it will give you the information you need to make intelligent choices.

Any compromise that involves reducing penetration in favor of any other factor is usually a poor choice unless you have special needs, such as being an air marshal and requiring ammunition that produces large, shallow wounds. Since adequate penetration is usually more important than expansion, especially when trying to reach critical tissues that are protected by bone, adequate expansion should be your primary concern and good expansion your secondary concern.

Because the Hague Convention of 1899 prohibited the use of expanding bullets in international warfare, the U.S. military generally uses ammunition with full-metal jackets (FMJ), which is also called *ball ammunition*. Based on extensive research, there is no doubt ball ammunition will cause incapacitation or death. Contrary to what some people believe, FMJ bullets with good penetration are more effective than JHP bullets with poor penetration, especially if the JHP bullets fail to expand, which is often the case.

Although expansion tends to reduce penetration, some companies produce ammunition that provides both adequate penetration and good expansion, and any reputable company that claims to be producing high-quality defense ammunition should also be able to tell you what standards its ammunition meets. Most of the best defense ammunition meets at least some of the FBI penetration standards.

As a rule, increasing the velocity of a bullet tends to increase the recoil, but a handgun that does not have enough recoil to knock the user over is unlikely to have enough force to knock people over who get shot. This includes the famous *Dirty Harry* .44 Magnum, which is a very difficult handgun to manage because of recoil and is not likely to knock anyone over except on television or in the movies.

Since one-shot stops are rare unless you penetrate the brain stem or upper cervical spine, causing incapacitation usually requires one or more follow-up shots. If you are unable to make these follow-up shots with speed and accuracy because you cannot manage the recoil your handgun produces, you are putting yourself at a serious disadvantage. Heavy recoil can also put you at a disadvantage when facing multiple adversaries and trying to make two or more quick, consecutive shots.

If you are choosing between a 9mm and a .45 ACP and you cannot manage the recoil from a .45 ACP, the 9mm is a better choice. Two well-placed follow-up shots from a 9mm are more combat effective than one poorly placed follow-up shot from a .45 ACP. If you are using a handgun with a heavy recoil that causes shaking, flinching, or blinking, even the first shot from a 9mm might be more accurate than the first shot from a .45 ACP.

If you are going to use defense ammunition you believe will outperform ball ammunition, you need to be familiar with what you are using. This means you need to know what it feels like to shoot it, and you need to know whether it's accurate and reliable when used in your self-defense handgun. Since defense ammunition tends to be expensive compared to practice ammunition, many people practice with cheap ammunition but then load their handguns with defense ammunition they have never fired.

Being in the middle of a gunfight is the wrong time to discover your defense ammunition has more recoil than you can easily manage or it causes your gun to malfunction. Police officers who qualify using inexpensive practice ammunition are often surprised to find the ammunition they normally carry on duty behaves much differently from the ammunition they used to qualify. For a qualification to have any meaning, you need to qualify with the ammunition you carry on duty. This could partially explain why there is no correlation between the ways police officers perform on the range and how they perform during a deadly confrontation.

Despite some of their excellent qualities, even the best hollowpoints cannot guarantee immediate incapacitation unless the bullet hits the brain stem or the upper cervical spine. Since the brain and body may continue to function for 10 to 15 seconds after the heart stops, there is more than enough time for someone to return fire. In *Gunshot Wounds*, Dr. Vincent Di Maio, a forensic pathologist and gunshot wound expert, discusses a case where a man whose heart was shredded by a shotgun blast still managed to run 65 feet before he collapsed. A bullet that penetrates the brain stem or upper cervical spinal cord causes immediate incapacitation and eventual death, but a bullet that penetrates the frontal lobes of the brain, which are behind the frontal bone (forehead), may give someone enough time to return fire.

A bullet that punctures the heart or severs a major artery may not cause any degree of incapacitation until blood loss reaches about 20 percent to 30 percent of the body's total blood supply, and it seldom becomes life-threatening until blood loss reaches about 50 percent. Incapacitation and death from hemorrhaging can occur anywhere from seconds to hours, and handgun bullets are much less likely to cause severe hemorrhaging than high-velocity rifle bullets or shotgun slugs.

Ammunition effectiveness has been a controversial topic for many decades, and countless hours have been spent arguing over stopping power or one-shot-stops. Many of these arguments are based on hearsay more than scientific facts.

Rather than recommend specific companies, this book is going to establish some basic guidelines that will help you decide which kind of ammunition is best for your situation. Such companies as Speer, Federal, Remington, Winchester, Cor-Bon, or Hornady make a wide variety of defense ammunition that will satisfy almost anyone's needs, and they are constantly improving their products.

Much of the confusion relating to handgun ammunition is based on the mistaken belief that high-velocity rifle bullets and high-velocity handgun bullets travel at similar speeds and produce similar wounds. The bullets from a rifle can travel faster than 3,000 fps and they pulverize tissue, whereas the bullets from a handgun seldom travel faster than 1,500 fps and they crush tissue.

To grasp what you can reasonably expect from a handgun bullet, you need to understand the factors that affect performance. The primary factors are penetration, permanent wound cavity, temporary wound cavity, and caliber. The secondary factors are expansion, fragmentation, tumble, muzzle energy, and recoil. Some of these factors—including penetration, caliber, expansion, and recoil—were briefly discussed elsewhere in the book.

Combat effectiveness is determined by shot placement and how a bullet interacts with human tissue as it travels through a body. Other than bullets that penetrate the brain stem or upper cervical spinal cord, two identical bullets hitting similar tissues might not have the same effect because of differences in anatomy, physiology, emotions, general health, or drug use. Even the best shot placement with the best ammunition can produce unexpected results.

Shot placement can refer to the first shot or follow-up shots. In most cases, a tactical shooter should try to fire at least one rapid two-shot burst at each target, such as one heart shot and one head shot or two head shots.

Primary Factors

1. Penetration: distance bullet travels through human tissue.
2. Permanent wound cavity: area caused by the bullet crushing the tissue.
3. Temporary wound cavity: area caused by the bullet stretching the tissue.
4. Caliber: diameter of bullet measured in inches or millimeters.

Secondary Factors

1. Muzzle energy: the kinetic energy a bullet has when it leaves the barrel.
2. Expansion: increase in diameter as a bullet travels through tissue.
3. Tumble: tilting of a bullet's long axis as it travels through tissue.
4. Fragmentation: secondary missiles caused by bullet or bone fragments.
5. Recoil: backward momentum (kick) that equals a bullet's forward momentum.

PENETRATION

You cannot damage critical tissue unless your bullet has enough penetration to reach it. At least 12 inches of penetration in 10-percent ballistic (ordnance) gelatin is a minimum standard for defense ammunition, but more than 18 inches of penetration would probably not increase combat effectiveness.

Less penetration might be acceptable if you are shooting at the heart while facing the front or back of the target. If you are facing the side of your target and a bullet needs to penetrate the dense bone in the upper arm (humerus) to reach the heart or your target is abnormally large, muscular, or fat, less than 12 inches of penetration might prevent the bullet from reaching the heart.

Having a bullet reach the heart is essential, but having a bullet perforate the heart will increase potential tissue damage. When a bullet perforates the heart, it not only enters the organ, it also exits it. Bullets that enter and exit are more likely to pierce both walls in a heart chamber or pierce several heart chambers than bullets that penetrate far enough to reach the heart but stop before they exit.

The risk of penetrating a target (overpenetration) and hitting a bystander is relatively small compared to the risk of missing a target and hitting a bystander with a bullet or bullet fragment. Even if a bullet exits the body, it might not have enough kinetic energy left to injure another person. When passing through a human body, JHP bullets normally lose kinetic energy faster than roundnose (elliptical ogive) bullets, and bullets are often trapped in the body because their velocity is not sufficient to overcome the resistance offered by skin.

PERMANENT WOUND CAVITY

The permanent wound cavity is the cavity produced by the crushing force of a bullet as it travels through human tissue, and the size of this cavity is a good measure of how much tissue damage a bullet has caused. Enhancing penetration can increase the length and volume of the permanent wound cavity.

If penetration is the same, you can increase the size of the permanent wound cavity by increasing the caliber of the bullet or by using bullets that expand as they pass through tissue. The increases in tissue damage you get from using a larger caliber or a bullet that mushrooms are usually less than those you get by increasing penetration. Bullets also need good penetration to reach critical tissues.

A 9mm hollowpoint bullet that mushrooms can reach the same diameter as a .45 ACP that does not expand, and a .45 ACP bullet that mushrooms will have a larger diameter than a .45 ACP that does not expand. Since 9mm hollowpoint bullets do not always expand, the most reliable way to produce a slightly larger permanent wound cavity is to use a .45 ACP bullet instead.

Hollowpoint bullets do not always expand because materials, such as heavy clothing, fill the opening in the tip of the bullet. To keep this from happening, Hornady has developed an ammunition line called Critical Duty that reduces the risk of not having expansion if a bullet passes through clothing or other barriers before it hits human tissue. To encourage expansion, the bullet has a special soft tip that initiates expansion by being pushed into the hollow cavity upon impact. As the soft tip is being pushed inward, it swells and expands the opening in the bullet.

A .45 ACP that expands can give you a larger permanent wound cavity, but it can also create a problem if you cannot manage the heavy recoil produced by most .45 ACP hollowpoints. Since one-shot stops are largely a myth—with the exception of a well-placed brain stem or upper cervical spine shot—you will normally need to fire more than one shot if you want to incapacitate someone with any handgun. If heavy recoil prevents you from firing follow-up shots accurately and quickly, you will probably be more combat effective with a caliber that produces less recoil. A good compromise for many people is a .40-caliber S&W, which is only .05-inch smaller than a .45 ACP and usually has less recoil.

Since most of the primary targets for shot placement are protected by bony structures—such as the cranium, sternum, rib cage, or spinal column—hollowpoint bullets must be able to penetrate both soft tissue and bone. Bullets that flatten on the skull but fail to penetrate are unlikely to cause incapacitation. Unlike with penetration, there is no minimum standard for how much a bullet needs to expand.

TEMPORARY WOUND CAVITY

A temporary wound cavity is created by a penetration of a bullet and spreads away from a bullet the way ripples spread away from a stone dropped in water. A temporary wound cavity is also called a *temporary cavitation* because the bullet forms a temporary cavity in the tissue for about 5 to 10 milliseconds. Whereas a permanent wound cavity forms when a bullet crushes tissue, a temporary wound cavity forms when a bullet stretches or tears tissue. The temporary cavity made by a handgun bullet might not be large enough to cause significant tissue damage.

Increasing the amount of kinetic energy a bullet expends within a target will increase the size of the temporary wound cavity and a bullet's potential for causing tissue damage if other factors—such as shot placement, penetration, caliber, weight, bullet composition, or bullet design—are equal. Hollowpoint bullets usually lose kinetic energy faster and produce a larger temporary cavity than solid bullets.

Besides increasing the size of the temporary cavity, increasing velocity may increase the fragmentation of a bullet or bone. The stretching that results from increasing the size of the temporary cavity can make tissue, such as muscle or nerve tissue, more vulnerable to being damaged by bullet or bone fragments.

Gunshot wound trauma is the tissue damage that results when the transfer of kinetic energy from a bullet causes tissue derangement or destruction. If all other things are equal, increasing kinetic energy potentially increases tissue damage. A bullet cannot release all its kinetic energy in a body unless it stops before it exits the body. If a bullet perforates the body, any kinetic energy that is not expended before the bullet exits the body will not increase tissue damage.

A standard roundnose bullet tends to produce a wound channel that is the same size or even slightly smaller than the diameter of the bullet. For this reason, and despite pressure by activist groups, most law-enforcement agencies have stopped using roundnose bullets and now use hollowpoint bullets, which if they expand can create a permanent wound cavity that is larger than the bullet's diameter.

Another problem that may result from using a roundnose bullet is deflection. A roundnose bullet that hits the head is more likely to glance off the skin or the skull than a flat-nose bullet with straight sides. To increase the probability of penetrating the skull with a roundnose bullet, hit the skull at or close to a 90-degree angle. Lightweight bullets need more velocity to penetrate the skull than heavier bullets. According to Officer Cirillo, wadcutter bullets, which have a flat nose (meplat) and straight sides, are excellent for making head shots.

A temporary wound cavity is produced by stretching, and the displacement of tissues may not last for more than 5 to 10 milliseconds; but even so, tissue damage will occur if the magnitude of the stretching exceeds the elastic limits of the tissues being stretched. Like a rubber band, human tissues have an elastic limit. If you do not stretch a tissue far enough to reach the limit, it returns to its original shape after the forces that cause the stretching are removed. But if you stretch a tissue beyond its elastic limit, it will tear, and it will not return to its original shape.

It's doubtful the temporary cavity made by handgun bullets traveling at less than 1,000 fps will cause much tissue damage, but handgun bullets traveling at 1,600 fps might cause serious damage if they pass through fragile tissues that have a very low elastic limit and are easily damaged by stretching, such as brain, spinal cord, liver, spleen, kidney, or pancreatic tissue. Bullets from high-velocity military rifles traveling at 3,000 fps will cause massive tissue damage in structures that have high elastic limits, such as muscles, bowels, lungs, or blood vessels, but it's possible that the temporary cavity made by high-velocity FN 5.7x28mm handgun bullets traveling at 2,350 fps may also damage tissues that have high elastic limits.

Handgun bullets produce a visible permanent wound cavity, and increasing the diameter of a bullet might increase the size of the permanent wound cavity, but the permanent wound cavity made by a 9mm can look about the same as the permanent wound cavity made by a .45 ACP. A high-velocity rifle bullet can shatter bones or pulverize organs, but it's unlikely a handgun bullet will have the same effect unless the handgun bullet produces the same recoil as the rifle bullet.

CALIBER

Since the temporary wound cavity made by handgun bullets might not cause tissue damage, the effectiveness of a handgun bullet is usually measured by the size of the permanent cavity. If all other things are equal, the size of the permanent wound cavity made by a .45 ACP is slightly larger than the one made by a 9mm because the diameter of a .45 ACP is about 1/10 of an inch larger than that of a 9mm.

Even when other things are not equal, the difference between the tissue damage caused by a 9mm and a .45 ACP can be hard to detect. Dr. Di Maio pointed out in *Gunshot Wounds* that if a 115-grain FMJ 9mm military cartridge with a muzzle velocity of 1,140 fps is compared to a 230-grain FMJ .45 ACP with a muzzle velocity of 850 fps, there are no appreciable differences between the damage caused by the 9mm and the .45 ACP. He also stated that studies conducted by the military, civilian government agencies, and private individuals have found no appreciable difference in effectiveness between the 9mm and the .45 ACP.

Heavier JHP bullets tend to have more penetration than lighter JHP bullets. The 147-grain 9mm tends to have more penetration than the 115-grain 9mm, and a 230-grain .45 ACP tends to have more penetration than a 185-grain .45 ACP. When the 147-grain 9mm is compared with the 230-grain .45 ACP, both bullets have at least 12 inches of penetration, but the 9mm, which is smaller in diameter and lighter than a .45 ACP, has about 2 inches more penetration than the .45 ACP.

Scientific data can tell you a lot about the quality of defense ammunition, but it is not always accurate because of the way it's collected and the fact that personal opinions have been known to override statistics. The 9mm usually has less recoil than a .45 ACP, and a 9mm magazine usually carries more rounds than a .45 ACP magazine. On the other hand, some people will never have confidence in a 9mm, and looking down the barrel of a .45 ACP tends to impress people more than looking down the barrel of a 9mm.

Without damaging the brain stem or the upper cervical spinal cord, neither bullet is going to be a one-shot man-stopper.

If your aim point is the center of mass, which is almost like having no aim point, and you can manage the recoil from a .45 ACP, the .45 ACP will probably give you a slight advantage. If your aim point is the heart and you normally use one or two follow-up shots, the 9mm will probably give you a slight advantage if having less recoil than the .45 ACP improves your shot placement.

If shot placement and penetration are equal, it's unlikely a .45 ACP would hit critical tissues that a slightly smaller 9mm would miss. In *Shooting to Live*, Captains Fairbairn and Sykes reported a case where a robber was shot six times with a .45 Colt, including once near the heart, and he was still standing until he was knocked unconscious by being hit over the head with the butt of the revolver.

MUZZLE ENERGY (KINETIC ENERGY)

Since many of the conversations about ammunition will include discussions about muzzle energy and foot-pounds, it might be helpful to understand what these terms mean. *Kinetic energy* is the ability to do work by virtue of motion, and the formula for kinetic energy is one-half the product of an object's mass multiplied by the square of its velocity (kinetic energy = 1/2 mass x velocity squared). Kinetic energy is measured in foot-pounds, and a *foot-pound* is the energy that would lift a 1-pound weight 1 foot. When discussing ammunition, kinetic energy is often referred to as *muzzle energy*. Let's review some basic facts:

- Increasing kinetic energy tends to increase tissue damage.
- Kinetic energy is needed to penetrate skin or bone and reach critical tissues.
- Passing through dense human tissue can rapidly reduce kinetic energy.
- Minor flesh wounds will not cause a major decrease in kinetic energy.
- Kinetic energy is expended when a bullet deforms or expands (mushrooms).
- Penetration determines a bullet's effectiveness more than kinetic energy.

Increasing the kinetic energy a bullet expends before it exits the body will increase the bullet's potential for causing tissue damage. How much incapacitation the transfer of kinetic energy causes will depend on what kind of tissues or organs are affected. A transfer of kinetic energy is more likely to damage nerve tissue than muscle or connective tissue, and damaging an organ such as the brain will usually cause faster incapacitation than damaging an organ such as the heart.

Two factors that affect the velocity and muzzle energy of a bullet are the quality and quantity of the propellant (gunpowder) and the length of the barrel. A longer barrel usually produces more muzzle energy than a shorter one.

Before presenting a formula that you can use to calculate kinetic energy if you know the weight and velocity of a bullet, you need to understand that even though increasing the kinetic energy of a bullet may increase potential tissue damage, this relationship can be affected by variables, such as shot placement or penetration, and by human factors, such as the physical or mental characteristics of your adversary. It is well documented that extensive tissue damage often has no visible effect on highly aggressive people who fail to notice their injuries.

The two factors that usually increase combat effectiveness more than kinetic energy are shot placement and penetration. A bullet needs to hit the right aim point and it needs to have enough penetration to reach the critical tissues at which you are aiming. In some cases, too much kinetic energy can decrease a bullet's ability to expand or can cause overpenetration, which endangers innocent bystanders.

If you know a bullet's weight in grains and its velocity in fps, you can calculate the bullet's muzzle energy by using the formula below. Muzzle energy is the same as kinetic energy, and velocity is measured in fps.

Muzzle energy = weight x velocity squared ÷ 450,240

Using 450,240 converts grains (gr.) into pounds (grains divided by 7,000 equal pounds) and pounds into mass (pounds divided by 32.16 equal mass). The number 2 divides mass times velocity squared in half.

7,000 ÷ 32.16 x 2 = 450,240

Here's an example of how to calculate muzzle energy using the formula:

Muzzle energy = weight x velocity squared ÷ 450,240

SS190 FN 5.7x28mm ammunition has a 31-grain bullet (weight) that travels at 2,133 fps (velocity). To calculate the muzzle velocity using the above formula:

Muzzle energy = 31 x velocity squared ÷ 450,240

Muzzle energy = 31 x (2133 x 2133) ÷ 450,240

Muzzle energy = 31 x 4549689 ÷ 450,240

Muzzle energy = 313.25 foot-pounds

Being able to calculate muzzle energy can be useful when trying to evaluate ammunition. The SS190 has a diameter about the same as a .22 Magnum, and, like a .22 Magnum, it has good accuracy and penetration and low recoil. The SS190 can also defeat body armor that would stop most handgun ammunition. Whether such light bullets ever replace heavier bullets for self-defense remains to be seen.

The militaries in some countries are already using the FN 5.7x28mm in a FN Five-seveN pistol, which is manufactured by FN Herstal and has a 20-round magazine. Until more information is available on the FN 5.7x28mm cartridge, we are still going to recommend four minimum standards that we believe should be applied to most of the self-defense ammunition being used in a handgun:

- Minimum penetration: 12 inches through 10 percent ballistic gelatin.
- Minimum caliber: somewhere between 9mm and a .45 ACP.
- Bullet design: some type of JHP bullet.
- Function: ammunition must be reliable and reasonably accurate.

EXPANSION

Expansion can increase the diameter of a bullet as it passes through human tissue, which tends to increase tissue damage. If a bullet does not hit critical tissues, having a bullet mushroom may increase tissue damage, but the increase in tissue damage might not increase incapacitation. Hollowpoint bullets do not always expand when they pass through tissue, but if you have good expansion, the expanded diameter can be 50 percent to 60 percent larger than the bullet's original diameter.

Bullets that consistently expand about the same way when they pass through 10 percent ballistic gelatin, which has a uniform (homogenous) consistency, might not expand the same way when they pass through the human body, which has a mixed (heterogeneous) consistency. Bullets that pass through adipose (fatty) tissue might not expand at all, and bullets that hit a bone might have asymmetrical expansion.

Most JHP bullets are covered by a metal that is different from the core of the bullet and have an open hole at the tip. If that hole becomes filled with solid material before it hits human tissue, the bullet may not expand. In Hornady's Critical Duty ammunition, a soft material in the opening keeps the cavity from clogging and helps the bullet pass the FBI's Ballistic Test Protocol, which includes (1) 12 to 18 inches of penetration when passing through ballistic gelatin or common materials such as heavy clothing, plywood, wallboard, auto glass, or 20-gauge hot-rolled steel; (2) at least 50-percent expansion; and (3) 100-percent weight retention of the bullet after it passes through gelatin or other barriers.

Increasing expansion tends to reduce penetration, and adequate penetration is usually more important than expansion. If you are shooting at someone who is facing you and your aim point is the heart, 10 inches of penetration might be sufficient because the body has a smaller front-to-back dimension than side-to-side dimension. A bullet that has 10 inches of penetration through 10-percent ballistic gelatin might not penetrate 10 inches after passing through heavy clothing or bones, such as skull, spinal column, or sternum, which protect the brain, spinal cord, or heart, respectively.

If your aim point is a heart shot, which includes the heart and thoracic spine, your bullet must penetrate the thoracic vertebrae to reach the spinal cord. A poorly designed bullet that needs to penetrate both clothing and bone might expand, lose its kinetic energy, and stop before it penetrates the spinal cord.

Significant and predictable expansion is a good quality for ammunition to have if it also has adequate penetration. When deciding on how much penetration you need, the FBI barrier standards are a good starting point, and a reputable company will tell you if its ammunition meets any or all of the standards. If you don't believe your ammunition needs to meet all the FBI standards, you might change your mind if you get in a situation where one of the barriers you thought was unimportant is stopping your bullets or making them ineffective.

TUMBLE

Tumble, which is a tilting of a bullet's long axis as it travels through tissue, often creates a larger wound channel than the bullet would make if it didn't travel sideways (yaw) and then tumble. Unlike .45 ACP ball ammunition, which has a bullet that tends to create a straight wound channel when it travels through soft tissue, the FN 5.7x28mm bullet tends to tumble as it passes through soft tissue, which can increase the size of the temporary or permanent wound cavity.

FRAGMENTATION

Fragments from a bullet or fragments that result when a bullet strikes a bone can be propelled outward from the bullet and sever tissues that are outside the permanent cavity. Secondary missiles that result from bullet or bone fragments can weaken tissues and increase the tissue damage caused by temporary cavities.

Bullet or bone fragments are possible when using high-velocity handgun ammunition, such as a JHP .357 Magnum, but high-velocity rifle bullets normally produce much more fragmentation than high-velocity handgun bullets. Handgun ammunition that is designed to fragment is not suitable for most self-defense applications because it has limited penetration and it seldom reaches vital organs.

RECOIL

Recoil is the backward momentum (kick) that equals a bullet's forward momentum, and the impact of a bullet on the body is directly proportional to the recoil of the weapon. Even if your bullet misses critical tissues, the impact from a bullet might give you enough time to improve placement of your next shot.

The impact from a bullet hitting a bullet-resistant vest may cause blunt trauma because the vest will absorb most of the kinetic energy from the bullet. Wearing a metal or ceramic shock plate can help you spread the kinetic energy over a larger area because the plate functions as shock absorbers. Canting your hand when you shoot transfers the kinetic energy from recoil to the arm and shoulder and lets them function as a shock absorber. If you are not off balance at the time of impact, a handgun bullet that hits your vest or penetrates your body will not knock you over, but you may throw yourself to the ground or fall over backward after being shot.

The ported compensators people use in the target-shooting sports to reduce or control recoil (muzzle flip) are not a good choice for people who use a handgun for self-defense because of the sound, flash, or pressure waves that are directed to the side or back toward the shooter. Because of the flash, using a compensator at night may blind or burn you and make it difficult to stay focused on your target.

SELECTING AMMUNITION

Bullet Summary

The following apply if penetration and other things are equal:

- No single factor affects tissue damage more than accurate shot placement.
- Increasing the caliber from 9mm to .45 ACP tends to increase tissue damage.
- Expansion (mushrooming) of a bullet tends to increase tissue damage.
- Increasing velocity, weight, or kinetic energy tends to increase tissue damage.
- Bullets that produce bone or metal fragments tend to increase tissue damage.
- Increasing the size of the temporary wound cavity may increase tissue damage.

Factors that can help you decide which caliber of handgun is best for you include recoil, the size of handgun you prefer, and the handgun's capacity to hold ammunition. Most of the ammunition used for self-defense by law enforcement or military personnel will be 9mm, .38 Special, .357 Magnum, .357 SIG, .40 S&W, or .45 ACP. A .380 caliber is usually considered too small, although militaries have used .380s in the past, and a .44 Magnum is usually considered too large because of its heavy recoil and overpenetration. For special duties, such as undercover work or when using a suppressor, a .22 caliber might be a good choice.

Unless you are willing to give up magazine capacity, a small handgun that shoots 9mm ammunition might be a better choice than a small handgun that shoots .45 ACP. You may also find that using a handgun that shoots .40 S&W is a good compromise if you feel a 9mm is too small and a .45 ACP is too large.

For reasons that are often difficult to identify, some guns are more reliable or accurate when used with specific brands of ammunition. If your handgun fits in this category, using ammunition that helps you avoid malfunctions is more important than using ammunition that gives you the tightest groups.

Although police departments often prefer to have all their members use the same kind of ammunition, this probably doesn't affect most civilians unless you have a group of people who want to split the cost of a large quantity of ammunition to get the volume discount.

In addition to everything else, you need to pick a caliber with which you are going to be happy. If you are convinced that a 9mm is totally ineffective despite all the data to the contrary, rather than carry a caliber that you believe is ineffective, choose a caliber that will give you a greater feeling of confidence. Many of the studies conducted in the 1980s indicate the temporary wound cavity caused by handgun bullets does not increase tissue damage, but modern ammunition has higher velocities and produces more kinetic energy than it did in the 1980s. It also appears that the studies in the 1980s did not consider head shots.

RECOMMENDED JACKETED HOLLOWPOINT AMMUNITION

The figures below are guidelines because bullet technology is always changing and new designs might favor a weight that is different from the ones listed. Try to avoid bullets that do not have 12 to 18 inches of penetration in 10 percent ballistic gelatin and try to avoid bullets that weigh less than 110 grains, such as a .380 ACP or a .22 Magnum. When selecting JHP ammunition, penetration and expansion are far more important than velocity or muzzle energy, and you should avoid ammunition that has more recoil than you can easily manage.

9mm Luger: 124-, 135-, or 147-grain JHP

.357 SIG: 125- or 135-grain JHP

.357 Magnum: 125- or 145-grain JHP

.38 Special: 110-, 125-, or 129-grain JHP

.40 S&W: 165-, 175-, or 180-grain JHP

.45 ACP: 185-, 220-, or 230-grain JHP

••

JHP bullets are less likely to wound innocent bystanders than an FMJ bullet because they (1) lose velocity faster than an FMJ bullet when they penetrate body parts and (2) are less likely to ricochet when they strike a hard surface. Unlike high-velocity rifle bullets—which can pulverize tissue—handgun bullets crush or shred tissue. If all other things are equal, increasing the weight of a JHP bullet may increase penetration, but increasing velocity may accelerate expansion and decrease penetration.

••

All the ammunition listed above has JHP bullets, but JHP bullets are not always more effective than FMJ bullets. Three problems that JHP bullets sometimes have are (1) insufficient penetration because of the expansion, (2) failure to expand, and (3) failure to feed. An FMJ bullet that has good penetration is a better choice than a JHP bullet that has insufficient penetration, and an FMJ bullet might cause slightly more tissue damage than a smaller caliber JHP bullet that fails to expand. An FMJ bullet that feeds properly is always a better choice than a JHP bullet that causes malfunctions. If JHP bullets will not feed properly, jacketed-soft-point (JSP) bullets usually have more expansion than FMJ bullets and they seldom cause malfunctions. Compared to FMJ bullets, JHP and JSP (jacketed soft-point) bullets are less likely to exit a body or ricochet.

If other factors are equal, a JHP bullet that has reliable expansion and good penetration is usually more combat effective than an FMJ bullet. One possible exception would be FMJ bullets that tumble. The tissue damage caused by FMJ bullets that tumble can be greater than the tissue damage caused by JHP bullets that expand. A 5.8 X 27mm FMJ bullet is more likely to tumble than the JHP bullets used in most handguns. Since some of the 5.8 X 27mm bullets are also hollowpoints, they might expand and tumble but not have adequate penetration.

HANDGUN
SAFETY

The importance of handgun safety cannot be overstated, and even experts can make fatal mistakes if they ignore handgun safety rules. Cars and guns both serve a useful purpose, but both devices can result in fatal injuries if used improperly. For people who would rather surrender to vicious criminals than defend themselves with deadly force, a whistle or wasp spray might be more useful than a handgun. On the other hand, if you believe using a handgun is a reasonable way to protect yourself against an imminent deadly threat, it is your responsibility to learn how to store, transport, and shoot the gun safely and without violating any laws.

The only thing that most people believe is more important than protecting themselves is protecting their family, and having a handgun and children in the house at the same time can present difficult problems. If you need to choose between making a handgun easily accessible when you need to use it and making it unavailable to children, we believe your first concern needs to be making it unavailable to children, who might accidently injure themselves or someone else.

Children are very clever when it comes to finding things you hide, and they can spend days or weeks looking for things they were told not to touch. Believing that hiding your gun one place and the magazine or ammunition another will keep children from finding and loading the gun is also being overly optimistic.

Because of television, movies, and video games, even young children know you need to load a gun before you can use it, and the next thing they usually look for after they find an empty gun you have carefully hidden is the ammunition. Believing a child will not be able to load a gun is also being overly optimistic.

Locks and safes can be defeated, but most children do not have this level of competence. Devices that lock the trigger or action and make a gun inoperable will stop most children from firing the gun. If you use these devices, carefully read and follow the instructions provided by the company that manufactures the device. None of these safety devices will work if you forget to use them.

A gun safe is a good investment for anyone who owns a gun. Not only will it keep children away from your guns if you keep the combination secret, but it will also keep most criminals from stealing your guns. When entering the combination to open your safe, a touch pad will give you faster access to your guns than a dial. High-quality gun safes also protect you against both burglary and fire.

If a gun safe is too large for your bedroom and you want to keep a gun in at room, you can use a high-quality steel lockbox that's operated by a key. A lockbox that's less than 150 pounds and not bolted to the floor will not give you much protection against theft because some burglars will simply steal the whole box and try to open it later. If you use a lockbox that's opened by a key to deter children from gaining access to a gun, try to keep that key with you at all times.

Besides keeping guns away from children and preventing theft, having a gun safe or a lockbox can prevent illegal intruders from arming themselves with one of your guns. Most criminals are happy to provide their own guns, but the guns they find hanging on your wall or at the bottom of your sock drawer might be even better than the ones they brought with them. The situation will be even worse if criminals happen to find your only gun.

Never store a gun in a place that is going to be easy for criminals to find. Since many criminals prefer to dump the contents of a drawer on the floor or on a bed rather than search the drawer, carefully covering guns, money, or jewelry with various items of clothing is not going to make much difference. Most criminals who break into a house to support their drug habit are not especially intelligent, but they are often very good at finding where you hide your valuables.

Storing a handgun safely is very important, especially if you have children in the house, but having access to a functional handgun if you need to use it is also critical. Regardless of how you store a handgun, it should not take more than about one minute to make it functional. If you store a loaded gun in a safe or lockbox that uses a touch pad or key, getting the gun should take less than a minute. If you store an empty gun in a safe that uses a combination lock and you load the gun with a magazine or speed loader, it might take more than a minute.

Another issue that relates to having access to your handgun is periodically checking it to make certain that rust has not affected its functionality. If you live in a humid climate or near saltwater, the moving parts of your gun can rust and become dysfunctional or your ammunition may corrode and not fire. More than a few police officers have been surprised to find their revolvers or pistols malfunctioned because of rust or corrosion when they tried to qualify.

Even if you live in a place that tends to be environmentally friendly toward guns, do not store your handgun in a leather holster because the leather attracts moisture. Also use a lubricant or rust inhibitor, such as silicon spray, that protects against moisture. Wipe off your ammunition with a soft, clean cloth, but avoid using lubricants or rust inhibitors because of possible damage to the propellant or primers. Even if you do not shoot your handgun more than a few times a year, you should check it for rust at least once every few months.

If your handgun has attachments, such as laser sights or a tactical light, you should periodically check these items to make certain they are functional. Other items that can help you protect your family and yourself if you are ever attacked in your home by an illegal intruder are a high-intensity flashlight, a good first-aid kit, and a fire extinguisher. These should also be checked periodically.

The stress of having someone break into your home can make it difficult to think clearly, and you should make it easy for yourself to find the things that might save your life. This includes access to a telephone so you can call the police.

RULES FOR USING A GUN SAFELY

It's customary for most firearms instructors to give you a list of rules that will help you avoid hurting yourself or others, and many of those rules will be similar to the six rules below.

Basic Safety Rules
for Nontactical Situations

1. Treat all guns as if they were loaded until you can verify otherwise.
2. Prevent unauthorized use of any gun you own or control.
3. Always point your gun in a safe direction (control your muzzle).
4. Do not put your finger on the trigger until you are ready to shoot.
5. Consider the path your bullet may travel before you decide to shoot.
6. Verify your target before you pull the trigger.

Rules 2, 5, and 6 are good all-purpose rules, but rules 1, 3, and 4 need to be modified when dealing with tactical situations.

Rule 1: *Treat all guns as if they were loaded until you can verify otherwise*. This is a good one, but before you get involved in a tactical situation, you also need to verify that any gun you are using for self-defense is properly loaded and being carried safely. Indications that you have violated the second part of this rule include leaving the gun range and forgetting to reload your gun before you go on duty, forgetting to replace practice ammunition with duty ammunition, forgetting to fasten the retaining strap on your holster, and forgetting to make certain your magazine is properly seated. Any of these mistakes can have fatal consequences.

Rule 3: *Always point your gun in a safe direction*. This might not apply if you are using a gun for self-defense. If someone is trying to kill you, you may need to point your gun in a direction that will be unsafe for the person who is trying to kill you. It's also hard to avoid pointing your gun in an unsafe direction if your flashlight is next to your gun or you are using a gun-mounted light. Keeping your gun and light pointed at the same place will decrease your response time.

Rule 4: *Do not put your finger on the trigger until you are ready to shoot*. This rule applies to target shooters more than tactical shooters. Police officers often put their finger on the trigger when pointing a gun at someone who has a gun, but in most cases they will not need to shoot. In a self-defense situation, the wording for rule four should be: *Do not put your finger on the trigger until you verify the target and you are ready to shoot if necessary*. When your flashlight is pointing in the same direction as your gun or you are doing a building search, you still refrain from placing your finger on the trigger until target verification is completed. The last thing you do before you shoot is verify your target again.

Research conducted by the FBI clearly shows keeping your finger off the trigger until you decide to shoot can increase the time it takes to shoot.

According to Dr. Di Maio, keeping your finger off the trigger can increase the time it takes to shoot by about a third of a second. According to Captains Fairbairn and Sykes, who wrote *Shooting to Live*, taking longer than a third of a second to fire your first shot can get you killed. Keeping your finger off the trigger is a good policy because it can help avoid accidental discharges that might cause unintentional injuries. But on the other hand, not touching the trigger until you are positive you are going to shoot increases the time it takes to shoot by about a third of a second.

If you have your finger on the trigger when someone who is threatening you drops his gun and surrenders, take your finger off the trigger but keep your gun aimed at him. If you are using a target focus and not shifting your focus back and forth between the target and your front sight, you should not lose more than a fraction of a second if your adversary suddenly reaches for a gun that was hidden in a back pocket and you need to shoot before you get shot. Using a continuous target focus makes it easier to detect even small signs of aggression.

Any organization that tells people not to put their finger on the trigger until they are going to shoot should require its agents or officers to use this technique each time they qualify. People who have never been trained to shoot this way have a tendency to slap the trigger and miss their targets. Poor marksmanship could be more of a threat to your survival than the time you lose when you start with your finger off the trigger. Many of the instructors who teach this technique do not use it themselves when dealing with targets that might shoot back.

The best way to keep your finger off the trigger is to have it pointed straight forward along the bottom edge of the frame of your gun. Some people have suggested that keeping your trigger finger bent and touching the frame with the tip of your finger is also an option, but this can result in hitting the side of the trigger when you try to make contact with the trigger or dropping your finger behind the trigger if you are using a double-action handgun. Keeping your trigger finger pointed straight forward along the bottom of the frame also gives you a sense of where your gun is pointed because of its alignment with the barrel.

Good training can help you avoid having an accidental discharge. You should not put your finger on the trigger until you have a verified target and the probability is high you will shoot, and you should not put your finger on the trigger when you draw your gun. If you have your finger on the trigger, shooting single action instead of double action will increase your risk of having an accidental discharge. An accidental discharge that occurs because you had your finger on the trigger before you had a verified target might be called a *negligent discharge*.

EMPTY GUNS

No one gets shot by an empty gun, but more than 20 police officers have been accidently killed during training exercises by guns they thought were empty. This kind of accident is preventable if safety protocols are stringently followed.

When handling a semiautomatic pistol, you will not know if the gun is empty until you have removed the magazine and visually and physically checked the gun to make certain the chamber is empty. You can physically check the chamber by locking the action open and feeling the mouth of the chamber with your finger. The most common mistake people make when unloading a semiautomatic pistol is to drop the magazine and forget to check the chamber.

After you unload a double-action revolver by swinging the cylinder out and ejecting all of the ammunition by pushing on the ejector rod, you should visually check the chambers and then physically check each chamber with your finger. Many people do not believe physically checking the chambers of a cylinder is necessary, but if a round fails to eject for some unexpected reason and you have poor lighting, physically checking the chambers is a good precaution.

When unloading a single-action revolver, you may need to open the loading gate, put the hammer at half-cock, unload one chamber at a time, and then go back and physically check each chamber. Use the ejector rod that runs along the barrel to push a round out that does not fall out. As with any gun you are unloading, always keep the barrel pointed in a safe direction and keep your finger away from the trigger. You should also read the owner's manual that comes with your handgun and follow instructions.

Some people like to activate the slide on a pistol they believe is empty as a final check to make certain the gun is empty. If you do this, always have your gun pointed in a safe direction and never have your finger on the trigger. If your pistol has a decocking lever, always have your gun pointed in a safe direction and your finger off the trigger when you activate the decocking lever to drop the hammer.

Anyone who has been involved in law enforcement for a long time has probably seen people shoot the ground or themselves with a gun they thought was empty. Another time an accidental discharge may occur is when people who like to practice pulling the trigger when the gun is empty (which is called *dry-fire* practice) forget to unload the gun before they start. Bottom line: any gun not actively being used for self-defense should always be pointed in a safe direction.

Even if someone you trust hands you a gun and tells you it's not loaded, always check the gun yourself to verify. Since the person holding the gun is responsible for any damage that results from an accidental discharge, most people will not object if you check to see if a gun they handed you is empty, as long as you point the gun in a safe direction when you check it.

VERIFY TARGET

The last of the six rules for using a gun safely states that you should verify your target before you pull the trigger. Despite the obvious reasons for following this rule, it is often violated, and the consequences can be catastrophic.

As most law enforcement officers who have been involved in a situation where someone is shooting from the window of a house should already know, the next person to look out of a window or walk out of a door might not be the person who was shooting the gun. Failure to verify your target in these circumstances can result in shooting a hostage or family member who tried to escape the gunman by running out the back door.

If poor lighting makes it difficult to verify your target, you can normally remedy this situation by using an external light source. Police officers sometimes use the headlights of a vehicle to light up a dark area instead of flashlights because it's safer to position yourself away from the light source than behind it. Regardless of what you are using for a light source, having enough light to identify and verify your target is always better than shooting a target that cannot be verified. When searching areas that have dim light or no light, a light mounted on a handgun and used correctly can blind or illuminate potential targets.

Another situation that can result in hitting an unverified target is shooting through a closed door or a wall. If you cannot see the target but you decide to take a shot because you believe the person is a deadly threat, the risk you are taking is about the same as it would be if you were doing a field search and shot at something you could not identify because it was moving in the bushes.

Some people would argue that you have a right to shoot people through the door if you believe they are trying to illegally enter your house and you also have a right to shoot people who are moving around in your house if you believe they have entered illegally. What the outcome will be if you do either of these two things is difficult to say.

If it turns out the person you shot was armed and in the process of trying to commit a home-invasion robbery, you might not be arrested. If it turns out you shot a neighbor who was knocking on your door because of a medical emergency or the person you shot inside your house was a son or daughter who came home early from vacation, the legal consequences might be the least of your problems.

From a tactical standpoint, if robbers are clearly trying to enter your house by breaking down a door, shooting through the door before you can see them can still be a bad choice. If you miss, the robbers may decide to change their tactics and try to attack you from several different directions at the same time. On the other hand, if you wait until you can verify your targets, you might get hits instead of misses, which may cause robbers who are physically able to flee the scene.

HANDGUN
SKILLS
THE PORTER METHOD

The Porter method was created by examining tactical shooting techniques that evolved over the past several hundred years. Some of the major milestones in tactical shooting occurred because of dueling and World War II. Some people argue the target-shooting techniques police officers are being taught are effective, but it's hard to understand what these people consider effective when the average hit rate for police officers is about 20 percent.

Field testing has proven all the techniques used in the Porter method are combat effective, such as using a target focus during close-quarter combat when the targets are moving or canting the hand. Most police firearms instructors have recognized the value of target-focused shooting for decades, but most departments emphasize front-sight-focused shooting and largely ignore target-focused shooting unless they are training tactical units that handle high-risk assignments. This is unfortunate because most of the police officers killed in the line of duty are uniformed officers handling disturbance calls, working traffic, or making an arrest.

One of the less common techniques used in the Porter method is the cant. In most cases, the hand is canted inward when doing one- or two-handed shooting, although it may be canted outward just after you draw your gun from a holster to keep the slide of a semiautomatic pistol from hitting your clothing or body.

Colonel Applegate realized using a canted grip was an option but used a vertical grip, locked elbow, and vertical lift when raising a gun. The Porter method uses a canted grip, has the elbows bent when moving the gun up or down, and after a gun reaches the desired elevation, pushes it outward by extending the elbows or pulls it inward by flexing (bending) the elbows. Whereas Colonel Applegate used a vice-like convulsive grip and made using a crouch mandatory, the Porter method uses a firm but not extremely tight grip and makes using a crouch optional.

Jim Cirillo, Jeff Cooper, and Paul Castle, who was a police officer in

England and developed the central axis relock (CAR) shooting system, also used a cant. According to Colonel Applegate, the inward, canted grip was being used by target shooters back in the 1940s. The way the Porter method uses the cant is different for several reasons:

- The cant is used when shooting with one hand or two.
- The dominant eye is normally used when shooting with the dominant hand.
- When using an inward cant, the arm and forearm are usually about horizontal.
- The arm and shoulder control recoil by acting as a shock absorber.
- The dominant hand's grip is the same when shooting with one hand or two.
- Canting the wrist helps you avoid bending it downward when shooting a pistol.

TACTICAL, BLADED, AND TARGET-SHOOTING STANCES

Since tactical shooters and target shooters have different needs, the Porter method uses an angled tactical stance or perpendicular bladed stance instead of a parallel (isosceles) target-shooting stance. A left-tactical stance has the left foot forward, and a right-tactical stance has the right foot forward. Tactical stances are usually about 45 degrees, but the angle can be increased or decreased to meet tactical needs. Tactical stances provide a good balance between stability and mobility, they work well on most kinds of terrain or during strong wind, they can be used when moving and shooting at the same time, and they make it easy to turn, look, and shoot to the side or behind you.

A bladed stance can be used when you have limited space, such as during a building search. A left-bladed stance has the left foot forward and a right-bladed stance has the right foot forward. Unlike a target-shooting stance, a bladed stance gives you good stability when trying to resist a frontal attack and good mobility when moving forward or backward. Both tactical and bladed stances facilitate handgun retention because your holster is usually to the rear, you can shoot with your gun close to your body, and you can use your support hand for self-defense.

Such terms as *point shooting, snap shooting, reflex shooting, instinct shooting*, and *unsighted shooting* are often poorly understood, which is why we break all shooting down into two categories: front-sight-focused

Left-Tactical Stance

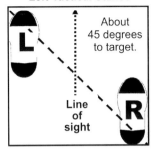

About 45 degrees to target.

Line of sight

Right-Tactical Stance

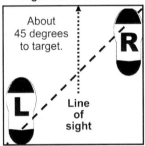

About 45 degrees to target.

Line of sight

Left-Bladed Stance

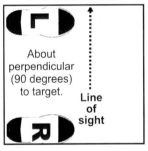

About perpendicular (90 degrees) to target.

Line of sight

Target-Shooting Stance

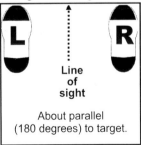

Line of sight

About parallel (180 degrees) to target.

shooting and target-focused shooting. Front-sight focused shooting means your focus is on the front sight, your rear sight is blurred, and your target is blurred. Target-focused shooting means your focus is on the target and both your front and rear sights are blurred. Front-sight-focused shooting is very effective when your target is stationary and you have good lighting but relatively ineffective when your target is moving quickly or poor lighting makes it difficult to see the front sight.

Front-sight-focus shooting is useful when teaching basic marksmanship, but it's almost useless when trying to defend yourself against someone who is armed with a gun or knife at close range unless the person is stationary and you have good lighting. Most police departments emphasize a front-sight focus more than target focus, which partially explains why the average hit rate for police is about 20 percent and also why there is no direct correlation between qualification scores and performance during deadly confrontations.

Having police officers stand stationary in a straight line and shoot stationary paper targets that are always facing the shooter might be an easy way to get people qualified once a year, but it will not do much to keep anyone from getting killed when facing a gun or knife. Some agencies and departments apparently realize this fact, which is why their specialized units, such as a special weapons and tactics team (SWAT) or a special response team (SRT), get much different firearms training than everyone else. Since most deadly confrontations are over before anyone has time to call for a specialized unit, the police officers who handle most of the dangerous situations are less likely to have good firearms training and are the most likely to get killed.

Even though your attention is on your target and not your front sight, target-focused shooting is not done without aiming or aligning your gun before you pull the trigger. With the possible exception of target shooters, who practice hundreds of hours per month and shoot thousands of rounds per year, people who use a target focus will be faster and more combat effective at distances of less than 21 feet than people who use a front-sight focus. Tactical target-focused shooting requires less practice than it takes to become a competitive target shooter because the movements are more natural and you are not required to learn nonessential skills.

According to the FBI statistics taken from 2001 to 2010, when the distance between officers and offenders was reported, about 85 percent of the officers killed with firearms were 0 to 20 feet from the offender. Since most gunfights are fought at less than 21 feet, being fast and accurate at a short distance (0 to 20 feet) is usually more important than being either fast or accurate at a longer distance.

LAW ENFORCEMENT OFFICERS FELONIOUSLY KILLED WITH FIREARMS

Distance Between Victim Officer and Offender, 2001-2010

Distance in Feet	Total	2001	2002	2003	2004	2005	2006	2007	2008	2009	2010
Number of victim officers killed with firearms	**498**	**61**	**51**	**45**	**54**	**50**	**46**	**56**	**35**	**45**	**55**
0-5	243	29	25	24	24	31	24	27	19	19	21
6-10	90	17	9	12	8	9	8	10	3	7	7
11-20	69	5	8	3	11	4	4	7	8	9	10
21-50	37	5	3	3	5	3	1	5	1	5	6
Over 50	29	3	4	3	1	2	4	4	2	2	4
Not Reported	30	2	2	0	5	1	5	3	2	3	7

Target-focused shooting is highly versatile and more likely to save your life in a gunfight than front-sight-focused shooting, but this does not mean front-sight-focused shooting is not used. Since many people never become skilled enough to use target-focused shooting much beyond 20 feet, front-sight-focused shooting can be used if the distance is greater than 20 feet, or it might be used at 20 feet or less if the target is stationary and very small. Very few tactical shooters are combat effective when using target-focused shooting at distances greater than 75 feet.

If you estimate front-sight-focused shooting might be effective in about 15 percent of all deadly confrontations involving a firearm, it seems logical that most of your training time should be spent on target-focused shooting—which makes it hard to understand why some of the people who say they are teaching tactical shooting spend most of their time teaching people to shoot with a front-sight focus.

Unless you have unlimited time and resources, it is not practical to have tactical shooters spend much time practicing at distances over 50 feet. Even though the chart on the previous page applies to police officers, based on news reports, the number of private citizens killed when the distance between the shooter and victim is more than 50 feet is very small. Target shooters practice shooting targets at 150 feet.

The Porter method is based on research and practical experience, and most of the handgun techniques are different from the ones you would use if you wanted to win a shooting match. Tactical shooting is not a sport—your main goal is being able to make combat-effective shots as quickly as possible under combat conditions. In competition shooting, your main goal is to score the most points and beat the other shooters. If you want to be a tactical handgun shooter, you need to combine combat-effective shooting skills with realistic practice.

The Porter method was built from the ground up, but many of the techniques we use were tested and proven by tactical shooters back in the 1800s. What makes this method unique is the way the most effective techniques used by tactical shooters have been blended together. Techniques that are not effective, regardless of whether they are strongly endorsed by other tactical shooters or target shooters, have not been included, and we have tried to give credit to the handgun experts who originated or popularized the shooting techniques we do recommend. This was not always easy because many of the most effective handgun techniques were used by one person before they were popularized by someone else.

If this was a perfect world, police and military personnel would not learn much from reading this book because their organizations would already be giving them realistic training. Based on FBI statistics, national hit rates, and news reports, most police officers are not getting realistic training, and even if the reason for failure to train is not deliberate indifference, the problem needs to be fixed.

Tactical shooting is not difficult to learn, but some shooters do not practice enough to master basic marksmanship. Most police officers practice just enough to meet minimum state standards, and this lack of practice partially explains their poor performance during deadly confrontations. Unlike some federal agents who qualify four times per year and shoot about 300 rounds per qualification, most police officers qualify at most once a year and shoot about 50 rounds.

It's unrealistic to expect tactical shooters to shoot as many rounds per year as competition shooters, but it's also unrealistic to believe you can maintain or improve your tactical skills without practice. This book can give you information that helps you develop tactical skills in the shortest possible time, but you will not make much progress unless you study, learn, and practice these tactical skills.

To help make progress, what we can do is give you some cost-effective ways to practice your tactical skills at home in your free time, such as dry-fire practice or laser practice. This kind of practice can help you improve your tactical skills when going to the range and firing live ammunition is not practical. You can use visualizations and mental practice to improve both handgun and tactical skills.

The fundamentals for tactical shooting and target shooting are similar—grip, stance, alignment, and trigger pull—but the advanced skills for tactical shooting and competition shooting are much different. Tactical shooting is about survival, whereas competition target shooting is about scoring enough points to win. The first shooting match tactical shooters lose might be their last chance to compete.

- Grip: how you can use one or two hands to hold a handgun.
- Stance: how you position your body when you shoot a handgun.
- Alignment: how you aim the handgun at your target.
- Trigger pull: how you activate the mechanism that fires the handgun.

GRIP

Grip refers to the way you use one or both hands to hold a handgun. When gripping a handgun with one hand, your index finger (trigger finger) will be used to activate the trigger, your other three fingers will be wrapped around the grip, and your thumb will be wrapped around the grip and pointed downward about the same way it points downward when you make a fist. Competition target shooters may point the thumb upward or forward, but this is a weaker grip and not a grip that would give you much control if someone tried to grab your gun.

A strong grip is also very important because it can help you align the gun. All three fingers and your thumb should apply a firm, steady pressure on the grip, but not enough pressure to fatigue your muscles or make your hand shake. When your index finger activates the trigger, your hand should not progressively clutch the grip, which can make it hard to release the trigger quickly so it can reset itself.

In tactical shooting, you should not need to reposition your one-handed grip if you change to a two-handed grip. The hand holding the grip is the dominant hand, and the hand reinforcing the dominant hand is the support hand. If you go from a one-handed grip to a two-handed grip, the four fingers of the support hand should wrap around the knuckles of the dominant hand, and the thumb of your support hand should wrap over the thumb of your dominant hand and point forward or downward. Tactical shooting can be done with one or two hands.

When using a two-handed grip, both hands should compress the grip, and you should not push the gun forward with one hand and pull it back with the other. Some tactical shooters might use this grip (Weaver grip), but it's easier, safer, and more effective to use a handgrip that uniformly compresses your gun's entire grip.

We do not recommend a convulsive grip, which is what you might use if you were climbing a rope with just your hands. We are also against using a very light grip, which might be used for target shooting when the gun is held in a stationary position and handgun retention is not a concern.

Competition shooters often use large target grips that are hard to conceal and special accessories, such optical sights, compensators, and muzzle brakes, that most tactical shooters do not use. If you carry a gun for self-defense, practice with the same gun you normally carry. Target shooters often switch from one gun to another depending on the course they are shooting, but tactical shooters are usually more combat effective if they consistently use the same handgun.

When listing the fundamentals, target shooters often list stance before grip because they take a stance and then put their hand on the grip. In tactical shooting, it is often beneficial to have a good grip on your gun before you take a stance. If a deadly threat suddenly appears, this will shorten the time it takes to draw your gun. If your holster has a retaining strap, release it as you grip the handle.

Most of the holsters used in competition shooting do not have a safety device that must be released before you can draw the gun. In tactical shooting, this kind of device can be useful because it may prevent someone from grabbing your gun or your gun from falling out when you are running.

If the holster you normally carry your gun in has a safety device, do not practice drawing with a holster that does not have the same kind of device. Just as you should try to practice with the handgun you normally carry, you should also try to practice with the holster you normally use when you carry the gun.

More than a few police officers have forgotten to release the retaining strap on their holster before they tried to execute a quick draw. Sometimes the strap breaks, but other times it keeps you from drawing your gun. This might not be a problem for target shooters, but it can be a serious problem for tactical shooters.

If you are holding your gun in two hands and your dominant hand is using a thumb-down grip instead of a thumb-up or thumb-forward grip, you should be able to remove your support hand without affecting the grip you have on the gun with your dominant hand. This keeps you from temporarily losing control of a gun because you need to change the way your dominant hand is holding it when you go from a two-handed grip to a one-handed grip. You should also be able to go from a one-handed grip to a two-handed grip without changing your one-handed grip.

Handguns are seldom used to inflict blunt trauma, but they can be used this way if your gun malfunctions or you run out of ammunition. A thumb-down grip is more likely to give you the kind of grip you will need if you want to hit someone with your gun than a thumb-up or thumb-forward grip.

We have never found a valid reason for pointing one or both thumbs up in the air when using a handgun, but having both thumbs forward might be useful if you have a gun-mounted light and you can use the thumb of your support hand to activate the light. If thumb pressure activates the light and releasing pressure extinguishes the light, the thumbs-forward position works very well when using a technique called *flash and shoot*, which means you activate the light for a fraction of a second, shoot if you have a target, and release pressure to extinguish the light.

Having both thumbs pointed forward is also a good grip when using a front-sight focus, and many of the best target shooters use this grip and get excellent results.

The Porter method favors a canted grip over a vertical grip for most tactical shooting, but using a vertical grip would be acceptable if you have a difficult time getting a sight picture when using a front-sight focus. Most target shooters use a vertical grip, although a few top competitors have used a canted grip so they can use their dominant eye (master eye) when shooting with their weak hand. For example, if you are right-handed and your dominant eye is your right eye, you might gain some advantage by canting a gun you are holding in your left hand to the right, which will make it easier to aim with your dominant eye (right eye).

If you do not know which eye is your dominant eye, point the index finger of the right hand at a distant object with both eyes open. After you have your finger aligned with the object, close your left eye. If your finger and the object are still aligned, your right eye is your dominant eye.

If the object is not aligned after you close your left eye, open your left eye and close your right eye. If the object is aligned when your left eye is open, your left eye is your dominant eye. The dominant eye for most people is on the same side as the dominant hand, but a few people are cross-dominant, which means the dominant hand is on one side of the body and the dominant eye is on the other.

When canting a handgun, you can use your dominant or nondominant eye to align the gun. Most people prefer using their dominant eye regardless of which hand they are shooting with, but this is a personal preference. Using a cant reduces the tendency to bend your wrist downward when you extend your gun outward to shoot, and it creates a more natural alignment between your gun and your body. When people reach out to point at something with their index finger, they normally cant the hand inward instead of keeping it vertical.

The inward cant can also help you manage recoil because your shoulder will be in a better position to act as a shock absorber than when your hand is vertical. The normal inward cant when shooting with one or two hands is 15 to 45 degrees. Two possible exceptions are when one arm is fully extended and you prefer a vertical grip or when you shoot just after you draw and use an outward cant.

Most tactical shooters can use a target focus or front-sight focus when the gun is canted inward, but you may want to cant a gun outward when you are shooting a semiautomatic pistol and it's close to your body. Canting the gun outward can reduce the risk of having the slide hit clothing or your body. If your right hand crosses in front of your shoulders so you can shoot out of the driver's window, canting the gun outward can help avoid having the slide hit your face.

When using the Porter method, it would be rare to have both arms fully extended. This arm position, which is often referred to as the isosceles position, is very stable, but lacks the kind of mobility you need for tactical shooting. Bending the elbows when using the isosceles position will improve mobility, but not enough to justify using this position for tactical shooting. People who use the isosceles position seldom use a canted grip and normally use a front-sight focus.

The point shooting Colonel Applegate taught was combat effective, but it had one flaw: even when you lock your elbow and use a vertical arm lift to raise the gun, you tend to bend your wrist and point the gun downward—and some guns tend to point downward more than others. This can be corrected by canting the gun inward and keeping your elbow bent and close to the body when you raise the gun. When shooting two-handed, the gun is canted, and both elbows are bent. The deep crouch Colonel Applegate used can also be used in the Porter method.

The canted grip can be used when shooting around barricades, and using your right eye when shooting from the right side of the barricade or your left eye when shooting from the left side of the barricade will expose less of your head than using your left eye when shooting from the right side of the barricade or your right eye when shooting from the left side of the barricade.

For a tactical shooter, the best method for shooting around barricades is to use a two-handed cant and keep the gun behind the barricade so the barrel does not stick out in front of the barricade. Target shooters normally brace the gun in some way against the side of the barricade and let the barrel stick out.

If you are using a front-sight focus because of the distance or because you need more accuracy, you can stabilize your handgun by pressing your support hand against the side of a barricade. For example, if you are shooting around the left side and your gun is in your left hand, you would press your right hand against the barricade. If a barricade is unstable, you are usually better not to use it for support. The same principles that apply when shooting around a barricade also apply when shooting around corners, walls, or cover that has a vertical edge.

Some people find that it's easier to sight over the top of a handgun when the gun is canted than when the top of the gun is flat. This might be especially true when doing target-focused shooting and using the upper silhouette of your gun as a visual reference point. You will also see more of your target when a handgun is canted than when it's vertical. Jim Cirillo taught the silhouette technique.

If canting a handgun caused a major decrease in accuracy, champion target shooters, such as famous Brian Enos, would not use this method. Canting a sniper rifle when shooting targets at 300 yards is more likely to decrease accuracy than canting a handgun when shooting targets at 75 feet or less.

Shooting with a cant is usually easier for beginners to learn than for people who normally use a vertical grip when shooting a handgun. This is call *negative transfer* because your previous method of shooting is having a negative effect when you try to learn a new method of shooting. Regardless of previous training, some people are more affected by negative transfer than others. Since tactical shooting is about survival, you may need to use old and less effective methods of shooting until you become proficient with newer and more effective methods.

Many of the movements in the Porter method resemble those used in boxing or fencing. The tactical stances are diagonal when facing an adversary, and you can shoot when your gun is held close to or away from your body. Regardless of whether the top of the gun is aligned with your line of sight (high position) or is below your line of sight (low position), your gun can be pulled inward (retracted) by bending one or both elbows or pushed outward (extended) by straightening one or both elbows.

STANCE

Most competitive target shooters try to settle into a solid stance before they shoot because they know having a good foundation tends to improve their accuracy. This is why they spend hundreds of hours perfecting and practicing their stances. A tactical shooter has a different perspective. In the real world, the most important thing is using the best stance you can under the circumstances so you can shoot as quickly as possible and achieve combat-effective accuracy.

If you are standing on uneven ground, you may need to shoot with most of your weight on one foot, and, even though it tends to decrease your accuracy, you may need to shoot while moving. Getting into a perfect stance is not a luxury you can afford when you are shooting for survival and not for points.

When you see police officers lined up along a firing line and carefully settling into a stance while they wait for the range master to give the order to fire, it's easy to understand why the average police officer misses about eight out of every ten shots he fires at a human target. If you want to see the people you are training become competent tactical shooters, you need to teach practical-shooting skills, not target-shooting skills.

Unlike a target shooter who is facing targets that do not shoot back, a tactical shooter needs to use a stance that makes it easy to duck, dodge, or dive for cover. Target shooters are not concerned about mobility unless they lose points for not doing such things as using cover or shooting from different stances or locations.

Some of the competitions that attempt to include tactical shooting skills are very lenient when it comes to enforcing such things as the proper use of cover, and some of the requirements are not realistic enough to make them useful in tactical situations.

If paper targets shot back or tried to grab your gun, target shooting might look a lot more like tactical shooting. Most target shooters do not understand the need for tactical shooting because they have never used a handgun against a deadly threat.

Most competition shooters use target-shooting techniques that maximize points and try to avoid tactical techniques that reduce accuracy unless penalties are given for not using tactical techniques. Most police officers learn target-shooting techniques in the academy, and that's what they use during annual qualifications.

When officers are instructed to shoot at 7 feet without focusing on the front sight, you will often see a large number of them focusing on the front sight if no penalties are given for using it. Focusing on the front sight might give some of the officers a tighter group when shooting at stationary targets, but it will hurt their chances of survival if they try to use the same techniques when shooting at a target who is armed, dangerous, and moving. If you want to survive in the real world, you need to learn skills you can use in the real world, and most police departments do not even try to offer reality-based training.

Understanding what defines a stance will be easier if you break a stance down into four parts: upper extremities, thorax, waist, and lower extremities. If you think of the body as a gun turret, the waist would be the pivot point that allows the gun to move up or down along a vertical line or side to side along a horizontal line. When the hips are stationary, spinal extension (leaning back) provides the upward movement, spinal flexion (leaning forward) provides the downward movement, and spinal rotation provides the side-to-side horizontal movement.

- Upper extremities: shoulder girdle, upper arm, forearm, wrist, and hand.
- Thorax: chest cavity, which includes heart (mediastinum) and lung cavities.
- Waist: area between thorax (ribs) and hips (pelvis).
- Lower extremities: pelvic girdle, thigh, leg, ankle, and foot.

The reason for mentioning these four parts is to emphasize that a stance is not a single unit, but rather a combination of four different units, and these units can be combined in many different ways. When people talk about the isosceles stance, it usually means your feet and chest are parallel to the target and your arms are straight, level, joined together by the hands, and held in front of the chest. The word *isosceles* is used because the angles between the arms and chest are the same.

When target shooters use the word *isosceles*, they are usually describing the entire stance and not just the arm position. The phrase *modified isosceles stance* can be used to describe any stance that is not the traditional isosceles stance, but it is largely meaningless without a definition. Some people use modified isosceles stance to describe a stance where the feet are not parallel to the chest, the arms are bent instead of straight, and the angles between the arms and the chest are not the same. Most police officers use the traditional isosceles stance.

The traditional or modified isosceles stance is often the most-effective stance when doing competitive target shooting, but it's the least-effective stance when doing tactical shooting. It lacks mobility, you can be knocked over if pushed from the front or back, it exposes more of your body than a tactical or bladed stance, and it makes it possible for you to be hit in both the heart and spinal cord with one shot.

Some people claim the isosceles stance gives more protection than a bladed stance if one is wearing a ballistic vest. This argument is weak for three reasons: (1) criminals have access to high-powered rifles and armor-piercing ammunition that will penetrate a standard vest, (2) criminals may use head shots if they believe their target is wearing a vest,, and (3) a vest with side panels will protect the sides of the chest. Furthermore, a bladed stance makes it unlikely one bullet will hit both the heart and spinal cord, and a bullet needs to have more penetration when it enters from the side than from the front. A parallel stance also exposes more of your body than a bladed stance, and it may expose your heart to blunt trauma.

Basic Tactical Stance

If you have both feet on a straight line, you can change an isosceles stance into a basic tactical stance by stepping back with one foot so your back foot and shooting hand are on the same side of the body and the angle between your ankles and a target in front of you is about 45 degrees. Using a tactical stance will give you more mobility, make it easier to avoid being knocked over if pushed from the front or back, and expose less of your body.

Shifting from a parallel (isosceles) stance into an angled (tactical) stance will force you to reposition your upper body if you want to keep the gun pointing forward. As your foot moves back, the shoulder on the same side will move back, the arm on the same side will straighten, and the support arm of the opposite side will bend. When your foot moves back, adjust your lower body so it feels natural. If you were standing upright before you shifted into a basic tactical stance, you can bend your knees and lean slightly forward to improve your balance.

You could also move into a basic tactical stance by stepping forward with the foot that is on the same side of your body as your support hand, but moving back will move your gun away from someone who is attacking from the front. Compared to the isosceles stance, using the basic tactical stance will make it easier to see what's behind you or to start running if you need to move quickly. You can also drop down into a kneeling stance without repositioning your feet, and you can drop your back shoulder and roll if you need to lower your body quickly and shoot.

The position of your feet when using this tactical stance will depend on personal preference or the condition of the terrain on which you are standing. The most common positions for the feet are both facing forward or the front foot facing forward and the rear foot rotated outward to the side. A few people like to angle the front foot slightly inward and point the rear foot almost to the front. You should try to keep both feet flat on the ground and not stand on the ball of either foot.

Tactical stances can be used when shooting with one or two hands. When shooting with one hand, your nonshooting hand can be used for balance if you are moving or placed on the knee that's on the same side of the body and used as a brace to increase stability if you are stationary. When a target is moving, you might be more accurate if you move closer and flank or get behind the target before you shoot. If a target is stationary, you might be more accurate if you shoot from a stationary position, but you will also make yourself an easier target.

The basic tactical stance is similar to the Applegate stance but differs from the advanced tactical stance because the elbow is locked instead of bent, the hand is vertical instead of canted, and the gun is raised by swinging the entire arm upward instead of keeping it close to the body while it's being raised. Despite its flaws, the Applegate stance is more combat effective than a target-shooting stance.

Advanced Tactical Stance and Bladed Stance

Stance is not the only factor that distinguishes a tactical shooter from a target shooter, but it's one of the most visible factors. Since most target shooters are not familiar with tactical shooting skills or tactical terminology, it might be helpful to provide some basic definitions:

- *Retraction:* the gun is pulled in close to your body.
- *Extension:* the gun is pushed away from your body.

- *High position:* the top of the gun is level with your line of sight.
- *Low position:* the top of the gun is below your line of sight.
- *Canted:* your hand is angled 15 to 45 degrees inward or outward from vertical.
- *Speed:* shooting fast enough to avoid serious injuries or death.
- *Combat effective:* causing immediate or timely incapacitation.
- *Accuracy:* shooting with just enough precision to be combat effective.
- *Win:* incapacitating a deadly threat before you are wounded or killed.

The advanced tactical stance is more effective than the basic tactical stance because the gun is canted inward, the position of the arms makes it easy to manage recoil, and the stances can be adjusted to deal with a wide variety of deadly threats. To convert the basic tactical stance into an advanced tactical stance, cant the gun inward 15 or 45 degrees, bend the elbow of your dominant arm, and raise it until it's about level with the top of your dominant shoulder. Having your elbow in this position will help your body act as a shock absorber when managing recoil.

If you are using a two-handed canted grip, the angle between your dominant forearm and your support forearm will be the support angle, extending the gun will decrease the support angle, and retracting the gun will increase the support angle. If the distance between the gun and your body stays constant and the distance between the top of the gun and your line of sight stays constant, the support angle will stay about the same when you raise the gun, lower the gun, rotate the gun to the side, or tilt (side bend) your upper body to the side. If the support angle stays about constant, the angle of the cant will usually stay about constant.

You can usually align a gun faster by using spinal movements than by repositioning your feet or pivoting on the balls of your feet. If your feet are stationary, the vertical and horizontal movements will be similar to the movements of a gun turret. The basic spinal movements are flexion, which is downward vertical movement when you lean forward; extension, which is upward vertical movement when you lean backward; rotation, which is horizontal movement when you turn to the side; and side bending, which tilts the upper body to the side.

The spine has about 90 degrees of forward flexion, which lets you shoot straight down without repositioning the arms, but not enough backward extension (about 30 degrees) to shoot upward without repositioning the arms. When rotating to the side, the spine can rotate the shoulders about 45 degrees in either direction, but if you need more rotation, you can pick up another 45 degrees of rotation by rotating your hip joints, which gives you enough rotation to see and shoot what's behind you. You can also increase the rotation of your shoulders by pivoting on the ball of one or both feet or by repositioning one or both feet.

Some people find it helpful to understand what body parts are moving when they are learning how to move their gun in a vertical or horizontal direction, but with practice, these movements will become automatic and you will not be consciously aware of what body parts are moving. If your gun is pointed forward and you need to turn quickly to one side or the other and shoot, spinal and hip joint rotations will be almost simultaneous, and you will need to focus on acquiring the target and aligning your gun on it.

After you understand vertical and horizontal movements, the next step is understanding retraction and extension. By definition, retraction is pulling the gun in close to the body, and extension is pushing the gun away from the body. Having the gun retracted makes handgun retention easier, and having the gun extended tends to improve accuracy. If you need to draw and shoot quickly, shooting with the gun retracted will be faster than waiting until the gun is extended.

A gun can be retracted or extended when it is held in a high or low position. A high position means the top of the gun is level with your line of sight, and a low position means the top of the gun is below your line of sight. The term *line of sight* refers to an imaginary straight line between your eye and your target.

Unlike your line of sight, which is a straight line, the trajectory of a bullet is a curved path. Although snipers may need to adjust their sights to compensate for distance or windage, a tactical shooter can be combat effective without making these adjustments. Most tactical handguns do not have adjustable sights, and the bullet drop when shooting at close range will not decrease combat effectiveness.

You can shoot with the cross-dominant eye—which means when you shoot with the right hand, you aim with the left eye, and when you shoot with the left hand, you aim with the right eye—but people prefer aiming with their dominant eye unless the side of a barrier you are shooting around and your dominant eye are not on the same side. If your dominant eye is your right eye and you are shooting around the left side of a barrier, you might aim with your left eye. In this situation, using your nondominant eye will expose less of your head. If you are shooting around the left side of a barrier, using a right-tactical stance and leaning sideways will help you avoid exposing your left leg. Shooting with both eyes open in a tactical situation is almost essential unless you are making a long-distance shot.

When you combine retraction and extension with high and low positions, you have four combinations, and each one has advantages and disadvantages:

- High-position extended: maximum accuracy and slow from draw.
- High-position retracted: good accuracy and moderate speed from draw.
- Low-position extended: moderate accuracy and fast from draw.
- Low-position retracted: limited accuracy and very fast from draw.

After the gun is in your hand, you can use a high or low position and extend or retract the gun as needed. Straightening the elbow will extend the gun, and bending the elbow will retract the gun. The most common ready position is a low position just below eye level with the gun retracted. If suddenly attacked, you can shoot from the retracted position and continue shooting if you extend the gun outward to improve your accuracy. If you are moving the gun in and out along a straight line, you can have combat-effective accuracy as the gun moves in and out.

If a threat is potential but not verified, you can hold a canted gun just below eye level and scan the area, which will give you a larger unobstructed field of view than holding a vertical gun at eye level. If you are concerned about handgun retention, using a two-handed grip and keeping the gun in a retracted position close to your chest will make it easier to protect your gun. Then if you have a target, you can shoot from the retracted position. If your gun is extended and someone tries to grab it, you can retract the gun, move away, and shoot at the same time.

If you need to increase your accuracy, raise your gun into your line of sight, keep your eyes focused on the target, and extend the gun outward while keeping your elbows slightly bent. If you want to use a front-sight focus instead of target focus, you can keep the gun canted or use a vertical position. If you straighten your dominant elbow when you use a front-sight focus, your arm will not function as a shock absorber, and it may increase the time it takes to make follow-up shots. Using a front-sight focus when a handgun is canted will not decrease accuracy.

When you are moving along a wall, it might be practical to shift from a tactical stance into a bladed stance because standing sideways makes you a smaller target. The bladed stance keeps your gun to the rear more than a tactical stance, which means it might be useful if you reach out with your support hand to open a door or check to see if someone has a weapon. Because it protects your midline targets, such as your heart and descending aorta, it can also be useful during a knife attack.

Walking and shooting at the same time can be combat effective when using tactical or bladed stances if you hold the gun about midway between retraction and extension and just below eye level. To improve accuracy, keep your knees partially bent and shoot when your front foot is firmly on the floor and your rear foot is barely touching the floor. If possible, avoid shooting while running.

If you are using a one-handed advanced or bladed stance with the gun in your right hand and your left foot forward and you want to make your left hand your dominant hand, rotate the gun to a vertical position, shift it from the right hand to the left, and cant the gun inward. Since an inward cant is toward the body, an inward cant with the right hand would be a counterclockwise cant, and an inward cant with the left hand would be a clockwise cant.

If you are using a two-handed tactical or bladed stance, follow the same procedure, but after the gun is properly canted, make your right hand your support hand. After you have made your left hand your dominant hand, you can change the angle of the stance by moving your right foot to the front. Regardless of which of the three stances you are using—basic tactical, advanced tactical, or bladed—having the left foot forward will make the stance a left stance and having the right foot forward will make the stance a right stance.

In tactical shooting, grip, stance, and alignment are usually performed as one continuous movement. After you see a target, the movements needed to grip the gun, settle into a stance, and align the gun should be automatic. Unlike target shooters, who would rather shoot slower and have a tight group than be the first person to shoot, tactical shooters prefer to shoot faster and have a larger but combat-effective group than let someone else shoot first. Even if you shoot first and miss, you may have time to fire a follow-up shot before your adversary shoots.

If you are shooting with one hand and you need to rotate your body so you can shoot to the right or left or behind you, retract the gun and keep it close to your chest until you stop rotating. Then you can shoot while the gun is still retracted or extend the gun and shoot. If your arm is extended while your body is rotating, angular momentum will make it hard to stop the gun before it swings past your target. Even though using a two-handed grip makes it easier to control momentum, retracting the gun before you rotate your body tends to improve accuracy.

If someone is running at you with a gun and you cannot make a head shot, it will be hard to stop the person from returning fire or colliding with your body unless you can get behind cover and shoot, or sidestep and shoot. Even if a bullet stops the attacker's heart, incapacitation will take at least 10 to 15 seconds.

If someone is running at you with a knife, retreat is not possible, and you cannot make a head shot, you can try to get behind cover and shoot, or sidestep and shoot. If someone knocks you down, you might be able to stop the knife with your feet and shoot, but this will not work unless you are on your back and you can keep your feet between you and the knife until you can shoot. A bladed stance is more effective against a knife than a tactical stance because your heart is farther from the knife and you can use the hand closer to the knife to defend and the other hand to shoot. If you have a knife or nightstick, you can use it in your nonshooting hand. Because of the need for immediate incapacitation, try to make a head shot.

Even though a large percentage of gunfights require one-handed shooting, two-handed shooting tends to be more combat effective because the support hand helps you steady the gun, especially when making follow-up shots. If you have multiple targets who are very close together, you may be able to hit all of them by keeping your feet stationary and rotating your body. Rotating your body like a gun turret can be very effective against multiple targets, but to make yourself less of a target, do not remain stationary any longer than absolutely necessary.

It's possible to shoot when your gun is moving into extension or retraction, but shooting while the gun is moving tends to be less accurate than shooting after the gun has stopped moving. Being able to shoot with combat effectiveness while moving your gun in or out along a straight line requires practice. When you are extending a gun along a straight line, the movement is similar to using an electric drill to bore a deep hole in a vertical wall with your hand canted inward. When you are retracting a gun along a straight line, the movement is similar to pulling a drill bit straight out while your hand is canted inward. Deviating from a straight line when pushing a drill bit in or pulling it out just makes the hole crooked, but deviating from a straight line when extending or retracting a gun will usually make you miss your target.

To practice simultaneous movement, walk in a predefined area and take a shot when a target appears. To improve target discrimination, use both shoot and don't-shoot targets. To improve your response times, targets should appear and disappear within 1.5 seconds. Some of the standard methods for making a target disappear are to rotate the target so only a thin edge is visible and to have the target drop behind cover. When progressive training is used, you can start with larger targets, such as a 6-inch circle, or longer time limits, such as a three-second time limit, and progressively reduce one or both until you reach acceptable levels of performance.

If you want to be a good tactical shooter and have reliable shot placement, after your gun is already in your hand you need to hit a 4-inch circle at 21 feet or less within 1.5 seconds after the target appears. If your speed and accuracy are not at this level, you need to improve your reaction time or movement time to decrease your total response time. If this exercise is done with the gun already holstered, you need to allow extra time for gripping and drawing the gun. Experienced police officers usually have their guns drawn before they need to use them.

Tactical shooters will not draw as quickly as fast-draw artists who use stances and holsters that maximize speed, but tactical shooters can gain a fraction of a second advantage when they draw by using simultaneous movements. If you are standing erect and your goal is to draw your gun and raise it to eye level, draw the gun as you lean forward from the waist and bend your knees. Leaning forward will move your hips back at the same time your hand is moving your gun up and forward and will lower your eye level at the same time you are raising your gun. Bending the knees improves your balance and makes you a smaller target.

If speed and accuracy are not as good as you would like, use larger targets and be satisfied with slower times until your speed and accuracy improve. Anyone who has the basic handgun skills needed to start learning how to become a tactical shooter should be able to hit 6-inch paper plates at 21 feet or less when using a front-sight focus and a generous time limit.

A 4-inch group with two hits will always be combat effective when making head shots, and it might be combat effective when making heart shots. A 4-inch group with two hits will usually cause limited incapacity when making pelvic shots if you hit the spinal cord or a major blood vessel. When making a center-of-mass shot, a 4-inch group with two hits might not have any effect until hours later. Anything less than a head shot makes simultaneous movements, such as shooting and moving, moving and shooting, or shooting and moving at the same time almost essential. If you stand in one place and continue shooting the way you do when shooting paper targets, you will make yourself an easy target.

If you are trying to make a heart shot and you group two shots within a 4-inch circle over the aim point, you might not cause timely incapacitation. If two shots hit one lung, people might not know they were shot, and you might not see any change in functionality for several minutes. Many of the internal organs do not have pain receptors that notify the body when bullets cause tissue damage.

After you are satisfied with your level of accuracy, you should start working on your speed. Since being accurate implies your body movements are reasonably correct, you need to reduce your total response time, which is calculated by adding your reaction time and movement time together.

A safe way to improve your reaction time is to point your index finger at a target as soon as it appears. This will improve your situational awareness and your target acquisition. You can also use a pistol that fires a laser beam when you pull the trigger. If someone is faster with a laser pistol than with a pistol that shoots live ammunition, try to identify the cause. Some people convulsively tighten their grip on a handgun or flinch because they fear the recoil or the sound.

If you want to make aligning (mounting) a gun fast, you need to eliminate unnecessary movements that increase the distance your gun travels and avoid pauses that increase the time it takes to complete the essential movements. Try to make your movements feel smooth, continuous, and natural before you try to make them fast, and try to breathe normally and stay relaxed when you practice. Correct and regular practice is the best way to improve both performance and confidence.

To achieve the fastest possible response time, practice until the movements become almost automatic. If you need to think about stance or alignment before you shoot, you will increase your response time. Practicing speed drills with live ammunition is necessary, but you can use mental practice, dry-fire practice, air guns, or laser training guns to improve your speed without going to a gun range.

Shooting over a shoulder is a good way to practice simultaneous movements and make them almost automatic. A two-handed canted grip and shooting with the gun extended are preferred, but you could use a one-handed canted grip or shoot while the gun is retracted. If a gun is not already retracted before you rotate your body and you shoot after the gun is extended, the basic movements for shooting over either shoulder can be described as *pull in/spin/push out/shoot*.

If you are using an advanced left-tactical stance with a two-handed grip and the gun is in your right hand, to shoot over your *right* shoulder: (1) keep the gun canted inward, (2) retract the gun inward toward your chest if it's not already retracted, (3) rotate your body until you are looking over your right shoulder, and (4) extend the gun outward and shoot. If you need more rotation, lift your left heel off the ground and let your feet pivot to the right or step to the left with your right foot before you lift your left heel and pivot to the right. Shooting over your right shoulder is usually faster and easier if you shoot with just your right hand.

If you are using an advanced left-tactical stance with a two-handed grip and the gun is in your right hand, to shoot over your *left* shoulder: (1) keep the gun canted inward, (2) retract the gun inward toward your chest if it's not already retracted, (3) rotate your body until you are looking over your left shoulder, and (4) extend the gun outward and shoot. If you need more rotation, lift your right heel and let your feet pivot to the left, or step forward and to the left with your right foot at the same time you pivot to the left on your left foot.

Hip Shooting

A few people are combat effective when hip shooting at 21 feet, but most tactical shooters should not fire when the gun is next to the side of the hip if they have time to move the gun in front of their body. It's hard to see a gun when it's next to your hip because your central vision is focused on the target and the gun is usually outside your peripheral vision. When you have the gun in front of your body, you can focus on the target with your central vision but also see the gun with your peripheral vision, which tends to improve accuracy.

Hip shooting might be your only option if you need to shoot just after your gun clears the holster, and canting the gun outward can help you avoid having the slide on a semiautomatic pistol hit your clothing or your body. If you draw with your right hand, step back with your right foot as you draw the gun, which will move you into a tactical stance and move the holster back as you pull the gun forward. Stepping back can make handgun retention easier if it moves the gun away from someone attacking you from the front. If your adversary is close, you can use your nonshooting hand for self-defense. If your adversary tries to grab your gun, switch to a two-handed grip and use good shot placement.

Summary of Stances

Basic Tactical Stance
(feet at least slightly angled forward)

- Hands or hand: canted inward 15 to 45 degrees.
- Can be vertical when using front-sight-focused shooting.
- Lower body: angled about 45 degrees (diagonal) to target.
- Upper body: usually angled slightly less than 45 degrees to target.
- Dominant arm: usually about straight with elbow pointing outward.
- Support arm: bent with elbow pointed in a downward direction.

Advanced Tactical Stance
(feet at least slightly angled forward)

- Hands or hand: canted inward 15 to 45 degrees.
- Lower and upper body: angled about 45 degrees (diagonal) to target.
- Dominant arm: elbow bent, pointed outward, and about shoulder level. Angle of bend in elbow depends on distance of hand from shoulder.
- Support arm: elbow bent and pointed in downward direction.
- Angle between dominant arm and support arm: about 90 degrees.

Bladed Stance
(feet at least slightly angled forward)

- Hands or hand: canted inward 15 to 45 degrees.
- Lower and upper body: bladed (almost perpendicular) to target.
- Dominant arm: elbow bent, pointed outward, and slightly above shoulder.
- Angle of bend in elbow depends on distance of hand from shoulder.
- Support arm: elbow bent and pointed in downward direction.
- Angle between dominant and support arm: about 90 degrees.
- Can be with one-handed bull's-eye-shooting position (off-hand position).

Hip Shooting
(if you step back with one foot as you draw the gun)

- Hand: canted outward 15 degrees just after draw.
- If time permits, to improve accuracy, shift into the advanced tactical stance.
- Lower body: angled about 45 degrees (diagonal) to target.
- Legs might be parallel to target when you draw the gun.
- Upper body: parallel or angled about 45 degrees to target.
- Dominant arm: elbow bent and pointed outward.
- Support hand: on top of thigh as brace or used for balance or self-defense.

Reducing Fatal Errors Related to Stance

1. The worst mistake poorly trained tactical shooters make is believing they need to have a good stance before they get a good grip, align the gun, and pull the trigger. The real world is not a target range, and the ground you are standing on might be uneven, soft, rocky, or slippery. Get the best stance you can under the circumstances and try to get a hit before your adversary has a chance to shoot.

2. A good tactical stance will not be perfectly parallel or perpendicular to your target under normal circumstances. This level of perfection might win target-shooting competitions, but it can get you killed in a gunfight. A tactical stance will not always have the feet at a 45-degree angle to the target, but it will normally be angled to some extent. If necessary, you can shoot while standing on one foot.

3. A good tactical stance will make it easy to switch from one-handed shooting to two-handed shooting and back to one-handed shooting if needed. When you are using a tactical stance, the shoulder of your shooting hand should be to the back, which will make handgun retention easier, and the shoulder of the other hand should be to the front, which will make it easier to use that hand for defense.

4. When using a tactical stance, you normally hold the gun in your dominant (strong) hand, but learning to use the nondominant (weak) hand can be a valuable asset. If your dominant hand is injured, you may need to shoot with your nondominant hand. This is a skill that goes beyond basic tactical shooting, but if you are right-handed and are forced to shoot around the left side of a barricade or wall, you will expose less of your head if you shoot with your left hand, using your left eye. It's possible you might need to shoot with both hands at the same time in a military situation but very unlikely in a nonmilitary situation.

5. Being prone can reduce body exposure more than standing or kneeling, or it can give you more stability when shooting at targets 150 feet away. However, a tactical shooter seldom uses a handgun at 150 feet, and a prone position reduces mobility. Rolling a short distance with reasonable speed might be possible, but you cannot run until you get back on your feet. A prone position can make it possible to use a curb for cover, but it can also put you at risk because of ricochets.

6. The traditional isosceles stance is better for target shooting than tactical shooting. Even people who learned the straddle stance (horse stance) when they studied martial arts normally use a boxer's stance during a street fight. The traditional isosceles stance has even less tactical value than a front-sight focus.

7. Try to avoid remaining stationary after you stop shooting. If you don't want to make yourself an easy target, change location or get behind cover after you shoot. If you are standing and cover is not available, you can move and drop down into a stance that makes you a smaller target, such as a kneeling, sitting, or prone stance. On the negative side, lowering your stance can reduce your mobility.

Stances Used for Tactical Shooting

High diagonal stance.   High diagonal stance.

Low diagonal stance.

High diagonal stance.

High bladed stance.

High bladed stance.

High diagonal stance.

High diagonal stance.

Shooting behind back.

Shooting behind back.

Right barricade.

Left barricade.

High diagonal stance.

High diagonal stance.

Racking slide.

Ready position.

Low bladed stance.

Kneeling stance.

Club defense.

Canted carbine position.

Transition to handgun.

Knife defense.

Knife defense.   Supine stance.

ALIGNMENT

Despite all the terms used to describe the different methods for aligning a handgun with a target, if a handgun has iron sights, all methods of alignment are either a target focus or a front-sight focus. Using a target focus means you focus on the target, and using a front-sight focus means you focus on the front sight.

Terms such as *point shooting, instinct shooting, quick kill, sighted shooting, aimed shooting,* and *snap shooting* are often difficult to define because they mean different things to different people. Jeff Cooper might have defined a target focus as unsighted shooting and a front-sight focus as sighted shooting.

Aiming is simply the process of aligning a gun with a target, and human physiology forces people to make one of three decisions when aiming a gun that has a front and rear sight: focus on the target, focus on the front sight, or focus on the rear sight. Because of the way the human eye is structured, we cannot focus on more than one object at a time. Most tactical shooting is done with a target focus, and most target shooting is done with a front-sight focus. You could focus on the rear sight, but this would make aligning the gun with your target very difficult.

One example of unaimed shooting would be to shoot blindly into an area to degrade your enemy's ability to return fire. This is sometimes called *suppressive fire* or *covering fire*, and the military is more likely to use this kind of unaimed shooting than law enforcement officers or private citizens.

People who promote target shooting are more likely to recommend using a front-sight focus for tactical shooting than people with extensive police or military experience. A tactical shooter may use a front-sight focus on rare occasions, but most tactical shooting with a handgun requires a target focus because the targets are usually close and moving, and your shooting needs to be fast and accurate.

If a tactical shooter is well trained, target-focused shooting can be used at distances up to about 45 feet. For a tactical shooter who has minimum training, target-focused shooting can be used at distances of up to about 21 feet. Tactical shooters who cannot use target-focused shooting at 21 feet should hope their luck is better than their training. Most shooting beyond 45 feet uses a front-sight focus.

Police departments often use 21 feet and 45 feet when training or qualifying police officers, but FBI statistics are usually based on 20 feet and 50 feet. Most of the distance numbers that relate to tactical shooting are somewhat arbitrary. Jeff Cooper considered 60 feet the maximum distance for target-focused shooting.

A front-sight focus is normally used when the distance is more than 75 feet and is often used at distances between 45 and 75 feet. Using a front-sight focus at less than 45 feet can be dangerous if the target is moving, the lighting is poor, or you need to shoot quickly. A front-sight focus might be used for precision shooting at close range if the target is small and you are not under pressure to shoot quickly.

Research done by optometrist Edward C. Godnig indicates it's very unlikely anyone could focus on the front sight during the first few seconds of a gunfight because the stress will make it hard for the eye to maintain a focus on close objects. Anyone who has faced someone who is holding a gun or knife will know that taking your eyes off that person is almost impossible. Not only is focusing on your target necessary to make certain the person has not surrendered before you shoot, but staying focused on the target will help you determine whether the person is moving as well as which way or how fast. When lighting is limited or inconsistent, moving targets are easier to see but harder to hit than stationary targets.

At the risk of being repetitive, we'd like to reiterate the following: when you look at FBI statistics, it becomes obvious that most tactical shooting is done at a distance of less than 21 feet, which means most tactical shooting should be done with a target focus. Since most police officers have not been trained to use a target focus, their departments are clearly a large part of the reason they often perform poorly during deadly confrontations. Until training becomes more consistent with reality and scientific research, improvement seems unlikely.

The main variations you find in front-sight focused shooting are focus on the top edge of the front sight, focus on the entire front sight, and shift your focus back and forth between the front sight and the target, which can be used to verify the alignment of your gun when shooting at a stationary target who does not pose an immediate threat. If the threat is immediate, the time you lose jumping back and forth from the front sight to the target might get you killed.

The following target-focused variants are arranged in order of accuracy, which means the variant that is often the most accurate is at the top and the variant that is often the least accurate is at the bottom. While focused on the target:

1. Bring the gun into alignment with your line of sight, which is the imaginary straight line between your eye and a target. This can bring a gun into alignment with your line of sight while looking through the sights or while you are looking over the top of the gun. If the gun is canted and you are using a semiautomatic pistol, the top of the gun would be the right or left top edge of the slide.

2. Bring the top of the gun into alignment just below your line of sight. If you look at the front sight when your gun is slightly below your line of sight, it will appear to stick out above the barrel of the gun, but you should not be looking at the front sight if you are using a target focus. If your gun is correctly aligned on a target when you hold it slightly below your line of sight, keeping the gun in place and lowering your head so you can focus on the front sight should give you a nearly perfect sight picture and verify your target-focused alignment was correct. This is something you would do during a practice session, not during a gunfight.

3. Align the gun as you move it in front of your lower body. This is the method of target-focused shooting most of the Old West gunfighters used. It tends to be less accurate than the two methods described above, but anyone who has studied the history of tactical shooting would find it hard to deny the effectiveness of this method. What makes this method of alignment less accurate than the first two methods is that the gun is farther below your line of sight and

it's visible because of peripheral vision more than central vision. Since the gun has less distance to travel if it's drawn from a holster on the hip or lifted from a low-ready position, you might be able to shoot faster than you could when using the first two methods.

4. If the gun is not visible, hip shooting is the least accurate method of target-focused shooting. In the first three methods of target-focused shooting, you can use visual and kinesthetic (tactile) reference points to align (index) the gun. If you are hip shooting and you cannot see the gun, the only indicators you can use to align the gun are how the gun feels in your hand and how your arm feels against your body.

When using a target-focus approach, bringing your gun into alignment with your line of sight tends to improve accuracy, but your line of sight is not always at eye level. If your target is above your head, your gun will be above eye level if you bring the top of your gun into alignment with your line of sight. If you are standing and your target is on the ground, your gun will be below eye level if you bring the top of your gun into alignment with your line of sight.

People can get in the habit of raising their gun to eye level before they shoot because this is the way they shoot paper targets. If you raise your gun to eye level when searching a building, you might not see someone on the ground because you are looking straight forward or your gun and hands are blocking your field of view.

Besides keeping a gun below eye level when searching an area, do not bring it up to eye level the instant you find a target. If you raise the gun to eye level and the target ducks down, you will probably miss if you try to shoot, and you may lose visual contact with the target. If you keep the gun below eye level and the target ducks down, you may still see the target, and you can use a target focus if you need to shoot. If you miss, keep the gun below eye level, try to maintain visual contact with the target, and look for cover or shoot again if you see the target.

When searching an area with poor lighting, using a front-sight focus will be harder than it would be if you had good lighting. Poor lighting makes it hard to see the front sight, and it makes central vision, which is used with a front-sight focus, relatively weak compared to peripheral vision. When a gun is held below your line of sight, a target-focus uses peripheral vision more than central vision, and your hands and the gun will be blocking out less peripheral vision, which is better than central vision for detecting movement in a low-light environment.

If a suspect with a gun moves while a police officer is focused on the front sight, the officer may panic, switch to a target focus, and shoot before the gun is aligned on the target. Since most police officers have not been properly trained to use a target focus, the bullet is unlikely to hit the suspect or stop the suspect from returning fire and shooting the officer. If a police officer is using a front-sight focus and the suspect's movement was to drop a gun and surrender, it may result in the officer unintentionally shooting an unarmed suspect who is no longer a threat.

The best way to avoid the fatal consequences that may occur if using a front-sight focus causes an officer to miss a shot—or the legal consequences that may occur if using a front-sight focus causes him to shoot an unarmed suspect—would be to teach police officers how to use target-focused shooting. It makes no sense to teach almost nothing but front-sight-focused shooting when a target focus is usually effective if a target is close, moving, or partially hidden by darkness.

One method of target-focused shooting you should avoid is having your index finger parallel to the barrel and pulling the trigger with your middle finger. Using this method makes handgun retention difficult because it weakens your grip and lowers your ability to strike someone with the gun. If you wanted to keep your finger off the trigger and on the frame to prevent an accidental discharge, you would have two fingers on the frame and only two fingers on the grips.

If someone is closing in on your position very quickly, shooting when the end of the barrel is almost making contact with the person's body is an option. Heavy contact can push the slide back on a semiautomatic pistol and prevent the gun from firing, but pushing the slide forward with the palm of your nondominant hand before you pull the trigger can keep the slide on some pistols from moving back. Contact shots are easier to make with a revolver than a semiautomatic pistol.

Some people may find discussion about using a contact shot offensive, but tactical shooting is not about meeting some artificial concept of fairness. It's about using whatever options you have available that will save your life. If you have a legal right to shoot someone, your distance from him when you shoot should make no difference. If you limit your options—such as never making contact shots or never cutting someone with a knife—you also limit your ability to survive.

Nothing makes the problems associated with using a front-sight focus more obvious than stopping a knife from cutting or stabbing you and trying to position yourself so you can shoot at the same time. You cannot focus on the front sight when you are trying to keep your eyes on the knife, look for escape routes, look for a barrier that you can put between yourself and the knife, or look for an opening that might give you a chance to take a shot without getting badly cut. If you are highly trained and you try to deflect (parry), block, or restrain the knife so you can take a shot without getting cut, your eyes will be focused on your adversary or the knife and the one thing you should not be focused on is the front sight of your gun.

In most tactical situations, the visual index and the kinesthetic index work together: your eyes acquire the target; your body moves your gun into alignment with the target, which is called *mounting the gun*; and your finger pulls the trigger when your eyes and body confirm the alignment is correct. To be a fast shooter, you need to have fast eyes because you need reliable target acquisition before you can align your gun with a target. You can shoot only as fast as you can see.

If you are facing multiple adversaries, you will not be able to monitor what the targets are doing if you are shifting your focus back and forth from them to the front sight. When using a front-sight focus, the targets become blurred and less visible each time you focus on the front sight, and you can waste valuable time trying to focus on the front sight. If you are using a target focus, you simply pick a target, align the gun with the target, and shoot what you are looking at.

Most tactical shooting is done with both eyes open because you can follow a moving target more easily when using both eyes, it will improve your chances of being able to see multiple adversaries, and your depth perception will be better. Depth perception is usually most reliable when both eyes are open and you can use binocular cues, but people can judge depth to a limited extent with just one eye by using monocular cues. Even when doing tactical shooting with a front-sight focus, shooting with both eyes open is usually a better choice than closing one eye.

Focusing on the front sight can be difficult if you have low or inconsistent lighting. In a tactical situation, waiting to get the front sight perfectly aligned with the rear sight before you pull the trigger can have fatal consequences, and poor lighting can make it almost impossible to get a perfect sight picture anyway. Having a perfect sight picture means the top of the front sight is level with the top of the rear sight and the front sight is centered exactly in the middle of the rear sight. A front-sight focus and a sight picture are used in tactical shooting when precision accuracy is required or you are shooting at a long distance. If you can be combat effective without precision accuracy, it makes more sense to use a target focus, which is faster to use and does not require being able to see the sights.

Front-sight-focused shooting is used in most bull's-eye shooting because it offers a high level of accuracy when you are trying to hit small targets or shoot a tight group, and it's the only kind of shooting that will give you any chance of winning a practical or defensive target-shooting competition.

Colonel Charles Askins made it clear in *The Art of Handgun Shooting* that for most tactical shooting, a target focus is far superior to a front-sight focus. Colonel Askins was a champion target shooter, but he had enough combat experience to know the difference between target shooting and tactical shooting and to know being good at one would not make you good at the other. Colonel Applegate expressed exactly the same view in *Kill or Get Killed*. For reasons that are not clear, police departments seem to have a different view.

DISTANCE-SIZE-TIME CONTINUUM

Since tactical shooters may use a front-sight focus in a few situations, we are going to offer some guidelines that will help you decide when to use a front-sight focus instead of a target focus. As Michael E. Conti stated in his *The Officer's Guide to Police Pistol Craft*, when facing a deadly threat, your chances of being able to focus on the front sight instead of the target are slim to none.

Factors that help you decide what kind of focus to use are distance, size, and time. If the distance to your target is 20 feet or less, a target focus is usually more effective than a front-sight focus. At short distances, you do not have time to focus on the front sight or get a sight picture if your adversary is attacking you with a knife or gun. Good tactical shooters can use target focus at distances of more than 20 feet.

The second critical factor is size. In a hostage situation, people threatening a hostage with a gun might not have more than a small part of their body exposed. In a situation that requires precision accuracy, regardless of distance, a front-sight focus might be more effective than a target focus. Two things that can make using a front-sight focus easier in a hostage situation are having the hostage taker and the hostage stationary and not having the gun pointed in your direction. It is easier to use a front-sight focus when the deadly threat is being directed at someone else.

The third factor is time. If you have less than a few seconds to align your gun and take the shot, using a target focus will be faster than using a front-sight focus. Targets that move erratically or briefly expose themselves force you to shoot and use the best alignment possible under the circumstances or not get a shot.

When facing a deadly threat, such factors as distance, size, and time interact with each other and create a sense of urgency. Because of the way the human body functions, when a deadly threat creates a sense of urgency, people respond by keeping their eyes focused on the threat so they can see what he is doing.

You may have situations where the space between you and a person posing a deadly threat is less than 21 feet, but he does not create a strong sense of urgency because he has not detected your presence. If you are hiding behind cover when an armed robber enters a store and he does not see you, your sense of urgency should be relatively low and using a front-sight focus should be relatively easy, compared to a situation where you and the robber see each other at the same time.

Another way to lower your sense of urgency is to have your partner stay behind cover and give someone a verbal command to surrender. This will give you time to get a good sight picture before your partner issues the command, and you will not need to rush the shot if the person tries to shoot your partner.

You can also use a front-sight focus when trapping a target. If someone is shooting at you from behind cover, focus your front sight on where you believe a body part, such as the head, will be the next time it appears and then shoot as soon as you have a target.

TRIGGER PULL

When you pull the trigger, you need to do it in a way that does not disturb the alignment of your gun before the bullet has cleared the barrel. In competition shooting, this can mean staying sharply focused on the front sight until you see it rise when the gun recoils. In tactical shooting, you seldom use the front sight, and you are not likely to watch the front sight rise unless you are shooting a distance that is far beyond normal distances for tactical shooting with a handgun, such as 150 feet.

Different words have been used to describe how you should pull a trigger, such as *press* or *squeeze*, and how you should not pull a trigger, such as *jerk* or *snap*. We believe the best word for describing how to pull a trigger is *slide*. When you pull the trigger, think of sliding it back and then releasing it so it can move forward and reset itself. Do not try to determine exactly when the gun will fire, which is called using a surprise break, and do not try to release the trigger the instant it fires the gun. The pulling movement should be smooth and continuous, and your finger should not interfere with the trigger when it tries to reset itself.

One of the most-effective and least-expensive ways to improve trigger pull is to practice pulling the trigger when your handgun is empty (dry-fire). To use this method, use the sights to get a good sight picture, pull the trigger, and watch to see if the gun remains aligned on the target. Some degree of movement is normal, but you should keep the gun as steady as possible until you hear the click tell you the firing mechanism has been activated. Try not to let the gun move at all when you are sliding the trigger toward the back of the trigger guard.

If you do not have access to a shooting range, dry-firing is an excellent way to practice all the basic shooting skills: grip, stance, alignment, and trigger pull. Other cost-effective ways to practice include using a handgun that shoots BBs or pellets or using a handgun that activates a laser-beam device each time you pull the trigger. Some guns are designed to shoot nothing but laser beams.

Shooting skills, like most other motor skills, are degradable, which means failure to practice can result in a loss of skill. If self-defense is the reason you learned how to use a handgun, you should practice correctly and on a regular basis with your handgun for the same reason.

Before you dry-fire a gun or practice with a laser device that attaches to a gun, empty the gun, leave the cartridges in one room, and practice in a different room. Even if your gun is empty, always point it in a safe direction, such as in the direction of a backstop that will trap a bullet. Dry firing will not damage most handguns, but check with a competent source, such as the company that made your handgun, if you have any doubts. You will know you have perfected your trigger pull when aiming a gun, pulling the trigger, and hitting your target become almost automatic and you cannot remember exactly when you pulled the trigger.

LOAD AND RELOAD

If you try to make training and practice realistic, reloading would have a higher priority than weak-hand shooting and a lower priority than grip, stance, alignment, or trigger pull. If you get involved in a gunfight, it's unlikely that you will fire more than five shots, which means you will probably not need to reload even if you carry a relatively low-capacity handgun, such as a five-shot revolver.

If you carry a pistol that holds 10 or more rounds in the magazine, it's even more unlikely you will need to reload. Police officers are more likely to fire more than five shots during a gunfight than private citizens, but the number of shots fired may represent the total number of shots fired by all of the officers involved. Some studies indicate when two or more officers engage one subject in a gunfight, they often shoot more rounds per officer than if one officer engaged the subject in a gunfight. It also appears that officers who use pistols with high-capacity magazines fire more rounds per gunfight than officers who carry revolvers.

People should be able to reload any handgun they carry with reasonable smoothness and speed, and people who carry a handgun that holds fewer than six rounds should carry extra ammunition. Before semiautomatic pistols with high-capacity magazines were widely used by police officers, most officers carried six rounds in their revolvers, 12 rounds in belt pouches or speed loaders, and possibly 18 rounds in a plastic ammunition wallet in their back pocket.

Because of the many different handguns you can carry, we are not going to give specific advice on how to load or unload every handgun. The best source of information on how to load or unload you handgun is the owner's manual that came with it. If you do not have the manual, many handgun manufacturers make them available on the Internet or provide instructions on how to order one.

Regardless of what kind of handgun you carry, you should be able to load and fire one round at a time. To do this with a revolver, you need to know which way the cylinder rotates so the round moves into place behind the chamber when you cock the hammer. In a semiautomatic pistol, you need to know how to load one round in the chamber and rack or release the slide so you can fire the pistol.

Most people believe they can count the number of rounds they fire during a gunfight, but this is not supported by facts. If they fire more than one or two rounds, most people cannot tell you how many rounds they fired unless they know how many rounds they had in their gun and they fired until the gun was empty. In most tactical situations, you tend to lose fine motor control because of stress, and reloading your gun when you know it's empty is usually safer than trying to make a tactical reload, which means removing and saving a partially empty magazine and then replacing it with a fully loaded magazine.

If you are involved in a gunfight, it is safer to drop an empty magazine on the ground and replace it with a full magazine than try to put the empty magazine in your pocket after you replace it with a full magazine. No one wants to lose or damage a good magazine, but getting your gun reloaded as quickly as possible needs to be your main concern. Unless you carry loose ammunition, you could not reload the empty magazine if you wanted to. If you are in a military situation where good magazines are scarce and you have the ammunition you need to reload empty magazines, recovering a dropped magazine might be more reasonable.

If you believe you might need to do a tactical reload, these guidelines can be helpful. When you are ready to replace a partially used magazine, grasp a fully loaded magazine the way you normally do when you load your gun and place your hand below the magazine to be replaced. Some people run their index finger upward and along the side of the full magazine that faces the front of the gun and use it to guide the magazine into the opening of the magazine well, which is the open space between the grips of a gun that holds the magazine.

After you have the full magazine in your hand, activate your magazine release and drop the partially used magazine into the same hand that is holding the full magazine. While this is taking place, your dominant hand should have a firm grip on the gun, and the barrel should be pointed in the direction of your adversary. As the partially used magazine drops, catch it with the palm of your hand and hold it between your little finger and ring finger. If you believe you are going to drop one of the magazines, hold on to the full magazine and let the other one fall on the ground. Some people prefer to grasp the used magazine between their middle finger and ring finger, but both methods are acceptable.

Regardless of whether you are still holding the used magazine or have dropped it on the ground, load the full magazine and give the bottom a hard tap to make certain it's properly seated. If you have a live round in the chamber, there is no reason to rack the slide, but some people would rather rack the slide and lose the live round than risk having an empty chamber.

If you have loaded the full magazine and you still have the partially empty magazine in your hand, do not put it back in your magazine holder if you still have a full magazine in it. If things get very stressful and you need to reload again, you might mistakenly load the partially used magazine instead of the full magazine. Some people put partially used magazines in a back pocket.

If you need to reload during a gunfight, two things are very important: reload when you are behind cover if you can and keep your eyes on your adversary while you reload. These things are not essential when target shooting, but they are very important if someone is shooting at you. It's good to carry extra magazines when you knowingly enter a dangerous situation, such as a drug raid, but most people will not fire enough rounds during a gunfight to make reloading necessary.

MALFUNCTIONS

This will not apply to everyone who uses a handgun for self-defense, but if you have a backup gun, switching to the backup gun is usually faster than trying to reload or clear a malfunction in your primary gun. If all else fails and you need to deal with a malfunction, try to get behind cover before you start and look for escape routes in the event you cannot clear the malfunction and you need to retreat.

The best way to deal with malfunctions is to avoid them. Break in a new gun by shooting several hundred rounds before you use it for self-defense, and test the ammunition you are going to use when you carry the gun. Although it tends to be rare when using a modern handgun, a gun may function normally when using practice ammunition but malfunction when defense ammunition is used. Another good precaution is to keep any handgun you are going to use for self-defense clean and properly lubricated, especially if the gun gets wet because of perspiration.

Before you start looking for malfunctions, make certain that the gun is loaded and that none of the safeties on the gun are engaged. The chamber of a gun can be empty because you have fired all the ammunition or because of a malfunction that prevents rounds from feeding into the chamber. If a gun malfunctions, take immediate remedial action to make it functional.

Most modern revolvers do not malfunction if properly maintained, but some of the older ones would malfunction by not aligning the cylinder with the barrel when a gun was fired double-action. In some cases, a temporary fix for this problem was cocking the revolver single-action or rotating the cylinder by hand until it locked into place. Fixing this problem usually requires a gunsmith.

If a semiautomatic pistol fails to fire or a casing has been trapped in the ejection port, the first action you should perform is smack, rack, and roll (SRR). Smack means you give the bottom of the magazine a hard bump with the palm of your support hand to make certain it's properly seated. If you keep your fingers perpendicular to the barrel of the gun when you smack the bottom of the magazine, it should be easy to rotate your fingers around the grip after you smack the magazine and slide them into a support position when using a two-handed grip.

Rack and roll means you point the gun forward and in the direction of a potential target if you have one, slide your support hand over the top of the slide until you can grab the back of the slide with your palm and fingers, and pull the slide back (rack the slide). If an empty cartridge is sticking out the ejection port, which is called a *stovepipe*, sliding your hand back should dislodge the empty casing. As you rack the slide, tilt the pistol toward the ejection port. This will encourage any cartridge that gets ejected when you rack the slide to fall out because of gravity. When the slide is all the way back, release it and let it slam forward. Do not hold onto the slide (ride the slide) as it moves forward because this can weaken the forward momentum and cause another malfunction.

If you smack, rack, and roll, pointing your gun forward and in the direction of a potential target will decrease your response time if you need to shoot. If your target's location is unknown and you are not behind cover, try to get behind cover, keep the gun pointed forward, and scan the area for targets by carefully looking and listening. Avoid exposing more of your body than necessary when you scan.

If you point the gun to the side when you rack the slide, you may accidently shoot someone beside you, and if you point the gun up or down when you rack the slide, gravity cannot help you eject a spent cartridge and it will take longer to align the gun if your adversary is in front of you.

Grabbing the slide with your palm and fingers instead of your thumb and fingers will make the grip stronger. When using your support hand to rack the slide, your thumb should be pointed toward your body, your palm should be on one side of the slide, and all four fingers should be on the other side.

If smack, rack, and roll does not work, you may have two cartridges causing the malfunction because one cartridge did not eject and another failed to load (double-feed). To correct this problem, lock the slide back, remove (rip) the magazine, rack the slide, replace the magazine, and repeat smack, rack, and roll. If a double-feed occurs again, repeat the same sequence, but use a fresh magazine if you have one instead of the original magazine. If a malfunction occurs, the important thing is to get the gun working. Follow basic protocols, but do not try to determine specific causes for the malfunction.

DYSFUNCTIONS

You have a dysfunction when one of your hands is not capable of shooting or helping you reload the gun. Injuries to a body part—such as a shoulder, arm, or wrist—can make one or both hands nonfunctioning. If the gun is ready to shoot and you cannot use one hand, use the other. If the gun is empty, you can compensate for one hand being dysfunctional by using something else to hold the gun in place so you can reload the gun with your good hand. For example, put the gun under your other arm, behind one of your knees, or under your foot, knee, thigh, or buttocks, or put the gun in your holster or belt. After the full magazine has been inserted, bump the end against something to make certain it's seated.

If you need to rack the slide after the magazine has been properly inserted, use whatever you can find that will let you snag the rear sight and pull the slide back. Some of the possible options are the top of a holster or belt, the sole of your shoe, or the bark on a tree. After you snag the rear sight, push the gun forward hard enough to pull the slide all the way back and then pull the rear sight away from what you have it pressed up against and let the slide snap forward. Fixed iron sights are less likely to be damaged by this kind of abuse than adjustable sights.

PRIORITIZE

Tactical training needs to be prioritized and based on probable threats, unless you have enough resources to address all possible but unlikely threats. For example, if you are teaching tactical handgun shooting, most of the practice should take place at less than 21 feet, and much of the shooting should be done with one hand. Most tactical shooters will never need to shoot targets at 150 feet.

Despite various claims that police firearms training has made tremendous progress over the past several decades, the national hit rate for police officers was about 20 percent in 1986 when the infamous FBI firefight took place in Dade County, Florida, and it's still about 20 percent. In W. French Anderson's *Forensic Analysis of the April 11, 1986, FBI Firefight*, Special Agent Edmundo Mireles, Jr.—one of the FBI agents involved in this gunfight—observed: "The FBI has been compiling police-related statistics for several decades. What these statistics have shown is that in real-life police shooting incidents, only between 18 and 20 percent of the shots fired hit their target. Only 20 percent!" We continue to repeat this kind of information at the risk of being redundant because so many people continue to ignore the obvious fact that missing about 80 percent of the time indicates that most police firearms-training programs need to be improved.

It might be legally incorrect to say teaching people useless techniques that will get them killed is deliberate indifference, but people who were taught that most tactical shooting should be done with a front-sight focus stand almost no chance of protecting themselves during a gunfight. If you were taught that increasing the distance between you and your adversary to 36 feet puts you at a safe distance because it reduces your risk of getting shot and you give this a higher priority than running for cover or shooting while moving, you might be making a fatal mistake.

A shooting match is not a gunfight, and a gunfight is a lot more than just a shooting match. If gunfights were nothing but a shooting match, there would be a strong correlation between the scores police officers get on a shooting range and their performance during deadly confrontations that require using a handgun. In *Deadly Force*, authors William A. Geller and Michael S. Scott reported there is no relationship between the percentage of shots fired that hit their targets and qualifying scores. Massad Ayoob commented on the same lack of correlation between training and performance in his book *Combat Shooting*. In *The Officer Survival Manual*, Devallis Rutledge observed that target shooting promotes familiarity with your weapon, but it has nothing to do with winning a gunfight.

If police departments have an interest in officer safety, they need to worry more about making firearms training practical and less about making it politically correct or inexpensive. Most of the firearms training police departments offer is closer to being target shooting than tactical shooting, and many departments do not understand that poor training increases the risk of shooting innocent people. As Ed McGivern suggested in *Fast and Fancy Revolver Shooting and Police Training*, competent handgun training can save lives and prevent the "necessity of many killings." People with good tactical and handgun training are less likely to panic and shoot innocent bystanders than people who are poorly trained.

MULTIPLE TARGETS

Most police officers are not taught how to prioritize multiple adversaries. Simplistic guidance, such as "shoot the person closest to you first and never shoot anyone twice until you have shot everyone at least once," can get you killed when you are trying to defeat multiple adversaries. If you cannot avoid multiple adversaries by using situational awareness and recognizing danger signs, your best assets will be thinking fast, moving fast, not wasting shots, and having good luck. The five general principles that relate to multiple adversaries are:

- Make every effort possible to call for backup.
- You need 360-degree situational awareness to monitor the targets.
- Evasion or escape is usually safer than direct confrontations.
- Use a target focus and be prepared to shoot when you attack or retreat.
- Shoot the person who poses the most immediate deadly threat first.

Any plan for dealing with multiple adversaries is almost useless if it fails to consider incapacitation. People who recommend one shot per adversary might be right if the one shot is a head shot that causes immediate incapacitation, but three shots to the center of mass are useless if your opponent returns fire and kills you. In the 1997 North Hollywood shootout between police officers and bank robbers, unlike 650 center-of-mass shots, two head shots would have stopped the robbers.

One protocol for dealing with multiple adversaries is to scan the targets, shoot at the person who seems to be the most immediate deadly threat, and try to make a head shot or heart shot, depending on the circumstances and your training.

If a target continues to be an imminent deadly threat, you can shoot again, which makes you an easier target for your other adversaries, or you can try to get behind cover before you shoot again. If cover is not available, you can move and then shoot or move and shoot at the same time. Moving while shooting makes you a hard target to hit because you are not remaining stationary after you shoot. When you are moving, try to avoid falling down, exposing your back, being surrounded, or moving into an area with no cover or no exit routes.

No one can tell you exactly what you should do when dealing with multiple adversaries because success will depend partially on how quickly you adapt to a constantly changing environment and partially on luck. Using surprise based on mobility, speed, or deception is usually more effective than a bold frontal attack—but not always. If you're lucky, your adversaries will panic and make mistakes or flee when they see you have seriously injured one of their own. If you know you have multiple adversaries, avoid the fatal mistake of relaxing too soon.

QUICK DRAW AND HOLSTERS

The ideal way to win a gunfight is to subdue your adversary without getting hurt or firing a shot. The best way to do this is to stay alert and to have your gun in position to shoot before your adversary has a chance to draw. If your adversary has the drop on you, your chances of resolving the situation without getting shot are greatly reduced regardless of what you do.

As stated earlier, your brain is your most powerful weapon, but it's sometimes the one that is least used. A few examples of not using your brain include having your flashlight in the hand you use to draw your gun, taking your eyes off someone who might be dangerous, failing to watch someone's hands or what he is reaching for, or letting someone get behind you. If you let any of these situations occur, whatever quick-draw skills you have will probably be useless.

Having a fast draw can be useful if you are taken by surprise and you still have enough time to respond, but duty holsters and the ones used for concealed carry do not make it easy to draw and shoot quickly. Fast-draw exhibition shooters would be slower than normal if they had to deactivate a holster safety or remove clothing that is covering their gun before they could draw and shoot. Holsters are usually a compromise between maximum security and maximum speed.

Being fast on the draw will seldom save your life. Having someone grab your gun and use it against you, poor shooting skills, using the wrong aim point, or being indecisive is more likely to get you killed than being slow on the draw. Until you can shoot with speed and accuracy after a gun is already in your hand, having a smooth and reliable draw is more important than having a fast draw.

Having your gun aligned on someone who reaches for a gun will increase your chances of shooting first. Having the gun pointed slightly downward in a ready position but just a few inches from being aligned on your target is almost as good. If your gun is not already drawn, having situational awareness, recognizing danger signs, having your hand on your gun, and disengaging any safeties you have on a holster will give you some advantages if you need to draw and shoot.

Even in the Old West, bushwhacking and shooting people in the back was more popular than standing face-to-face and having a quick-draw contest. Most of the Wild West gunfighters realized face-to-face confrontations between two people of equal skill would usually result in both people getting shot and maybe killed. In most cases, running for cover before you draw your gun is a better option than having a fair gunfight unless you are very quick and your adversary is very slow. In the Old West, marshals and sheriffs tried to avoid fair fights—modern gunfighters, including police, should do the same. Being legal does not mean you need to give criminals who are trying to kill you a fair chance.

Rather than draw your gun when someone is rushing at you with a knife, try to put a barrier or distance between you and the knife and then draw your gun. The safest way to increase distance is to run in the opposite direction because backing away is too slow. If you remain stationary, the only shot that causes incapacitation fast enough to stop someone from cutting or stabbing you is a head shot. Even if you have used empty-handed knife disarms before, try to avoid having to use them.

If you parry (deflect) or block a knife, your safest option is to go for a head shot. Using a pelvic shot to instantly incapacitate aggressive people who are skillfully wielding a knife at close range is almost as hard as shooting the knife out of someone's hand or shooting someone in the knee. If you try to make a pelvic shot, simultaneous moving and shooting may help you avoid getting injured.

You do not need to be a quick-draw artist, but you should practice drawing your gun from a holster and not shooting, as well as drawing and then shooting. The reason for practicing both techniques is that automatically shooting after you draw your gun might be a good skill if you are planning to become a fast-draw artist, but in the real world, you are more likely to draw your gun and not shoot than draw your gun and shoot—which is why you need shoot-don't-shoot training.

Making the act of drawing and shooting your gun a conditioned reflex can have serious consequences because it can increase the risk of accidentally shooting someone in a no-shoot situation. You can make drawing your gun with your finger off the trigger a conditioned reflex, but your mind needs to consciously decide at what point your finger goes on the trigger and at what point you pull the trigger.

In your quest for speed, be careful not to let rushing a shot result in missing your target. Give yourself enough time to get your gun properly aligned before you pull the trigger. You may have times when you need to shoot from the hip, but that would normally mean your target is very close and you have very little time to respond. If you have time, move the gun into or slightly below your line of sight.

If you are trying to improve your draw, focus on safety, smoothness, and reliability before you try to improve your speed. If you are a tactical shooter, you should practice drawing your gun from the kind of holster or container—such as a purse or fanny pack—you plan to use when you carry your gun for self-defense.

For practice to be productive, it needs to be specific. If you want to increase your speed when drawing from a tactical holster, practice drawing from the same holster you are going to use. Specificity applies to most aspects of training. If you want to improve your combat effectiveness, your practice should closely parallel the tools, targets, and situations you are going to be dealing with in the real world. Two things that can help you increase the speed of your draw are good technique and frequent practice. A good technique will help you eliminate unnecessary movements that reduce your speed, and frequent practice will help you build the motor skills that make it easier for your body to move quickly.

If you are learning how to draw a handgun, make certain the gun is not loaded or pointing at your body when you draw and make certain your finger is not on the trigger when you draw the gun. Start with movements that are smooth and slow and work your way up to movements that are smooth and fast. Drawing in front of a mirror or filming your practice can help improve your draw.

A dominant-side holster (usually a right-side holster if you are right-handed) is the best option for most people, and these holsters can be worn inside or outside the belt. Holsters that might be useful under special circumstances include shoulder holsters, cross-draw holsters, pocket holsters, and ankle holsters, which are often used by people who carry a backup gun. You can also find deep-concealment holsters if concealment is your main concern, but some of these holsters can be hard to access and you may need to use two hands or unzip or unbuckle your pants to get your gun out of one of these holsters.

Regardless of what you use to carry your gun, your gun is not going to be of much value unless you can draw it quickly enough to counter any potential threat. Using a purse or fanny pack to carry a concealed handgun is perfectly acceptable if you can find and draw the gun when you need to use it. If you carry your handgun in a purse, shopping bag, fanny pack, or briefcase, make certain you don't need to feel around for the gun or move things out of the way before you can draw it.

Be very careful not to put your finger on the trigger when pulling your gun out of the holster or carrier. It is easy to see how jerking or tugging on a gun to get it out of a tight holster, purse, or fanny pack might result in an accidental discharge. If you are having this much difficultly removing your gun from a holster or any other container, look for another way to carry the gun.

One thing people sometimes forget when deciding what kind of holster they should use is comfort. A holster that's comfortable for a large or tall person might not be so for a shorter or heavier person, and a holster that works well for a man might not work as well for a woman. If you are not fairly certain about what kind of holster you need, you should wear the holster with your gun inside and see how it feels. If you are planning to use the holster for concealment, you should test the holster when wearing the kind of clothes you normally wear when you carry the gun.

Traditional leather holsters are still popular with many people, but they tend to absorb moisture and increase the risk of having your gun rust. Kydex and other synthetic materials are being used to make holsters, but price does not always indicate which ones are the best. Synthetic holsters are usually less likely to stretch, tear, crack, or be damaged by mold or mildew than leather holsters. If you always carry the same gun, you may need to change from one holster to another depending on what you are going to wear when you carry the gun. Tucking a gun in your belt or waistband instead of a holster is seldom a good idea.

TACTICAL SKILLS

Tactical skills are the art and science of using your handgun correctly when dealing with a deadly confrontation. From a self-defense perspective, good tactical skills can help you to avoid potentially dangerous situations or to deal quickly and effectively with deadly situations that you cannot avoid.

Unlike a military situation, in which guns are used for killing or wounding the enemy, in a nonmilitary situation guns are used to stop an imminent deadly threat by causing immediate or timely incapacitation. Causing incapacitation may result in death, but the reason for using deadly force is to cause incapacitation, not death. If someone is no longer an imminent deadly threat because of incapacitation, using additional force would not be reasonable or necessary—and it might be illegal.

Dangerous confrontations can be resolved by using nonphysical or physical skills. The two most common nonphysical skills are avoidance and negotiation. Avoidance is recognizing and staying away from dangerous situations, and negotiation is the process of using verbal skills to reach an agreement that prevents anyone from being seriously injured or killed.

Physical skills are body movements that give you a tactical advantage, such as flanking or getting behind adversaries, which makes you a harder target and them an easier one. You can also use movement to make yourself a harder target by not remaining stationary, increasing the distance between you and your adversaries, or repositioning behind cover. Moving quickly can surprise your adversaries and catch them off guard whether you attack, defend, or retreat. You can also move to a place that gives you concealment or a better field of view.

Unlike target shooting, which is won or lost because of marksmanship, most deadly confrontations against someone with a gun or knife are won or lost because of what happens *before* you pull the trigger. Experienced police officers can often resolve a dangerous situation without firing a shot because they know how to give themselves the upper hand and leave a suspect with only two options: submit or get shot. Most people would rather submit than face the possibility of getting shot.

This chapter will discuss some of the ways police officers use tactics to avoid the need for deadly force or to make deadly force effective. Many of the people who read this book will not be law enforcement officers, but the lessons these officers learned the hard way, or the mistakes they made that cost them their lives, are valuable sources of information for people who use a gun for self-defense.

The following discussion is based on tactical considerations, not local, state, or federal laws. It's your responsibility to know if using a certain tactic is legal or illegal. We have no way of knowing where you will be if you use deadly force, what the laws are for that jurisdiction, or how those laws will be interpreted. At a minimum, if you plan to use a handgun for self-defense, you should be familiar with the self-defense laws in your state. You should get any information your state provides that will help you understand your rights and responsibilities regarding the use of deadly force and self-defense. Since the self-defense laws are different in each state, you should get the same kind of information from any states you might visit. If you use deadly force to protect yourself, the laws for the state you are in will be the ones that are enforced. But remember that federal laws always apply regardless of which state you are in when you use deadly force.

It's possible the laws for the state you live in might be considered if the state you live in issued you a permit to carry a concealed handgun and a question is raised about your legal right to carry it in other states. If the state you are in when you use deadly force does not have a reciprocity agreement with the state that issued the concealed handgun permit, you might not have a legal right to carry a concealed handgun in the state where the deadly force was used.

Most people who carry a concealed handgun for self-defense will never use it, and issues relating to laws and jurisdictions will never become a concern. On the other hand, if you happen to shoot someone, you may regret not learning more about self-defense laws if a shooting you thought was legal turns out to be illegal.

Even if you have a basic understanding of the law, you should follow the same advice that most police unions give their members: do not give an official statement about a shooting or discuss the matter with anyone until you speak to an attorney. Most people do not remember exactly what happened during a shooting, and the statements they make just after a shooting are often confusing or incorrect.

If you shoot someone in self-defense, being in total compliance with the law does not guarantee you will not be charged with a crime or sued civilly. Police officers are often sued after the lethal force they used was ruled justifiable and they were not charged with a crime. Rather than fight the lawsuit, some departments settle out of court to protect themselves and let the officers pay for their own defense.

In his book *Blood Lessons*, Charles Remsberg pointed out that even if you do everything right during a shooting and afterwards, "there is still a high probability that there will be a lawsuit filed, and possibly a settlement or civil court verdict in favor of the suspect or his family." Two retired FBI agents named Urey Patrick and John Hall expressed this opinion in their book *In Defense of Self and Others*: "It should be apparent that it is impossible to avoid or prevent lawsuits in the aftermath of any use of force by a law enforcement officer. According to Kenneth Murray, who wrote the book titled *Training at the Speed of Life*, one of the officers who responded to the infamous North Hollywood bank robbery in 1997 spent more than $100,000 of his own money defending himself against a lawsuit that was filed after the robbery. Even if you kill someone in self-defense, you might be charged with murder or manslaughter because of public or political pressure.

If you would like a good overview of the laws different states use, a good starting point is *Self-Defense Law of All 50 States* by attorneys Mitch Vilos and Evan Vilos, but be sure to research the most up-to-date information in your jurisdiction, as laws do change. If you have a permit to carry a concealed weapon, many of the states can supply you with a copy of the state self-defense statutes that will help you understand your rights and duties.

As Sun Tzu explained in his classic book *The Art of War*, tactics are used to gain or maintain a position of advantage and control prior to and during a deadly confrontation. In most civilized countries, law-abiding citizens have a right to protect themselves when threatened by vicious criminals with imminent deadly force, but this right does not come without restrictions. You need to consider these restrictions and other possible liabilities when you select your tactics.

The four elements that increase the probability you will survive a dangerous confrontation are attitude, awareness, advantage, and accuracy.

- *Attitude* means you are willing to do whatever it takes to defend yourself.
- *Awareness* allows you to recognize, evaluate, and react to threats.
- *Advantage* means putting someone who is threatening you at a tactical disadvantage.
- *Accuracy* gives you the ability to be combat effective when you are using a handgun to stop a deadly threat.

Concepts like attitude, awareness, and accuracy are easier for most people to understand than advantage. A deadly confrontation with a criminal is not about fairness—it's about gaining advantages that give you the ability to win.

The seven basic ways to gain an advantage over a deadly assailant are to use decisiveness, determination, preparedness, movement, cover, concealment, and positioning to give yourself a tactical edge. If you are facing a dangerous criminal, your ability to be calm, cold, calculating, and ruthless may work to your advantage.

Decisiveness is needed to counter a major mistake that can get you injured or killed—hesitation. If you do not act before it's too late, it will be too late. If you wait for someone to hit you with a steel pipe, get within a few feet of you with a knife, or point a gun at you before you take action, it will probably be too late. Police officers have made all three of these fatal mistakes.

When you are facing a deadly confrontation, it is not a good time to wonder if you have a legal right to use deadly force or to have a moral dilemma with using deadly force. Most deadly confrontations are over within three to five seconds, which does not give you much time to analyze the situation and carefully consider the consequences.

Preparation can also help you avoid hesitation. Know the basic factors that justify the use of deadly force and decide how much risk you are willing to take before you are faced with a shoot-or-don't-shoot situation. Deciding to shoot is not an easy decision for most police officers because even if they are lucky enough to work for a department that has a written use-of-force policy, more questions are usually left unanswered than answered and lawsuits are almost unavoidable.

You have at least four possible options if you enter a room and someone is holding a gun pointed downward toward the floor:

1. Shoot without giving a verbal command (do this) and warning (or else).
2. Shoot immediately if the person disobeys your verbal command.
3. Shoot if the person disobeys your verbal command and raises the gun.
4. Do nothing if the person disobeys your verbal command and raises the gun.

All these options might be legal, but deciding which one is best depends on the circumstances. The first option is least likely to get you killed, and option four is most likely to get you killed because you are letting your adversary decide if you live or die. In most situations, police officers would use option three.

If a police officer with gun in hand responds to a bank robbery in progress and a suspect points a gun at the officer, the best option might be to shoot without giving a verbal command and warning, such as, "Lower the gun or I'll shoot!" In this situation, you might be dead before you complete the verbal command. If this case goes to court, the officer's side may argue that giving a verbal command and warning was not reasonable or necessary because it would have jeopardized the officer's safety, and the other side may counter that the suspect wanted to surrender but was shot by the police officer before he had a chance to do so.

Shooting someone who refuses to obey a verbal command and warning, such as, "Slowly put your gun on the floor or I'll shoot," regardless of whether you shoot 1 second or 15 seconds after the command is disobeyed, often results in criminal charges and civil liability—especially if activist groups demand you be arrested or the news media tries the case on television before the facts are known.

If the case goes to court, your side may argue that waiting longer would have increased your risk of being killed, and the other side may make the case that you should have waited longer before you decided to shoot, regardless of how long you waited. It's easy to understand why some people believe the criminal justice system protects dangerous criminals more than it protects police officers or innocent victims.

According to *Training at the Speed of Light* by Kenneth R. Murray, one police department in Florida took the position that anyone who refuses to drop a gun when ordered to do so is a lethal threat and can be shot if other alternatives are not available. This department was clearly putting the safety of the officer over that of the suspect who was holding a gun. Other alternatives might include a situation where the suspect is barricaded in a building and the officer can safely retreat and wait for a negotiator to arrive.

If an officer does not shoot until the suspect raises his gun, the officer might not have time to react and may get shot and killed before having enough time to shoot. Even if the officer has enough time to shoot, rushing the shot may cause him to miss, or poor shot placement may give the suspect enough time to return fire and kill the officer. Officers who shoot before someone starts to raise a gun might have time to make a head shot and cause immediate incapacitation, or time for two quick heart shots followed immediately by a head shot. This is one of those situations where being tactically correct can be legally precarious.

The worst option is to do nothing. Police officers who select this option are a danger to themselves because they are putting their life in the hands of an armed suspect. This does not mean doing nothing will always have a negative outcome. The suspect may decide to drop the gun or walk away, the gun might not be loaded or operational, or the suspect might shoot and miss. On the other hand, the suspect may kill the officer who did nothing, as well as his partner and any innocent bystanders or witnesses who might testify in court.

Attempting to disarm someone who refuses to drop a gun without using deadly force can get you killed, and sometimes the public fails to realize that what they see on television is not what happens in the real world. Situations in which a police officer might need to use a nonlethal disarming technique include not having enough time to draw and shoot, or having no way to shoot without endangering innocent bystanders. Using an electroshock device, such as a Taser gun, to disarm someone with a gun should be avoided unless you have no other option. Electroshock devices are not always reliable, and the strong, involuntary muscle contractions they induce might cause someone holding a gun to involuntarily pull the trigger.

Using electroshock devices to disarm someone with a knife is less dangerous than using them on someone who is holding a gun, but they are still more dangerous than using a handgun. If the device fails, you might not have enough time to draw your firearm and shoot. If you decide to use an electroshock device to disarm someone who is armed with a knife, have several people who are armed with guns backing you up and have medical responders available who can provide emergency care.

As a private citizen, you have one major advantage over police officers who are legally required to serve and protect the public by enforcing the law: you will not be charged with dereliction of duty if you end a deadly confrontation by walking away. Even if you have a legal right to stand your ground and fight, the legal consequences for standing your ground are usually worse than the legal consequences for walking away. Evil may triumph when good people do nothing, but doing nothing is less likely to get you sued or charged with a crime.

From a tactical—not legal—standpoint, retreat might be a better option even if you have a legal right to stand your ground and use deadly force. For example, retreating to cover and shooting from behind cover is almost always better than shooting at someone when you are standing out in the open. If you are not in a position to end a deadly confrontation quickly by firing a well-placed shot at close range, increasing the distance between you and your adversary may work in your favor, especially if you have better shooting skills than he does.

Self-defense laws may give you the right to protect yourself from a deadly threat, but they do not bestow the same arrest powers a police officer has. Using deadly force to protect personal property can be expensive. If someone is not threatening you with imminent serious bodily injury or death, you may face criminal charges if you use deadly force to stop someone from stealing property, and the legal expenses might be more than the value of the property being stolen.

Walking away alive after shooting someone in self-defense is often just the beginning of a long and unpleasant journey that includes criminal charges or civil lawsuits. As Jim Cirillo said: "In the end, it's all about politics." Mexico has had over 50,000 drug-related homicides, but some of its citizens still believe that getting murdered is morally superior to using deadly force to defend themselves.

Shooting someone in the back might be tactically correct or legal in some situations, but activists, the news media, and the lawyers defending the criminal you shot in the back will try to portray you as a cold-blooded killer. If the case goes to trial, the same people on the jury who believe police officers should shoot people in the leg instead of in the chest may also believe only a coward would shoot someone in the back, and what juries believe can send you to jail.

One of the hardest things for most people to understand is that dangerous criminals automatically have an advantage over innocent victims. Unlike law-abiding citizens, criminals are not concerned about the legality of having or using a gun, and they can pick the time and place for their crimes. Criminals do not worry about fairness, and about the only time they regret committing a crime is when they get caught. Without good training and good luck, it's hard not to be a victim.

If you do shoot someone in the back and the case goes to criminal court, you might improve your chances of being found not guilty if an expert witness can testify that your adversary was shot in the back because he was in the process of turning away from you when you fired the shot. For example, if someone who is facing you fires a shot at you and then turns away, the person's back might be facing you by the time your bullet hits the body.

Self-defense laws are not easy to understand, and different judges or prosecutors often interpret the same law in different ways. If you are using a gun for self-defense, learn enough about self-defense laws to avoid making serious mistakes that could have been avoided if you had at least a basic understanding of the self-defense law. If you would like to avoid prison or losing almost everything you own, get legal advice about when you have a right to use deadly force before you decide to use a handgun for self-defense. You may have the right to protect yourself against illegal deadly force, but these rights will not be the same in every state. If you really believe you always have a legal right to use deadly force when protecting personal property, you should definitely seek legal advice before you act on this belief.

PREPAREDNESS

Most people have heard the saying, "Ignorance of the law is no excuse," and this applies to self-defense laws. Special-interest groups are constantly challenging existing laws and trying to make changes that reflect their own personal values. Even though the average law-abiding citizen will probably not hear about any changes that result because of case law or changes in jury instructions, rewrites of an existing state self-defense law will usually draw enough media coverage to make people aware that the law has been changed. Seek legal advice if you do not understand how your safety will be affected by changes in self-defense laws.

Preparedness can also be applied to your equipment. More than a few police officers have been injured or killed because their handguns were not loaded or because they malfunctioned. If you are going to be effective during a deadly confrontation, you need to have a functional gun. If you have done everything possible to ensure that your gun will function properly and you have a malfunction, you need to know how to fix the malfunction as quickly as possible. Good preparation includes adequate ammunition and frequent practice.

Most modern handguns are extremely reliable and seldom require extensive maintenance, but even the most reliable guns should be checked at least once a week if they are being carried five or more days a week. Guns that are constantly exposed to perspiration have a tendency to rust, and they should always be wiped off and treated with a rust preventative, such as silicon spay, if they get wet. Contrary to popular belief, most stainless steel guns and guns with a rust-resistant finish are not completely immune to rust, and both revolvers and semiautomatic pistols can malfunction because of rust.

If you carry a semiautomatic pistol, you should periodically check both the gun and your magazines. Damaged magazines can cause malfunctions, and some magazines do rust. Malfunctions can also be caused by not having your magazine properly seated. Check to see if your magazine is properly seated after you put your gun in a holster, and if you have time, check whether it's properly seated before you use the gun for self-defense. Extra magazines are usually a good idea.

Ammunition can last for many years if it's not damaged by rust, corrosion, improper cleaning, or improper lubrication that damages the primers or propellant. That being said, shooting the ammunition you have in your gun every year and replacing it with new ammunition reminds you that defense ammunition has more recoil than most practice ammunition, and it also gives you a reason to practice.

You may also find that bullet technology has improved and decide to change to newer ammunition. Bullet technology improves at a faster rate than training improves. Modern hollowpoints are more effective than the earlier hollowpoint bullets because expansion and penetration are both good. Police training, on the other hand, is about the same as it was when police officers used roundnose bullets. Most departments do not give their officers time or ammunition for practice, and shooting is a motor skill that degrades without regular practice.

PROGRESSIVE AWARENESS

- Condition white: Maintain 360-degree situational awareness.
- Condition green: Scan for danger signs.
- Condition yellow: Look for potential threats.
- Condition red: React to verified threats.

Condition white is similar to the level of awareness you should have riding a motorcycle down a quiet country road. You may not have visible traffic, but you need to stay alert because you may discover deep holes or a cow in the road when you enter the next curve. As you get closer to a major city and traffic starts to increase, you should go to *condition green*. Even if there are no danger signs, you need to scan your surrounding environment with a higher level of alertness than you had before you started to merge with heavier traffic. As you get closer to a city, look for danger signs, such as traffic signals. If you see a danger sign, go to *condition yellow* and look for potential threats. A danger sign, such as a four-way flashing red light, becomes a potential threat if a car approaching the intersection from the side does not seem to be slowing down. If it becomes clear the person who was not slowing down is going to run the flashing red light, go to *condition red* and start taking evasive action. Recognizing the danger sign before the car is crossing in front of you will give you extra time to react. If you are on a motorcycle, your best option is usually to swerve to the side, brake hard, or brake and release and then swerve.

Most people walk down a street or enter a bank the same way they drive a car: distracted and with their brains on autopilot. In the car, the air conditioner is running full blast and the music is blaring. They probably don't know if they have cars behind them or next to them, and they seldom pay much attention to a traffic light unless it's yellow or red. If you enter a deadly confrontation with this level of awareness, your chances of being able to react fast enough to protect yourself and survive will be very small.

If you pay attention, you will often see danger signs that indicate a traffic accident or deadly confrontation is about to happen. Recognizing danger signs will give you more time to react than suddenly facing an unexpected threat. If you do not scan for danger signs and make them part of your early-warning system, you will usually have less time to react and fewer offensive or defensive options. Having more time enables you to plan and helps you make good decisions.

Many police officers have lost gunfights because of apathy or complacency. If you miss danger signs and potential threats, you may find yourself in a situation where luck will be your best hope for winning a gunfight. When you are suddenly faced with a deadly threat you failed to anticipate, it's hard to avoid panic or fear.

Some gunfights are hard to predict or prevent, and regardless of what you do, you may get killed. People without proper training often get killed in situations where people with better training would survive, but even good training might not protect you from a sniper, overwhelming force, or ambush. A bad scenario for anyone is to be outnumbered or outgunned by criminals who have killed before and will do it again without hesitation or fear. Even if you can think fast, move fast, and shoot with speed and accuracy, you might not survive.

FIND A WEAKNESS

Always look for a weakness in your adversary's defenses you can exploit. Being able to exploit this weakness requires handgun skills, tactical skills, and the right attitude. The most important handgun skill is being able to shoot with speed and accuracy when using a target focus, and the most important tactical skill is being able to recognize and respond to danger signs quickly and correctly. The most important attitude to have is a willingness to do whatever it takes to win without hesitation or regret.

As the great military strategist Sun Tzu noted: a brilliant general is one who can win without fighting. The same applies to law enforcement officers: the best way to stop a deadly confrontation is to stop it without firing a shot. If your only option is to shoot, try to do it before your adversary has a chance to shoot and try to make your first shot combat effective. You may not get a second chance.

If you need to draw quickly, having something in the hand you draw your gun with, such as a flashlight, can get you killed. When facing a deadly threat, if your gun hand is not empty, the only thing that should be in it is your gun.

One way to create a weakness you might be able to exploit is to change your position before your adversary has time to attack, such as to move to the side, behind cover, or behind your adversary (a flanking maneuver). Making a quick and unexpected movement can be effective, but you need to evaluate the situation so you can anticipate how your adversary will likely react.

If a nervous, desperate, or highly aggressive adversary is pointing a shotgun at you from six or seven feet away, you are probably too far away to risk using a disarming technique, and making a quick or unexpected reaction might cause your adversary to shoot. In some situations, doing nothing and waiting for a better opportunity to go on the offensive is better than making a move when the odds of coming out ahead are not in your favor. In some cases, verbal skills and the ability to evaluate your adversary might be more important than your shooting skills.

KNOW YOUR AIM POINTS

Aim points are areas of vulnerability in the human body, and hitting them will usually cause immediate or timely incapacitation. Shooting and missing might be better than freezing if you disrupt your adversary's plan, but hitting a reliable aim point is the only predictable way to cause immediate or timely incapacitation. Some people argue that shooting for the center of mass will increase your chances of hitting your target, but this logic is badly flawed. Five shots that penetrate noncritical tissue and fail to incapacitate someone are not much better than five misses. To stand a good chance of being able to cause immediate or timely incapacitation and stop a deadly threat, a bullet needs to penetrate one or more critical tissues.

CONFUSION: DECEPTIONS, DISRUPTIONS, AND DISTRACTIONS

The three best techniques for causing confusion are deception, disruption, and distraction. Deceptions cause people to make bad decisions because of false information, disruptions make it hard to think clearly because the brain is receiving more information than it can process at one time, and distractions divert people's attention from one place to another. Falsely telling people that your partner has a gun pointed at them would be a deception, asking too many questions at the same time may cause a disruption, and throwing a rock to divert someone's attention to the opposite side of the room would be a distraction.

Creating confusion can make it harder for people to process information correctly or react quickly, but it can also make people angry and cause them to be more violent than they might have been without the confusion. Using deception to cause confusion can be dangerous because most people do not like finding out that they have been deceived.

If someone is thinking about shooting you, asking a question such as, "Why don't we both just walk away and go home?" might disrupt any thoughts the person has about shooting at you and force him to think about other options. Ask questions that indicate you are trying to be reasonable and fair. If you are pointing a gun at someone who is pointing one at you, asking a question may give you a slight advantage if you shoot while the person is thinking about the question. If you make a center-of-mass shot, the person will probably have time to return fire, and the extra time you get because of asking the question might not make a difference. If you make a head shot, incapacitation would be immediate and asking a question may have saved your life.

You can create a diversion by turning a flashlight on and placing it where you would like a person to look when entering the room. If that person is looking at the flashlight and you are on the other side of the room, this could give you a tactical advantage or it may keep someone from entering the room if the flashlight is pointed at the doorway. Having a remote-control flashlight you could activate when someone enters the room could make the diversion more effective.

If someone is pointing a gun at you and your best option is trying to get behind cover that's fairly close, point the index finger of your nonshooting hand away from the cover, look where you are pointing, and ask a question, such as "What's that?" If the distraction works, the instant your adversary looks in the direction you are pointing, head for cover. As you move toward cover, draw your gun and get it pointed at your adversary. Shooting after you reach cover is usually safer and more accurate than trying to shoot and move at the same time unless your tactical training includes shooting while moving. Most police officers are not trained to shoot and move, move and shoot, or shoot while moving.

AMBUSH

You can use concealment to stage an attack that catches people by surprise and causes confusion. If a diversion is used before the ambush, surprise will occur on two levels: the diversion will cause one surprise, and the attack will cause another. Surprise is effective because it keeps an enemy from having enough time to set up a strong defense or launch a counterattack. In warfare, the two major elements of surprise are secrecy and speed.

Since ambush implies surprise, suddenness, and a lack of provocation, the best defenses against an ambush are awareness and prevention. If you detect a potential ambush, try to avoid the ambush by removing yourself from the danger zone. If you do not have an escape route, take the strongest position possible and call for backup. If you cannot get assistance, look for a point of weakness in the ambush and try to use it as your escape route. Be aware that some enemies will create points of weakness so they can funnel you into a secondary danger zone.

An ambush can also be used as a disruption because of the surprise and the confusion that follows. Unlike a military ambush, which usually involves more than one person, you may have areas in your home you can use as hiding places for staging an ambush. Rather than wait for a crisis to occur, you should study the floor plan in your house and select areas that you can use for an ambush if the need arises. In most cases, you will be more familiar with the layout of your home than a criminal intruder, which will give you a tactical advantage over the intruder. An ambush can be used when retreat is no longer safe or possible.

ACTS OF DESPERATION

Most people do not want to face a situation where they might get shot and possibly killed regardless of what they do. Old West gunfighters tried to avoid this kind of situation by not getting in a fair fight against gunfighters who were equally skilled. The outcome that often results when two people of equal skill get involved in a fair fight is mutual destruction that leaves both parties badly injured or dead.

If you are attacked by a criminal who wants to cause serious injury or death, you are not obligated to be fair or play by any rules. You can lie, throw dirt in his eyes, scratch, bite, or do whatever it takes to prevail. Since you didn't start the fight, you have a right to be ruthless if that's what it takes to keep from getting killed or seriously injured. When you go on the offensive, do it without hesitation and continue your offensive at maximum intensity until you win a decisive victory. People who illegally attack you with the intention of causing serious bodily injury or death are giving you the right to use whatever force is reasonable and necessary to protect yourself. If they die because you are defending yourself, it is as a result of their own actions.

Based on the number of police officers who fired shots at people who were less than 7 feet away and missed, it's possible the people who are shooting at you will also miss. Most criminals are not extremely skilled with a handgun, and the main advantage they have during a gunfight is the element of surprise. Good firearms training can give you an advantage over someone who is poorly trained, but early detection of a dangerous threat can give you an even greater advantage.

If the person who is shooting at you misses and you have a chance to shoot back, you should usually fire at least two shots. In most cases, the first aim point will be the heart, which is near the middle of the sternum. If those shots stop an adversary from moving forward but he is still holding a gun, then a head shot might be advisable if he is close and his head is stationary.

Most police departments do not teach their officers how to make head shots, but as we explained previously, penetrating the brain stem or the upper cervical spinal cord is the only way to cause immediate incapacitation 100 percent of the time. A head shot is not easy to make for people with poor shooting skills, especially when the head is moving, but it can make the difference between life and death in a gunfight. Tactical units within a police department might be taught how to make head shots and some federal agencies teach their agents how to make head shots.

As stated, poor training is one reason police officers miss about 80 percent of the time, but you also have police officers who believe firearms training is a necessary evil or a waste of time. These are often the same officers who don't believe they will ever need to use a gun or who carry guns that are dysfunctional because of corrosion. Handguns are like fire extinguishers—it is better to have one that works and not have to use it than to need to use it and find out it doesn't work.

The final question you need to ask yourself when dealing with a desperate situation is whether you would rather surrender and hope for the best or go down fighting regardless of the consequences. It's easy for someone to tell you that it's better to go down fighting, but no one can make this decision for you. Military statistics show that some people who decided they would rather go down fighting have been killed, and some people who decided they would rather surrender have survived. In the end, it comes down to doing what you think is right, and anyone with practical experience will tell you it's hard to know what you will do until you are facing the situation.

If someone has clearly expressed a desire to kill you or has a good reason for wanting to kill you, such as not wanting to leave any witnesses, almost anything you try will probably be better than giving up. If you do not see surrender or going down fighting as viable options, you might be able to use other alternatives, such as a tactical retreat (running away) or trying to reach a negotiated settlement that does not involve giving up your gun or getting killed. Even a vicious criminal may decide walking away is better than getting killed while trying to kill you.

EQUIPMENT

How much equipment is enough? This is another one of those questions that no one can answer for you. As a private citizen with a concealed handgun permit, you should probably carry extra ammunition if your handgun does not hold more than five rounds. If your handgun has a high-capacity magazine that holds eight or more rounds, you may not need the extra ammunition. Most gunfights are over in less than 5 seconds, with fewer than five rounds fired.

It's not uncommon to hear someone tell civilians: "If you need one handgun, you also need a backup gun because it's faster to pull out your backup gun than to reload your primary weapon." And if you need a backup gun, you also need a flashlight and a sharp knife. A few people may also suggest you wear a ballistic vest whenever you go out in public . . . and always carry two flashlights.

Deciding what kind of equipment you should carry is usually based on the kind of threats you are most likely to face. Extra ammunition might be reasonable if you anticipate facing multiple adversaries, but most people do not fire more than three to five shots during a gunfight. If you anticipate needing to reload, switching to a backup gun is usually faster than reloading an empty gun. If you work in a store that's frequently robbed, a ballistic vest might be reasonable.

Because of the hazards related to the job, it's almost always reasonable for an on-duty police officer to carry a primary weapon, extra ammunition, a backup gun, at least one flashlight, and a knife, and to wear a bullet-resistant vest. If a private citizen anticipates facing similar hazards, then having similar equipment and wearing a bullet-resistant vest might be reasonable. But most private citizens are not likely to face the kind of threats a police officer might, and having one gun and possibly extra ammunition is usually sufficient. If you go out at night, a small pocket-size flashlight and a small folding knife might be useful for reasons that are not related to self-defense. Most off-duty police officers carry a concealed handgun and possibly a knife, but most of them do not carry a backup gun or a flashlight or wear a bullet-resistant vest.

Many people who have a concealed handgun permit do not carry the gun when they leave home, and they seldom practice enough to improve their handgun skills. Investing in ammunition so you can practice at the range or investing in laser equipment so you can practice at home will probably keep you safer during a deadly confrontation than having a flashlight, knife, or ballistic armor.

Regardless of what equipment you buy, learn to use it correctly. Using any weapon incorrectly can increase your risk of getting injured or killed, and wearing a bullet-resistant vest does not make you invincible. If you bought a gun for peace of mind and you are not interested in learning how to use it properly—good luck. Having a gun and not knowing how to use it can be more dangerous than not having one.

STRATEGIES AND WHAT-IF SCENARIOS

If you have questions relating to tactics or strategies, speak to someone who has practical experience. Many of the tactics and strategies you see on television or in the movies will not work in the real world, where the bad guys use real guns. When creating what-if scenarios to prepare for dealing with deadly confrontations, use scenarios that resemble the kind of threats you are most likely to face, such as having your home robbed or getting robbed after cashing a payroll check. Two things a what-if scenario can help you do are find ways to avoid dangerous situations and find ways to survive dangerous situations.

This book can offer some principles for handling what-if scenarios, but real-life scenarios will seldom be exactly the same and you will need to modify some of these principles to meet your own needs. Anyone who has ever been involved in a deadly confrontation will understand the importance of being creative and flexible so you can make adjustments to compensate for unexpected circumstances.

The axioms below represent principles of warfare that have evolved over several thousand years. Many were first recorded by legendary Chinese strategist Sun Tzu, who wrote *The Art of War* around the end of the sixth century, and many he recorded are still being used in modern warfare. Military operations are different than nonmilitary operations, but many of the basic axioms that are used by the military when planning or dealing with enemy forces can also be used effectively by police officers and private citizens when dealing with dangerous criminals.

Basic Axioms

- Have confidence both in your plan and your ability to carry it out.
- Try to learn your adversary's plan and hide your own plan.
- If two plans seem equally effective, choose the simpler one.

- Complex plans are difficult to learn, remember, and use.
- Adjust your plan to be compatible with your resources.
- Have alternative plans in case your original plan fails.
- Plan for attack and defense at the same time.
- Discontinue a plan that is not working.
- Attack when strong and retreat when weak.
- Make your enemy an easier target than you are.
- Keep your enemy off balance by moving or standing still.
- Take a position that makes it easy to attack, defend, or escape.
- Use a plan that benefits from your strength and your enemy's weakness.

DANGER SIGNS

Look for things that might be potentially threatening. You cannot always identify criminals by how they look or dress; some criminals are very good at not looking suspicious. Rather than argue the good or bad points about judging people based on profiles or stereotypes, this book takes the approach that how people behave is more important than how they look. If a person or a group of people look suspicious, out of place, or dangerous, try to avoid making contact by changing direction and putting distance between you and the potential threat.

If your judgment was right and the threat was real, you may have avoided a deadly confrontation. If your judgment was wrong and the people you observed were not a threat, no harm is done. Unlike police officers, most people do not have the authority, training, or resources needed to investigate suspicious behavior, and your best option is to report something that looks suspicious to the police and let them investigate and do what they are getting paid to do. If you consider how many times trained police officers get killed, charged with a crime, or sued because of trying to protect the public, it should be obvious that private citizens who try to enforce the law are risking both their life and their economic future.

If you cannot avoid passing through dangerous areas, look for danger signs (red flags) that relate to criminal behavior. The first thing to watch is how people react as you approach. If people reposition themselves, take an interest in you, or try to make eye contact with you instead of ignoring you, this can be a danger sign. If someone is trying to make eye contact with you, return eye contact and then slowly look in a different direction. Not making eye contact by looking down or looking away can be viewed as a sign of weakness and make you a good potential victim, but making too much eye contact can be viewed as a sign of aggression.

A good tactic is to make eye contact when you get fairly close, smile or nod your head, and ask, "You doing all right?" The way people respond to a friendly greeting may help you decide whether you are going to have a problem. Being friendly can help you defuse potentially dangerous situations. Even if strangers appear to be friendly, do not drop your guard. If you are not a police officer, the best thing to do after getting a friendly response is to keep walking and try to increase the distance between you and the strangers. Someone who seems friendly may shoot you in the back, but it's not likely. Being followed as you walk away is a bad sign.

If people who were standing together separate as you approach, try to walk around them. Criminals often work together, and their separating could mean they are repositioning to get behind you or surround you. If retreat is not possible, take the best position you can if you are going to pass through them and look for escape routes or places you can use for cover. In some cases, stopping and waiting for people to leave might be your best option.

If you see obvious danger signs, reevaluate your ability to avoid danger. If you try to walk away and someone follows you, you might want to increase your speed or consider running instead of walking. If you increase your speed and it becomes obvious you are being followed, you might be facing a deadly threat, and you need to consider your options. If you doubt that you can reach a place that's relatively safe, such as a public area that has a lot of people and possibly a law enforcement or security officer, try to call for help any way you can. If an attack is imminent and you are armed, look for cover, have your gun ready, and be prepared to shoot. Do whatever you can to put your attacker at a disadvantage.

If your attacker continues to approach, issue a strong verbal command, such as, "Don't come any closer!" If the person continues to advance, do not wait until he is almost within arm's length before you defend yourself. If your only protection is a whistle, which some people claim is a better defensive weapon than a handgun, blow your whistle and hope someone hears it and then hope the person who hears it responds quickly enough to provide the kind of help you need.

If you carry a concealed handgun, it should be in your hand and ready to shoot. If you carry a semiautomatic pistol, make certain you have a round in the chamber. If you have the safety off, do not put your finger on the trigger until you are ready to shoot if necessary. Whether the gun can be openly displayed at this point or needs to be hidden may depend on the laws of the state you are in.

Waiting until someone is nearly on top of you before you draw your gun is a dangerous practice. Police officers who were trained to use handgun-retention techniques have gotten shot with their own guns because they waited too long. If a strong person gets a tight grip on your gun, using a knife to loosen the grip is often more effective than using conventional handgun-retention techniques. The best solution is to start shooting before someone has a chance to grab your gun.

Before the attacker gets within about 25 feet, give the command and warning, "Stop or I'll shoot!" If the person is a common thief, seeing the gun and hearing the warning might be enough to end the attack and give you a chance to escape. If the attacker stops advancing and starts talking, carefully watch the person's hands and do not let him get closer. If the attacker ignores your command ("Stop!") and your warning ("I'll shoot"), you might need to use deadly force.

On rare occasions, a criminal you have pointed your gun at will make a false police report and try to have you arrested for a criminal charge, such as reckless display or aggravated assault. Most experienced police officers will not arrest you if your story is credible, you do not have a criminal past, and the person who filed the complaint has no evidence. Some criminals seem to believe filing a preemptive complaint against you will stop you from filing a complaint against them or make the case against them weaker. What's more likely to happen is the person at whom you pointed the gun will walk away and look for a less dangerous victim.

The statistics are hard to verify, but some people suggest criminal predators abandon their attacks 98 percent of the time if they know you have a gun, which also means 2 percent continue the attack and you may need to use deadly force. Having a gun will not deter criminals who don't believe you will use it, and not using a gun when you should can get you or someone else killed with your gun.

If a person is not persuaded to leave because you have a gun and continues to advance, you are quickly reaching a point where you need to decide if you have a right to shoot. This decision might be easier if the person had a visible weapon, such as a gun or knife, but you might not be able to see a weapon or he might not have one. Where state laws are often unclear is when a criminal is large, strong, or young and the victim is small, weak, or old. Even without a deadly weapon, a powerful criminal can be a deadly threat to a weaker victim.

If criminals are bold enough to advance when you are pointing a gun at them and you decide not to shoot, you may get shot with your own gun. Letting people get close enough to take your gun can be fatal. In some cases, police officers who continued giving verbal warnings until the suspect took their gun have survived, but in other cases they were killed with their own guns.

It seems reasonable to believe anyone who illegally tries to take your gun is an imminent deadly threat, but being reasonable does not guarantee you will not be charged. It's possible the person you shot will say he walked up to you to ask you a question and you panicked and pulled the trigger. If you cannot produce witnesses or physical evidence to show that you had reason to believe he was trying to grab your gun, you may be charged with a crime, and you may have a hard time proving your innocence.

If you use deadly force to protect yourself against a deadly threat, you will need to explain why deadly force was justified. When you have witnesses who can testify you didn't shoot until you were shot at and the police find the gun, it's unlikely you will go to jail. When you have no witnesses and a gun is not found, you may go to jail if you cannot provide credible evidence to verify your story and justify the use of deadly force. Despite the possibility of legal consequence, do not let too much analysis (paralysis by analysis) prevent you from defending yourself.

After you decide to shoot, the only thing you need to focus on is stopping the deadly threat. This can be done by firing one or more shots that incapacitate your adversary, cause him to flee, or give you a chance to escape. If you are not a police officer, you are not required to apprehend dangerous criminals.

Even if using deadly force was the only way you could protect yourself against a deadly threat, very few people completely avoid the legal, financial, or psychological consequences that result when they kill someone in self-defense. These consequences are unfair and often unnecessary, but the only guaranteed way to avoid them is to do nothing and risk getting killed when a criminal attacks you.

ACTION AND REACTION

Quickness depends on a combination of two factors: reaction time and movement time. *Reaction time*, which is also called *scan-and-react time*, is the time it takes to perceive and interpret what you see and decide how to respond. *Movement time* is the time it takes to complete the response. The total time it takes to complete an action from start to finish (reaction time plus movement time) is called the *response time*. If circumstances change, you will need to reevaluate the situation and make a new decision (reaction time) and then make the movements that are required to implement the new decision (movement time).

You can decrease movement time by frequently and correctly practicing a movement until it becomes automatic, and you can complete the entire movement without conscious thought. Making a movement automatic may require hundreds of repetitions. To achieve maximum speed, make the essential movements as small as possible and remove nonessential movements (economy of movement).

A process is a series of movements that perform a specific function. When creating an automatic process (motor program), the stimuli that trigger a process need to be carefully defined. A draw-and-shoot motor program might be correct if someone reaches for a gun, but a draw-and-wait motor program would be correct when you are not sure whether you have a shoot-or-don't-shoot situation. Making a process automatic does not mean you cannot consciously stop the process if circumstances change and continuing the process might be detrimental.

Some people have better reflexes than others because of genetics, but most people can shorten their reaction times when drawing a gun by using training that improves threat recognition, which means they are quicker to react because they are quicker to recognize circumstances that would cause them to draw a gun. It also appears the same training that improves movement time may also improve reaction time because of an increase in neuromuscular efficiency.

Decreasing the time it takes to shoot with accuracy when your gun is already in your hand is usually more important than decreasing the time it takes to draw and shoot with accuracy. A good tactical shooting exercise is to start with your gun in your hand and try to shoot a surprise target that suddenly appears and disappears within 1.5 seconds. This is a shooting skill that can save your life. You can increase the difficulty of this exercise by having the disappearing targets pop up at different locations or having multiple targets pop up at the same time.

People are often slow to react when faced with danger, but the reasons are not always the same. Some people are slow to react because of poor training, and police officers are often slow to react because they are sleepy, preoccupied with personal problems, or unwilling to use deadly force. According to the FBI, 85 percent of the police officers who get killed in the line of duty do not fire their weapons.

Action is not always faster than reaction because of variables that are often ignored, such as the time or distance required to complete the action compared to the time or distance required to complete the reaction. If an adversary tries to draw a gun and shoot you (action) when your gun is already in your hand, you might be able to shoot (reaction) before your adversary has time to draw and shoot.

When someone initiates an action, being able to anticipate the action and react quickly and correctly can offset the advantage that often results from being the person who initiated the action. Another way to offset this advantage is to use a technique called *action-distraction*. If someone starts to draw before you have your hand on your gun, rather than react by doing what your adversary expects you to do (draw your gun), leap forward and block or parry (deflect) your adversary's gun with one hand while you draw and shoot with the other hand.

If your knife is easier to access than your gun, you can block or parry the gun with your knife and then attack with the knife. To improve your speed, use economy of movement: make your block or parry and knife attack one continuous movement. In fencing, defense and attack are often combined into one movement.

Anticipating an action can help you defeat the action before it's completed. To a large extent, the ability to anticipate an action depends on your situational awareness and experience. If you anticipate a deadly threat, your gun needs to be in your hand, not in your holster. In the Old West, a professional gunfighter might get the first shot off when going up against an amateur who draws first, but this requires a level of skill most people who carry a gun for self-defense do not have.

If you are armed and you see someone is drawing a gun but you are not close enough to block the gun, your best option might be to move in a lateral or diagonal direction or to get behind cover. Targets moving in a lateral or diagonal direction are harder to hit than targets moving directly away from you, and getting behind cover will make you a smaller target and may give you a chance to shoot.

Many people get confused by quick movements that give the impression you are going to do one thing when your intention is to do something else or nothing. Boxers often pretend to throw one punch (feint) in order to create an opening for another punch. If an army pretends to retreat so it can draw the enemy into an ambush, the tactic is called a *feint retreat*. When you are facing an overwhelming force, attacking as you retreat is often more effective than using a frontal attack.

If someone threatens you with a gun and you decide to use verbal skills instead of physical skills, ask questions that might cause him to think about something other than shooting you. Negotiating with someone who is pointing a gun at you might work if he has not already decided to shoot, but even when you believe you can negotiate your way out of a dangerous situation, look for ways to defend or attack if negotiations fail. In some cases, just trying to negotiate may give your reinforcements time to arrive.

A scientific principle known as Hick's law states that increasing the number of options you have to choose from will increase the time it takes to make a decision. If you want to improve your chances of being able to overcome the advantages your adversary gains by acting first and forcing you to react, you need to limit the number of decisions you must make before you can react.

For example, when using a front-sight focus, you need to decide whether to focus on the front sight or on the target, because you cannot do both. When you focus on the front sight, you cannot focus on the target and get a clear image of what the target is doing. When using a target focus, you don't need to decide whether to focus on the front sight or the target and then decide if you need to shoot, you simply focus on the target and shoot if you need to shoot.

Making the wrong decision quickly can be just as dangerous as taking too long to make the right decision. If you were trained to use a front-sight focus when someone is close, you might panic, shoot, and miss because there is no time to get a sight picture (doing the wrong thing quickly). If you realize a front-sight focus is useless and you switch to a target focus, you might get shot because it took you too long to shoot (taking too long to do the right thing).

Hick's law can also work against your adversary. Increasing the number of decisions your adversary needs to make also can increase the time it takes for him to make a decision. For example, asking an attacker if you should raise your hands or kneel down—even if you have no intention of doing either—can increase his response time because he will need to make decisions. Many of the techniques that are designed to buy you extra time involve asking multiple-choice questions that force people to think about the questions before they answer.

Since acting in self-defense implies someone else committed the first act of aggression, the best way to defend yourself is to use a combination of defensive and offensive maneuvers. If your position is weak because you are being forced to react to your adversary's actions, try to create an opening that will let you attack by doing something that forces your adversary to react to your actions.

Physical actions, such as moving quickly, can increase your adversary's response time by forcing him to make decisions and react to something you have done. By making him react to your actions, you can make the assumption that actions are always faster than reactions and can work in your favor.

Anything that makes it harder for you to hit a target will also make it harder for most other people to hit a target. The easiest human targets to hit are the ones that are stationary and facing the shooter, which is why standing still and facing a gunman does not make much sense. The hardest targets to hit are the ones that are moving, standing sideways, or partially concealed, which is why it makes sense to move, angle your body, or use cover if someone is shooting at you.

LIGHTING

Gunfighters in the Old West took advantage of lighting by trying to have the sun at their back if they fought during the day or to hide in darkness if they fought at night. Many of the felons who kill police officers also use darkness to gain a tactical advantage. What has changed since Old West gunfights is the availability of flashlights that produce high-intensity light.

Gunfights are characterized by poor lighting and moving targets, but police firearms training is characterized by good lighting and stationary targets. This is another unfortunate case where there seems to be an obvious disconnect between reality and training. Bad training can get you, members of your family, or innocent bystanders killed and result in criminal charges or civil lawsuits against you.

Before night-vision technology was developed, darkness could be used for concealment, and the two main things that would make you visible were incorrect use of your flashlight and muzzle flash when you fire a shot. Because of modern technology, using darkness for concealment is much more dangerous than it used to be, especially when police officers who are not issued night-vision equipment are up against criminals who do use such equipment.

If darkness is the only advantage you have, you need to use it. To avoid detection, do not let a light source that's behind you silhouette your body, wear something shiny that reflects light and reveals your location, or let your flashlight expose your body, your location, or your direction of travel.

To defend a secure location, you can create a deadly funnel by using a high-intensity flashlight to illuminate doorways or hallways that lead to where you are. This forces your adversaries to pass through a narrow passage that's well lit and in your line of fire. The flashlight can be visible, but you should be concealed behind cover and not directly behind the flashlight or illuminated by it.

A bright flashlight can be dangerous if it makes you visible or lets someone track your movements, but it might be the only way you can verify a target. Using a bright flashlight for a fraction of a second to verify a target just before you shoot is called *flash and shoot*. When using a gun-mounted light, you would use a short burst of light to illuminate the area in front of your gun, shoot if you have a target, and quickly change your location. Flash-and-shoot is not usually effective unless you are using a target focus, and the trigger is usually pulled while the target is still visible, although a small number of highly trained tactical shooters can pull the trigger just after the light goes out and still maintain combat-effective accuracy. In most cases, the sudden flash of bright light will cause your adversary to pause long enough for you to shoot. Since action is usually faster than reaction and the target may be temporarily blinded, the risk of having your light draw fire before you have a chance to shoot and move is relatively small.

If you obey the half-second rule (a gun-mounted light is turned on for 0.5 second or less), most people will not be able to react fast enough to shoot at your light before you turn it off, and those shooters who do return fire will probably miss. To make the risk of being hit by return fire even smaller, you can move in a lateral direction after you shoot and use flash-and-shoot again after you stop. Shooting from behind cover will also reduce your chances of being hit. Repeat the flash-and-shoot sequence until the threat has been neutralized or you can safely retreat. Unlike shooting at a muzzle flash, flash-and-shoot lets you verify your target. If you are shooting in a low-light or no-light environment, be aware that your muzzle flash can make you visible if you shoot after your light has been turned off.

If you do not have a gun-mounted light, you can use flash-and-shoot while holding a flashlight in one hand and your gun in the other. Having a gun-mounted light will make it easier to use a two-handed grip than holding the light in one hand and the gun in the other. Most gun-mounted lights have a switch that makes it easy to flick the light on and off. If you are using a flashlight, make certain the on-off switch can be manipulated quickly enough to use flash-and-shoot.

Since competition shooters are more concerned about scoring points than winning a gunfight, they are not usually concerned about how long they keep a target illuminated before they shoot or about moving after they shoot. For tactical shooters who are trying to conceal their position, avoid being hit by return fire, and neutralize a deadly threat if retreat is not feasible, flash-and-shoot is very effective.

Since no two deadly confrontations are ever the same, there are times when you may need to improvise, adapt, and overcome. Using a muzzle flash to shoot at someone who seems to be shooting at you or shooting into the dark at a noise that sounds like a footstep is taking a dangerous risk. We are not going to say shooting at a muzzle flash or a noise has never saved someone's life, but using flash-and-shoot lets you verify your target before you decide to shoot. When using flash-and-shoot, keep your finger off the trigger until you have a verified target.

The partial blindness that follows having someone shine a bright light in one's eyes creates a disruption because it stops the brain from being able to process visual information. Since most gunfights occur when lighting is dim or inconsistent, having a high-intensity flashlight is a good addition to your arsenal. Competent tactical shooters do not need to see their sights to hit a target, but they may need to use a flashlight to locate and verify targets before they shoot.

Most tactical shooters are familiar with common sources of artificial light, such as flashlights and spotlights, but glow sticks have some interesting properties that can make them useful to a tactical shooter. Glow sticks do not use electricity or start fires, and the kind used by U.S. Navy SEALs are waterproof. A glow stick thrown into a dark room can illuminate the people in the room without illuminating the people outside the room who threw the glow stick.

MISSES THAT MIGHT COUNT

Some people say misses never count, but that's not entirely true in the real world. Misses do not count when target shooting, but they might have value in a gunfight. A missed shot may cause adversaries to run for cover, faint, flee, or prematurely discharge their gun before it's aligned with your body. According to Captains Sykes and Fairbairn, who trained Shanghai police officers and British saboteurs, a missed shot can give you as much as a two-second advantage over your opponent. Despite the advantage you may get from missing your target, hitting aim points that result in damage to critical tissue and cause immediate or timely incapacitation will give you a much greater advantage.

If an adversary responds to a missed shot by ducking behind cover, you may be able to use suppression fire to keep the person pinned down until your backup arrives. Using suppression fire so you can advance on someone's position is a risky proposition, but criminals have used this technique to kill police officers. Having a high-capacity, semiautomatic pistol gives you a better chance of being able to use suppression fire than having a five-shot or six-shot revolver.

If you miss the person you were aiming at, take advantage of any extra time you get. If your adversary is temporarily shocked or stunned, use the time to fire follow-up shots, reload if your gun is empty, or move to a safer location, such as one that provides better cover or a better view of your adversary.

Purposely missing a shot is a warning shot, not a missed shot, and warning shots are not allowed by most police departments because of the possibility you might hit an innocent bystander. Cases have occurred in which a suspect surrendered after a warning shot, which was a better outcome for the suspects than getting killed, but the safety of innocent bystanders needs to be your first priority.

To say that only hits count also implies that all hits count, which it not true. People who are shot in a lung or somewhere within the center of mass might not realize they were shot until they see blood or someone tells them. A shot that goes unnoticed or fails to cause incapacitation is not much better than a miss. For a hit to count, it needs to cause immediate or timely incapacitation or give you a tactical advantage, such as allowing you to use cover or concealment, fire more shots, reload, call for help, or retreat.

Psychological factors, such as rage or drug use, can play a role when hits and misses have the same effect, but a bullet that penetrates the brain stem or upper cervical spinal cord will cause immediate incapacitation regardless of what other factors are involved. If people posing a deadly threat continue to fight after taking multiple hits from a handgun, the only shot that causes immediate incapacitation is a head shot. Regardless of how much tactical armor someone is wearing, the eyes and the bridge of the nose are usually not covered by anything that stops bullets.

ADVANCE OR RETREAT

Factors that can make targets, including people, harder to hit with a bullet include the following:

- Being behind cover can make targets harder to hit.
- Small targets are harder to hit than large targets.
- Moving targets are harder to hit than stationary targets.
- Fast-moving targets are harder to hit than are slow-moving targets.
- Decreasing exposure time can make targets harder to hit.
- Unpredictable movements can make targets harder to hit.

Even with these principles, you cannot design a plan that fits every situation. If you advance on people who are behind cover, flanking or getting behind them is usually safer than a frontal attack. If you must approach from the front, try to use cover as you advance because moving from one protected area to another reduces your risk of getting shot. Try not to expose the front of your body and make your movements quick and unpredictable. If the distance you need to travel is very short, running in a straight line to reduce your exposure time might be safer than using a zigzag pattern to make your movements less predictable.

If you decide to advance rather than retreat, be decisive. When police officers get killed by people armed with a pipe because they hesitated to use deadly force when the suspect approached, indecision and hesitation caused their death, not poor shooting skills. If you are not a police officer and it's not safe to stay where you are, it's usually better to retreat than try to advance. Even if you have a legal right to stand your ground, you might not have a legal right to conduct a frontal attack or pursue criminals who attempt to flee. If you are a law enforcement officer, wait for backup units and the right kind of equipment before you advance.

If your adversary decides to advance on your position, take your time and wait for a good shot. If you are low on ammunition, your chances of getting a good shot improve the closer your adversary gets. You may get your best shot when your adversary tries to cross the last open space before reaching your position, especially if you are protected by cover and your adversary runs straight at you. If you waste ammunition, you may run out or get shot while reloading.

If you try to shoot while retreating, stopping before you shoot is usually more accurate than shooting while you are walking or running. Running lets you cover ground faster than walking, but running on rough terrain may increase your risk of falling and getting injured. Using cover when you retreat may give you a chance to set an ambush if your adversary is getting too close. To increase the speed of your retreat, use a route that avoids obstacles.

MOBILITY

Good mobility will increase your chances of winning a boxing match or a deadly confrontation. Remaining stationary makes you an easy target, and being in motion makes you a hard target. If you are facing a knife or a gun, quick lateral movements can give you a tactical advantage. If your adversary and you are both using the right hand to hold your weapons, moving to your left will usually make it easier for you to avoid his weapon and protect your gun.

If you do not have someone to protect your back, look for situations that will help you avoid being attacked from the rear, such as putting your back against a wall, backing into a room that you know is safe, or backing into a corner. When protecting your back, try to use an area that provides concealment or cover and has escape routes that can help you avoid being surrounded or trapped.

Whether you should shoot, shoot and move, move and shoot, or shoot while moving depends on the circumstances and your level of skill. If an adversary reaches for a gun, shoot from whatever stance or place you are in if you stand a good chance of being able to neutralize the threat. This is one time when standing out in the open and shooting from a stationary position might be reasonable.

If you are facing someone at close range who attacks you with a knife, you might need to stop the knife attack and shoot at the same time. If the knife and your gun are both being held in the right hand, you can try to parry the knife with your left hand as you step forward and to the left with your left foot. If you are not incapacitated by the knife attack, positioning yourself to the side or behind your adversary will put you in a good position for a lateral or posterior head shot.

If someone is trying to shoot you, moving in a lateral direction will make you a harder target than moving directly at the person or away from him. If you are running at or away from someone, zigzagging will usually make you a harder target than moving along a straight line, but moving along a straight line will let you cover distance faster than moving along a line that is angled or curved.

When the person pointing a gun at you is using a two-handed grip and has the top of the gun just below eye level, try to drop below the line of sight and move in a lateral direction. The time it takes him to lower the gun, look for you, and realign the gun may give you enough time to shoot or find cover and shoot.

SURRENDERING YOUR GUN

Surrendering your gun is hardly ever a good option, and doing it can lead to getting killed with your own gun. Do not surrender your gun unless it gives you a tactical advantage, such as being able to buy time or use your backup gun. You might be replacing the criminal's empty gun with your loaded gun.

Gambling on the possibility you are a better tactical shooter than your adversary or that he will not shoot is often a better risk than surrendering your gun. If you are lucky, you might be able to reach cover or increase the distance between you and your assailant. Increasing the distance usually favors the better shooter, although closing the distance may favor someone who is competent enough to disarm an assailant without getting killed.

If you get shot but retain control of your gun, you might have time to return fire that incapacitates your adversary. Because of the brain stem, upper cervical spinal cord, and other critical tissues in the cranium—such as the basal ganglia—a head shot is your best chance of being able to cause immediate incapacitation.

The ideal solution is being able to avoid dangerous situations so you are not forced to make difficult decisions that often depend on luck more than knowledge or skill. Maintaining situational awareness, recognizing danger signs, knowing places you need to avoid, not going out after dark by yourself, not talking to strangers, and using common sense can help you avoid dangerous situations.

RELAXING TOO SOON

Making a one-shot stop with a handgun is very unlikely without a head shot, and it usually takes more than one shot to stop a dangerous threat by shooting at the heart. Unlike target shooting, during which you might be able to "call the shot" and predict where a bullet will hit, in a gunfight you might not know if or where a bullet hits until after the fight. And even if you know where a shot landed, you might not be able to tell if it severely damaged critical tissues. If you were aiming at center of mass, a one-shot stop is almost impossible.

Profuse bleeding and visible trauma to the head do not always indicate severe tissue damage, and police departments have documented cases where both an officer and a subject continued to fight after being hit by multiple gunshots to the torso. In many cases, the exact cause for incapacitation will not be known until after a medical examiner completes an autopsy. A bullet that hits a lung might be less combat effective than a bullet that hits the thigh and severs the femoral artery.

A second reason for not relying on a one-shot stop is the possibility that your assailant is wearing ballistic armor. Because of the easy access criminals have to body armor, you can never assume the person you are facing in a gunfight is not wearing a bullet-resistant vest. Even if someone you shot in the chest at close range seems to be dead, do not assume that he is. Criminals often fake unconsciousness or death to gain a tactical advantage. Even if you have control of your assailant's gun, it's possible he has more than one gun, which is why—whenever possible—you should maintain a safe distance behind cover and wait for the police to arrive and do their job.

EXCESSIVE FORCE

Excessive force is an issue where legal interpretations and tactical anatomy might not be compatible. *Overkill* is a word that often evokes sympathy from people who have never been involved in a life-or-death struggle. When the only thing members of a jury can relate to is seeing a criminal on television fly through the air and die after being hit once with a shot from a handgun, it can be hard for them to understand why shooting someone five or six times might be necessary.

From a tactical standpoint, you should continue shooting until the deadly threat you are facing has been undeniably stopped. This means your bullets have caused enough tissue damage to stop someone from continuing to be an imminent deadly threat. As discussed earlier, if you were taught you should err on the side of caution and keep shooting until your gun is empty and then reload and shoot a few more times, be aware that any shots you fire after someone is no longer an imminent deadly threat can have serious legal consequences, including being charged with murder.

It's hard for someone who has not been involved in a deadly confrontation to know if the number of shots fired at someone was reasonable or excessive. Most police officers have no idea how many of their shots were hits or misses or which shot or shots stopped the assailant until they read the medical examiner's report. Shooting someone five or six times may seem excessive to some people, but police officers have been shot and killed even after they shot someone five or six times.

CRIME SCENES

Regardless of whether you believe the person you shot is dead or alive, use extreme caution, call for immediate police backup if the police are not already en route, and call for an ambulance if one has not already been called. If you handle a weapon that was used by the assailant, you might destroy physical evidence that could show you acted in self-defense, or you might cause prosecutors to believe you tampered with the crime scene to make it look like you acted in self-defense.

If you decide to move a weapon away from a body because of fear the person will regain control of it and use it against you, if possible, do nothing until you discuss your intentions with the police. Be aware that if the weapon is a gun, it may be loaded and incorrectly handling it may cause an accidental discharge that could shoot you or someone else.

Another situation that can create legal problems is having a bystander steal a gun that was used by someone who tried to kill you. Some people believe it's better to remove the gun yourself than try to explain what happened to the gun that you claimed was used against you, but because of the legal system it's hard to predict if taking possession of the gun will help or hurt your case in court.

THE IMPORTANCE OF TACTICAL SKILLS

Tactical skills are often more important than handgun skills because they can help you avoid deadly confrontations before they occur, help you escape if they do occur, or give you a tactical advantage if escape is not safe or possible. Television and movies would probably be boring if the good guys always avoided gunfights, but in the real world—where the legal consequences of winning a gunfight can be almost as catastrophic as the biological consequences of losing one—a gunfight avoided is a gunfight won, and this applies to police officers and private citizens.

Standing out in the open instead of shooting from behind cover might not have much effect on your shooting skills, but it can certainly increase your risk of getting killed. For people who are not involved in law enforcement, a tactical retreat is a better option than testing your shooting skills against an armed criminal. If someone is pointing a gun at you and your gun is still in its holster, running for cover or grabbing his gun might be a better option than trying to draw, aim, and shoot—and some police officers have learned this lesson the hard way.

Using deadly force as your last resort is rational for several reasons.

1. Even in states that allow law-abiding citizens to stand their ground against vicious criminals, it will usually be easier to claim self-defense if you tried to avoid using deadly force until you had no other choice.
2. When using a handgun to defend against a deadly threat, most of the outcomes will be partially determined by luck.
3. If you are absolutely certain you have done everything possible to avoid using deadly force, you are less likely to hesitate when you need to shoot, more likely to stay focused on your target until the threat is neutralized, and less likely to have regrets because your assailant gave you no other choice. Life is not fair, but neither is being killed by a vicious criminal. If you worry about regretting your use of deadly force, you can surrender and let criminals decide your fate.

Many of the tactical skills discussed in this chapter are the result of personal involvement in deadly confrontations. Most of the people who try to kill you are not expert marksmen, but they are aggressive, they use deception, and they seldom hesitate after they decide to kill you. Even if police officers recognize a deadly threat, they are often slow to react, which is part of the reason some of the officers killed in the line of duty are killed with their own guns or do not fire their guns.

ATTITUDE, AWARENESS, ADVANTAGE, AND ACCURACY

Most handgun survival tactics relate to attitude, awareness, advantage, and accuracy. If you are confronted by a deadly threat and you decide to fight, your attitude concerning the fight needs to be "in it to win it." If you are protecting yourself or your family from serious harm, this can mean "fighting to the bitter end." In some cases, staging a tactical retreat that prevents you or your family from being injured will be your best option, but retreat might not be possible if you are the victim of a home-invasion robbery or an armed carjacking.

Attitude

We are not suggesting that you need to be compassionate and forgiving when someone is trying to kill you. It might not be politically correct, but it's hard to be enthusiastic about brotherly love when someone is trying to cause serious bodily harm or death by beating you with a club, cutting you with a knife, or shooting you with a gun. The question you need to ask yourself is not whether you have a moral right to be angry or ruthless, but whether these attitudes will help you protect you or others during a deadly confrontation.

Most experienced police officers will tell you that staying cool and focusing on your adversary will produce better results than a wild display of emotion. Yelling insults and obscenities will not make you sound rational if a video of your performance makes the evening news, and it seldom does much to improve your chances of winning a gunfight. The only people who seem to benefit from this kind of behavior are the criminals who show the court that your behavior was irrational and you were out of control. This approach may work for criminals if the video shows only your actions but not the reasons for them.

Anger and ruthlessness might serve a useful purpose when they encourage you to keep fighting after the rest of your body feels like quitting. If strong emotions increase the production of adrenaline, the extra push it gives you might be enough to keep you in the fight long enough to save your life.

Fear is another problem that can put you at a serious disadvantage during a deadly confrontation, and being aggressive, angry, or ruthless can be useful if it does not impair your ability to think clearly and make rational decisions. People who have been through a large number of deadly confrontations will normally tell you that remaining cool and staying focused on your objectives usually produce better results than relying on motivation from rage, anger, or other strong emotions.

Most people experience fear, but fear is not something to worry about unless it makes you dysfunctional and prevents you from being able to defend yourself. In addition to staying focused on the threat and not wasting mental energy trying to evaluate all the possible consequences that might occur if you get hurt or shoot someone, a good defense against fear is having confidence in your abilities because of your reality-based training and having practiced what you learned.

If you have confidence in yourself—which might be unjustified if you are poorly trained—do what you were trained to do and let your adversary worry about the consequences. Make the best decisions you can, but bear in mind that hesitation to take action can get you killed just as quickly as making mistakes.

In the real world, the one who decides if you have a shoot-or-don't-shoot situation is the person trying to cause serious bodily injury or death. Your job is to react quickly and correctly and do what he is forcing you to do.

Awareness, Advantage, and Accuracy

Awareness is not easy to teach because it often involves early recognition of danger signs with which most people are unfamiliar. Hearing a window break in the middle of the night or seeing someone enter your backyard with a crowbar is an easy danger sign for people to recognize, but having someone knock on your front door who appears to be legitimate or having someone walk up to you in a parking lot and ask an innocent question might not be perceived as a threat. One of the best ways to improve your awareness is to study how criminals operate by listening to or reading news reports that discuss recent criminal activity.

Nothing is fair about a vicious criminal attacking innocent victims, and there is no reason for innocent victims to believe they owe a vicious criminal a fair fight. If you find yourself in a fair fight against a vicious criminal, you need to change your tactics because you are doing something wrong. Your job is to get a tactical advantage and make the fight as unfair as possible in your favor.

Four things that can give you a tactical advantage are using concealment, cover, deception, or disruption. If you are being attacked or pursued, using concealment means making yourself less visible to a criminal. Some of the ways you can do this are using darkness or camouflage, hiding behind an object, making someone look into the sun, or blending in with a crowd.

Unlike concealment, cover can hide all or part of your body and it puts a barrier between you and the criminal. If you are being shot at, cover should have the ability to stop bullets. Items that might be used for cover when being shot at by a handgun include a large tree trunk or an engine block. Car doors are not reliable cover because a handgun bullet can often pass through the weaker parts of a door.

Putting distance between you and your adversary can sometimes be used as a substitute for cover if none is available. Moving in a lateral direction will normally make you a harder target than backing away from your adversary, and walking backward as you move away from someone will increase your risk of tripping over an unseen object. If you are armed and you fall backward, you may be able to shoot from a supine position, but this tactic should be used as a last resort because you will have limited mobility and you may get injured by the fall.

Using deceptions (such as putting your hat on a stick or throwing a rock) or using disruptions (such as throwing dirt or shining a light in someone's eyes) can give you a tactical advantage that makes it easier to retreat, defend, or attack. If retreat and defense are not options, your attack needs to be swift and decisive, and having the element of surprise on your side can give you an additional advantage.

Even if attitude, awareness, and advantage are working in your favor, your attack will not be combat effective without accurate shot placement, and keeping your emotions under control makes clear thinking and good shot placement easier.

BASIC STRATEGIES

When acting alone, your survival often depends on your willingness to do whatever it takes to survive and on using the right tactics. Even if you need to react quickly, failure to use your brain before you use your gun will often result in failure. As stated earlier, your brain is your most powerful weapon, and everything else is secondary.

If you need to choose between fight and flight, fight when you have a strong position and retreat when you have a weak position. Rushing blindly into danger because you failed to analyze a situation or freezing because you overanalyzed it (paralysis by analysis) can get you killed.

If you have a choice, wait for backup. Tombstone courage has gotten police officers killed, and the reckless behavior by one police officer can also get other officers killed. If you have a burglar in your house and you try to apprehend him yourself rather than wait for the police to arrive, you may get the responding officers killed because they heard gunshots and rushed in to save you before they had time to evaluate or contain the situation.

No one can maintain a high level of situational awareness all the time without developing signs or symptoms of fatigue. Even the best soldiers need time for rest and relaxation and a place where they are not required to be on high alert. One situation in which your level of alertness needs to change quickly is when you leave an area of relative security and enter an area where your safety is less certain. As soon as you enter an area where you get the feeling that something is not quite right, you need to be extremely cautious and be prepared to react quickly.

Attacks involving a sniper, an ambush, or an unexpected or overwhelming force are difficult to overcome because of the element of surprise. If you do not realize you are under attack until it occurs and you are not incapacitated by the attack, you must react very quickly to avoid further assaults. You also need to be careful about how you react because the first attack might have been designed to funnel you from one killing zone to another.

Most snipers try to remain concealed after they shoot, and even if you know a shot was fired, you might not be able to locate the sniper because of concealment or because he has moved to a new location or fled. After a sniper attack, do not make predictable movements, such as running to your car; try to find cover that will stop a high-velocity rifle bullet; and watch for other snipers. When a sniper uses stealth to approach a target, the technique is called *stalking*.

If you are attacked by a drive-by shooter and you are capable of moving, try to get behind cover as quickly as possible. The attacks are normally brief, and you seldom have a good chance of hitting one of your attackers. A drive-by shooting is similar to a sniper attack if the shooters are not detected before they start shooting.

These guidelines can help you avoid getting injured or killed because of an unexpected attack when you enter a high-risk area:

- Scan from side to side and up and down.
- Use concealment to reduce your visibility.
- Use cover to reduce your vulnerability.
- Locate and use a safe escape route.
- Depend on stealth and speed more than strength.

If you are attacked on the street, running into a building can put you in a good position to attack, defend, evade, or retreat. Possible escape routes include back doors, windows, and punching a hole through a wall. Avoid getting trapped in a room or on a roof.

If you survive the initial attack, a counterattack is seldom the best option if you have other choices. The people who initiated the attack are often better armed than you are, and they might have contingency plans for dealing with a counterattack. Many of the powerful drug gangs operating in the United States and Mexico are better armed than most police officers, and they have had years of practical experience to test and validate their tactics by having conducted more than 50,000 drug-related homicides. Many of these groups use military tactics and weapons.

Retreat is usually safer than trying to attack, defend, or evade. If retreat is not feasible, evasion (staying out of sight) is usually safer than trying to attack or defend. Unlike retreat, evasion will not take you out of a danger zone, but staying concealed may keep you safe. To stay concealed, avoid unnecessary movements, bright lights, making noise, or letting shiny objects, shadows, or your silhouette reveal your position. If you cannot retreat, evade, or defend—counterattack.

If you're a private citizen, try to get help. If you call 911, start by giving your location, the nature of your emergency, and your name. This should be enough to get police units headed in your direction. Try to make the call from behind cover.

NIGHT-VISION TECHNOLOGY

Technology is constantly advancing, and you can no longer rely on darkness for concealment if your adversary has access to night-vision equipment, such as night-vision goggles, monoculars, or weapon sights. Night-vision devices that amplify available light or use infrared illumination if ambient light is not sufficient usually produce green images. Thermal night-vision devices detect differences in temperature, and animals or people, who often emit more heat than the surrounding environment, usually appear as highly-visible white, black, or red thermal images.

Night observation devices (NODs) can be very useful when trying to locate potential threats, but thermal night-vision scopes or scopes that detect infrared (IR) images are more likely to be used on rifles or carbines than on handguns. Invisible infrared laser-aiming devices produce a laser beam that is not visible to the unaided eye, and some of them can be used on a handgun. If you were using one of these devices, you would also need to use night-vision equipment that converts invisible laser beams to visible laser beams, such as night-vision binoculars or monoculars.

Unlike using a flashlight that produces visible light and makes it easy for adversaries to see where you are, using invisible infrared laser-aiming devices makes it easier to locate or target people who are using darkness for concealment and not be detected. If you use an infrared illuminator to intensify the images you are looking at through night-vision equipment, you increase your risk of being detected by anyone else who is also using night-vision equipment, and the light produced by some of infrared illuminators is visible to the naked eye as a faint red glow.

Be aware that it might be illegal for civilians to purchase or possess the kind of night-vision equipment that military or law-enforcement personnel use, but most companies will tell you what the laws are that relate to specific kinds of night-vision equipment. Aiming devices that emit an invisible infrared laser beam are more likely to be regulated than aiming devices that produce visible laser beams.

HOME
SECURITY

Most states give you more latitude when defending yourself inside your home because of the castle doctrine or stand-your-ground laws. If criminals are trying to enter your home or they have already done so and retreat is not possible or safe, having a safe room can improve your chances for survival. If you go to a safe room, take a defensive position and call the police as soon as possible.

A safe room should channel criminals into your field of fire and funnel them through a single opening before they can enter the room. Having something in your safe room you can use for cover and concealment if armed intruders try to enter it will reduce your risk of being shot. Some of the equipment you should have in your safe room includes weapons, ammunition, communications gear, first-aid supplies, a high-intensity light, and a fire extinguisher.

If possible, your safe room should have an escape route. As the situation evolves, you might get a chance to retreat, the intruders might set your house on fire, or you might not be able to defend your position because of overwhelming force. If you need to escape because your position is being overrun, a strong door with a high-quality dead-bolt lock might give you extra time to retreat.

The tactical skills you use after criminals enter your home would be similar to those used after an ambush because both ambushes and illegal entries are usually surprise attacks. Some illegal entries, such as a professional home-invasion robbery, resemble a deliberate ambush because the operation is carefully planned and executed, and other illegal entries, such as a cat burglary, might resemble an immediate ambush because burglaries are often crimes of opportunity committed randomly and with very little planning.

When possible and safe, retreat is usually the best option, but leaving your safe room may expose you to more danger than remaining inside if criminals catch you and your family out in the open where you have almost no chance of being able to mount a strong defense or attack. If the intruders attack you while you are in the safe room, shooting at them, whether you hit or miss, may cause them to flee. If the criminals are armed but poorly organized, you might get lucky, and they might shoot each other because of poor fire discipline or cross-fire. If this happens, you might be able to use the confusion to cover your escape.

Retreat is usually a better option than standing your ground and fighting to the bitter end, but surrender is a poor option unless you are certain the criminals will not kill you if you do surrender. Putting your family in the hands of criminals who have just invaded your home is a leap of faith most people would not make. It is not unusual for home-invasion robbers to kill all the witnesses. If retreat or surrender is not an option, try to defend your safe room until the police arrive.

Trying to stop a home-invasion robbery makes much more sense than trying to stop a bank robbery. Most bank robbers are more interested in stealing money and making a clean getaway than getting into a gunfight, and many of the people who rob banks and say they have a gun are not armed. If you walk into a bank and see a robber threatening a teller with a gun, using deadly force to subdue the robber may stop the robbery, but it may also trigger a sequence of events that gets innocent people killed, especially if the robber has armed accomplices of whom you are unaware. If a bank robber seems to be willing to take the money and run without using violence, armed intervention should normally be handled by on-duty police officers. If you are visibly armed with a gun but not wearing a law-enforcement uniform when on-duty police officers respond to a robbery-in-progress call, you might be misidentified as an armed robber and shot or killed by friendly fire.

Unlike bank robbers, home-invasion robbers are usually armed. After they enter your home, in addition to robbery, they often commit other crimes such as rape, homicide, arson, torture, or kidnapping. Even if you have a silent panic alarm, the police will probably not arrive soon enough to prevent the robbers from causing serious bodily injuries or death, and most people either don't have a silent alarm or they have one that can easily be defeated by most professional criminals. If you believe home-invasion robbers are attempting to enter or have entered your home, failure to act immediately can have tragic or fatal consequences.

Stopping robbers before they enter your home is usually safer than trying to resist after they have already entered. If you see someone armed with a gun entering your home through a broken window, this would be a good time to stop the intrusion. Some home-security experts may recommend wasp spray or a whistle, but most police officers will probably tell you that a handgun or a shotgun will be more effective if you are trained to use it.

If the intruder gets inside your home, escaping to the outside or retreating to a safe room is usually safer than having a face-to-face gunfight while both of you are standing out in the open. In addition to such options as stopping the intruder from entering your home, escaping to the outside, or retreating to your safe room, you can also use a counterambush tactic when a criminal unexpectedly enters your home.

If a robber who enters your home sees you run away, the normal reaction is to give chase, try to subdue you, and then restrain you. What most robbers will not expect is a well-staged ambush. If you have armed yourself and you can find cover and concealment, stay hidden and wait for the robber to enter your field of fire. As soon as you have a good shot, shoot as many times as needed to cause incapacitation and then move to a secondary ambush point or your safe room. Be aware that you might be followed if the robber has accomplices, or the accomplices might set an ambush for you if they can predict your direction of travel. Always be prepared to use force whenever you attack, defend, or retreat.

Poor planning often leads to tragic outcomes, and the key to home-security planning is to plan for the worst and be prepared to change your plan if something unexpected happens. A realistic home-security plan is a flexible guideline that points you in the right direction but makes it easy to adjust your timing or tactics.

People who plan and prepare for deadly confrontations, such as a home-invasion robbery, are more likely to survive than people who pretend nothing like this can ever happen to them. Good planning and preparation can help you stop home-invasion robberies from happening or help you survive if one does happen. Although it's secondary compared to protecting your family and yourself, good planning and preparation can also help you protect your personal property.

A good security plan for your home starts with good physical security. Most homes are not going to have the same security equipment that banks have—such as a walk-in vault, inside and outside surveillance, and multiple hold-up alarms—but just having good outside lighting, high-quality windows, and solid doors with burglar-resistant locks can be a strong deterrent to burglars and robbers. Most people are not enthusiastic about having steel bars on their windows or steel-bar doors, but home-security alarm systems and outside surveillance systems that give you protection against burglars or robbers have become more affordable. A good security system can warn you that your home might be under attack, which will make it easier to think clearly and react correctly when preparing for the attack.

Knowing that someone is illegally entering your home does not automatically give you a legal right to stop him. If you live in a jurisdiction where the law requires that you retreat to the farthest part of your house and hide or try to escape, stopping an intruder from entering your house or searching your house for an intruder might be against the law. It is easy to see where a lawyer could say that the criminal you shot would not have died if you didn't try to stop the illegal entry or look for the intruder. Many states give you the right to stand your ground when attacked in your home, but other states might strongly encourage or require retreat.

Even if you have the right to search for intruders, having a flashlight in one hand and a gun in the other will make you an easy target and probably give the intruder a chance to shoot. Most people walking through a house make enough noise to let intruders know where they are and where they are headed. If you think you have an intruder, it's safer to go to your safe room, defend your position, and call the police than try to search the house.

Police officers wait for backup before searching the house because doing a search without having people who are trained to cover their backs is dangerous. Even with backup, searching a building can result in police fatalities if the intruder hides and waits for a chance to ambush the officers. Having another person who can search with you will not make you safer unless the two of you have been trained to work as a team when entering and searching rooms or navigating stairs.

Defending your safe room is almost always a better choice than searching your house for intruders, but safe rooms have limits that need to be considered. The safe room you are likely to have in the average home will not give you much protection against high-velocity rifles and probably only limited protection against shotguns or high-velocity handgun bullets. Unlike high-security safe rooms that are often surrounded on all six sides by bullet-resistant steel, the floors, walls, and ceilings you find in most homes will not stop even low-velocity handgun bullets.

A few of the safe rooms found in average homes might use an outside door instead of an inside door to protect the entry point, but most outside doors are only slightly more bullet resistant than inside doors, which is why it's easy for criminals to shoot someone who is looking at them through a peephole in a door.

With these thoughts in mind, unless your safe room is fortified, making it your final stand might not be a good idea. In most cases, your safe room will be the place that gives you a better protection than any other place in your house. Since you might reach a point where you can no longer defend yourself in the safe room, you should always have an escape route. Unlike a concealed safe room that might have hidden passageways or escape tunnels, the average safe room is more likely to have a window or an escape hatch in one of the walls, the floor, or the ceiling that leads to another room or to the outside of the house.

Your decision to defend a safe room or use the escape route should depend on which choice makes you safer. Even if you can stop intruders from entering your safe room, they might set your house on fire and you may need to leave the safe room to avoid the fire. Leaving your safe room after the police are on the scene reduces the risk of being injured by the intruders or being held hostage.

In most cases, retreating to your safe room and demonstrating your ability to resist with deadly force will be sufficient to stop the attack. As emphasized earlier, if the intruders decide to flee and they are no longer a threat, you may face criminal charges if you chase them down and use deadly force to stop them from stealing your personal property.

If you are in your safe room and the dispatcher advises you it's safe to come out, be prepared for the possibility that a police officer may knock on the door of your safe room to tell you the same thing. Based on the safety rules, you should not shoot because you do not have a verified target, which usually implies being able to see a person. If you are under attack in your safe room and someone kicks a hole in the door, seeing the foot might be considered verification.

One thing you should always insist on before the police clear the scene is that they do a thorough search of your house before they leave. The last thing you want is for dangerous criminals to conceal themselves in your house while the police officers are present and then go back to business as usual after the officers leave. In most cases, the search should include adjacent buildings and the surrounding area. Seeing or catching one criminal does not mean other criminals were not involved.

PHYSICAL SECURITY

Physical security measures can help you prevent unauthorized access to your home by increasing the time or effort it takes to get in. Physical security is not a substitute for armed resistance because most homes, unlike fortified installations, do not have such security features as reinforced concrete walls, heavy steel doors, or bullet-resistant windows. What most people can do is use cost-effective security measures that psychologically deter criminals from trying to enter their homes or that give them more time to arm and defend themselves if criminals do try to break in.

- *Perimeter barriers*. Examples include fencing or walls
  that limit access to your home by acting as a physical or

psychological barrier. Chain-link fencing is relatively inexpensive, but it can be defeated by bolt cutters or other hand tools. High walls with a top guard that makes it more difficult to scale the wall are usually expensive but more effective than a chain-link fence. Fence alarms can be used to increase security.

- *Protective lighting.* Most lighting is relatively inexpensive, and it makes detecting intruders easier, which makes it a good psychological deterrent. If lights that are usually on suddenly go off, this may indicate you are under attack.
- *Alarm systems.* Home-alarm systems can protect you against intruders or fire. A monitored silent alarm can be very effective, but a local alarm that produces loud sounds and bright lights may scare criminals away before they enter your home.
- *Doors and locks.* Even if a door is locked, most outside doors will not stop a professional burglar for more than a few minutes, but this may give you enough time to arm yourself or reach your safe room. Home-invasion robbers are more likely to use deception to gain entry than break a door down. Since most criminals enter through a door and a chain is only as strong as its weakest link, it makes no sense to put a high-security lock on a low-security door mounted in a weak frame. Most outside doors are not bullet resistant, but they should be kick resistant.

Keep outside doors locked and do not open them until you know who is on the other side. If you don't know the people at your door, ask for identification you can verify by phone. To give you this information, they can speak through the door or hold their ID card in front of a window. If your door has a security doorstop or a mail slot, they can give you their ID card. Surveillance cameras that let you photograph, see, and speak with people outside your door can also be used. If you don't recognize the people outside your door and they look suspicious or ask you to come outside, you should keep the door locked, call the police, and tell them you called the police. Most criminals will not wait for the police to arrive.

STREET CONFRONTATIONS

The term *street confrontation* refers to any situation in which you are facing a potential threat because you are walking down the street or through an open area, such as a parking lot or a parking garage. Having a gun and the knowledge to use it properly is no guarantee you will not be seriously injured or killed, but it will give you more control over your own safety than agreeing to do what a criminal demands. Submission might be effective if a criminal's primary goal is to steal your valuables and flee, but if he tries to force you into a vehicle and you decide to submit rather than resist, you have probably decreased your chances of being found alive. Rape victims are often beaten or killed after being abducted.

A gun is not the only weapon people can use for self-defense, but it's usually the most effective. Some criminals might be deterred by wasp or pepper spray, but others might become more violent after being sprayed with chemicals. You might be able to use martial arts techniques to stop an attack if you are highly trained and you take your adversary by surprise, but most of these techniques are useless against criminals who are physically superior and good street fighters.

Street safety starts by recognizing these basic principles:

- Money or expensive items, such as jewelry, will attract criminals.
- Violent crimes are easier to commit in dark or secluded places.
- Avoid areas that make it easy for people to approach you without being seen.
- Walking too close to a blind corner can leave you vulnerable to attack.
- Seek help or flee if you believe you are being followed.
- Be suspicious of people who hide one or both hands or cover their faces.

- Always be aware of your surroundings and the people who are near you.
- Be cautious when strangers approach and offer or ask for favors.
- Do not talk to strangers who are in vehicles or near alleys.
- Any stranger who refuses to take no for an answer is a potential threat.
- Reposition yourself if people try to surround you or get behind you.
- Look inside a room for signs of danger before you enter.
- After you are in a room, watch the doors and other entrances.
- Traveling in a group is normally safer than traveling alone.
- Any stranger who tries to force you into a vehicle is a deadly threat.
- Most criminals prefer to attack people who look like easy victims.
- Be very cautious when entering or leaving your home or place of business.
- Unusual or unexpected people or things should raise your level of awareness.
- Trust your instincts and try to avoid situations that make you feel apprehensive.

The value of some of these principles will depend on the situation. Open spaces can help you maintain a greater distance between you and potential threats, but they can also make you more visible. For example, walking in the street might help you avoid walking close to people you believe might be dangerous, but it can also make you more visible to people who are looking up or down the street. If you see a potentially dangerous situation in front of you, turning around and going back in the direction you came from might be your best option. Taking a longer route, even if it makes you late, is better than being attacked because you took a shorter route.

Unless you are willing to throw fate to the wind, walking in areas that make it easy for someone to approach you should usually be classified as a condition-green situation unless something happens that elevates the situation to a higher threat level. When operating at condition green, you should always be alert for potential threats, but not to the point of paranoia.

Well-lit areas with high levels of pedestrian traffic and police or camera surveillance are not normally the kind of places someone would pick to commit a violent crime. On the contrary, most criminals prefer to commit crimes in places where easy detection is not possible. Unfortunately for private citizens, this is not always the case and some criminals commit violent crimes in front of multiple witnesses as a way to impress friends or fellow gang members.

As stated earlier, you have four levels of awareness:

- Condition white: Maintain 360-degree situational awareness.
- Condition green: Scan for danger signs.
- Condition yellow: Look for potential threats.
- Condition red: React to verified threats.

If you are in a large grocery store shopping, maintaining condition white awareness is probably sufficient. After you buy your groceries and enter the parking lot, you should raise your level of awareness to condition green and scan for danger signs. A car with backup lights on might indicate someone is getting ready to back over you and your grocery cart. The key to using condition yellow is being able to identify danger signs, which in most cases are characterized by someone doing something unusual or unexpected.

If you are loading groceries in your car and someone you do not recognize is walking directly toward you, this would justify condition yellow, which means you need to anticipate a possible threat. Make eye contact with the stranger to let him know that you see him coming and are not going to be submissive. If the stranger walks up and grabs your arm, go to condition red. Possible reactions include pulling your arm away and running back into the store. If you cannot break free, yell for help and strongly resist any efforts anyone makes to push you into your car. If you have a gun, do not expose it if you are close enough for your assailant to grab it. If you can break loose by scratching your attacker's eyes, by biting, or by other means, try to escape. If your attacker chases you and you can put about 21 feet or a barrier between you and him, you can draw your gun while running, stop, turn, and shoot if you have no other way to stop an imminent deadly threat. Most criminals try to avoid getting hurt, and even violent criminals, such as a sadistic rapist, are seldom suicidal. After criminals see you are not the submissive, defenseless victim they thought you were, they will often flee as quickly as they can rather than test your shooting skills or risk getting arrested.

Classical warning signs for a bank robbery are individuals wearing heavy clothing on a hot day, which may indicate that someone is concealing a weapon, or wearing a ski mask, which can be pulled down over the face to conceal the person's identity. A less recognized sign is one hand concealed in a pocket the entire time a person speaks to a teller.

Having someone who appears to be intoxicated approach you and demand money for food is clearly a warning sign, but not the kind you usually get from a dangerous criminal. In many cases, the person who is most likely to be dangerous will approach you with a smile and try to build rapport by complimenting you on something; posing innocent questions, such as asking for directions; offering to help do something, such as load your groceries in your car; or mentioning that one of your tires needs air. If this approach is successful, you will drop your guard and relax. Criminals who use this approach are often well dressed and reasonably attractive.

Some criminals are very good at creating situations that help them maneuver people into a position that makes it easy for them to commit crimes. Many of the police officers killed in the line of duty by criminals were carefully manipulated into a bad position before they were shot and killed. Three of the deadly errors police officers often make are apathy (lack of interest), complacency (lack of concern for safety), and preoccupation (lack of situational awareness).

If you have any doubts about strangers who start talking to you, end the conversation quickly, do not question their honesty or motives, and remain alert. To encourage people to go away, tell them you don't have the information they want, you do not need any help, or you don't talk to strangers. If the person hesitates or refuses to go away, the situation might be more serious than it first appeared, and you should look for help or a way to escape.

In some cases, your best option is to make certain your car is locked and walk to an area that appears to be safer than where you are. If you can safely enter your car without being followed into the car and abducted, lock your doors, drive away, and watch to see if a person or car is following you. Even if police officers do not have enough probable cause to make an arrest, telling them what happened might help them solve past crimes or prevent future ones.

If a criminal decides pleasant conversation is not working but still wants to steal your car, rob, or rape you, friendliness may change to aggressiveness, and the situation may change from condition yellow to condition red because you now have a verified threat. You need to act. If escape or getting rescued is not possible, the option of last resort might be using either nonlethal or lethal force.

If you have handled the situation correctly up to this point, you may be in a better position to resist than if you have ignored it. For example, if you anticipated someone might be a threat, you should have done everything possible to keep that person from getting behind you, since keeping a threat in front of you will make it easier to resist an attack. Other possibilities that can help you create or maintain advantages are increasing the distance between you and the potential threat or putting a barrier, such as a car, between you and him. If you get in a gunfight, you may be able to use the car for concealment or cover.

Depending on where you carry a gun, you might be able to put your hand on the gun or even draw and conceal it behind your back without attracting attention. This can save you time if you are faced with a sudden attack. Never carry anything in your hands you may need to drop before you can draw your gun.

If you kill someone, it may take years before the courts decide whether a decision you made in less than two seconds was justified. If the case does go to court, your best defense will be having convincing evidence that you were facing an imminent deadly threat and using deadly force was your last resort.

INDICATIONS OF DECEPTION

- Abnormal body movements: constantly moving or changing postures.
- Changes in breathing: rapid breathing, deep breathing, or holding breath.
- Changes in complexion: skin may become flushed or blanched.
- Changes in voice: the voice cracks or the pitch becomes higher.
- Dryness of mouth: asking for something to drink or licking the lips.
- Evasive, vague, or contradictory statements or answers.
- Excessive perspiration: may affect axilla (armpit), hands, or face.
- Excessive swallowing: may be indicated by movement of the larynx.
- Fidgeting: constantly touching or rubbing the face or hands.
- Head, neck, or shoulder movements that are stiff or mechanical.
- Nervous responses: inappropriate emotions, words, or hesitations.
- Rapid eye movement: moving the eyes or head and looking around.
- Restlessness: tapping fingers, clenching hands, or chewing lips or nails.

- Words or hand gestures not properly formed, synchronized, or used.
- Gestures or facial expressions that seem to be inconsistent with spoken words.

Indications of lying are usually based on emotional changes that result from guilt, and most criminals do not feel much guilt when they lie. It also appears the ability to lie without being detected improves with practice. While there is no guarantee you will always know if someone is lying, you can improve your chances of detecting that you are being lied to by recognizing the above-listed indications of deception.

Even if you cannot prove someone is lying, just believing he may be should be enough reason to elevate your level of awareness. Rather than accuse people the instant they say something you believe is false, it is usually better not to mention your suspicions and let them continue talking. If people believe they are doing a good job of deceiving you, they often get careless and make statements you know or can easily prove are false.

Refusing to look someone in the eye is often mentioned as an indication that someone is lying, but criminals are often very good at lying and looking you directly in the eye at the same time. If they are lying to you while doing so and you turn away, this is considered a sign of weakness on your part, which might encourage them to be more aggressive. Be very suspicious of people who look you in the eye and tell you how honest or religious they are.

Historically, criminals who specialize in con games seldom use physical violence, but violent criminals, such as robbers and rapists, sometimes employ the same kind of deceptions that a con artist uses to swindle victims. Look out for the following deceptions:

- Appear to be friendly, harmless, or helpless.
- Ask for information or for help.
- Offer a gift or favor to build friendship.
- Pose as someone you can trust.
- Use conspicuous honesty to build trust.
- Suggest a way to make or save money.
- Tell you how lucky you are.

•••

Rather than refusing to answer a question, a good con artist will ignore the question, truthfully answer part of the question, or answer a different question. After ignoring a question, he might change the subject or ask you a question.

•••

To counter these deceptions, do not make impulsive decisions, beware of strangers who offer something free, and avoid people who become overly friendly. Be very cautious of people who ask you to go with them for any reason or encourage you to get out of your car. If a stranger approaches your car and wants you to roll down the window, make sure your doors are locked and keep your windows rolled up. Be especially vigilant if a stranger starts a conversation, and while the two of you are speaking another stranger unexpectedly appears and tries to join the conversation. Con artists often work as a team, and one member of the team will usually pretend to be on your side. If a stranger unexpectedly sits down beside you, be cautious. If a stranger tries to enter your car, drive away if possible or move your handgun into a ready position if you cannot move your car.

TACTICAL TRAINING PROTOCOLS

Being able to draw, aim, and shoot a handgun without consciously thinking about the movements is called *unconscious competence*. After you start the draw, your body will automatically perform all the movements without additional thought unless something occurs that causes your brain to change from automatic behavior to conscious behavior, such as having someone surrender. This is the kind of competence you need to be effective during a deadly confrontation. After you decide to shoot, you need to stop thinking and start shooting.

If you know what skills and what level of competence you want to achieve, you can shorten the training time by setting goals for yourself. The most effective goals have all the elements that are represented by the acronym SATISFY.

S—Specific: Set goals that are clearly defined, measurable, and essential.

A—Achievable: Do not set goals that are beyond your ability to achieve.

T—Timely: Set goals that help you learn the essential skills at the right time.

I—In writing: Write your goals down and keep a record of your progress.

S—Simple: Make your goals easy to understand and easy to visualize.

F—Flexible: Modify your practice to improve your areas of weakness.

Y—You are responsible: Achieving your goals is your responsibility.

The goals for a tactical shooter include accuracy, speed, shot placement, and tactical skills. The accuracy needed to be combat effective will not make you a champion target shooter, but it will help you survive a gunfight. For tactical shooters, tactical skills are usually more important than handgun skills.

Tactical shot placement is not important for target shooters because points are seldom scored because of any direct relationship between hits and the location of critical tissues. Even if the size of an X-ring and the size of a tactical aim point are similar, most target shooters do not visualize human organs when shooting at the X-ring. If training is going to be realistic, tactical shooters need to visualize themselves damaging critical tissues or causing incapacitation, not scoring points.

Depending on the quality of your practice, one hour of practice can be an hour well spent or an hour wasted. Regardless of how many hours you practice, high-quality practice usually produces high-quality performance, and poor-quality practice usually produces poor-quality performance.

In law-enforcement training programs, it is common to see high-quality instructors offering low-quality training because of departmental policies or poorly designed state standards. Many of these instructors would never use the techniques they teach in class if they themselves were involved in a deadly confrontation, but these are the techniques the department or state requires them to teach if they want to maintain their teaching certifications.

Listed below are recommendations that can improve firearms teaching.

- Prioritize: Emphasize and teach realistic shooting skills.
- Explain: Describe the shooting skills being taught and provide instruction.
- Demonstrate: Show students what it looks like to perform the skills.
- Supervise: Detect, explain, and correct any mistakes made by students.
- Motivate: Encourage effort, patience, and perseverance.
- Confirm: Compliment students who perform a shooting skill correctly.

Two areas where police programs often fall short are content and repetition. Even if most of the shooting skills officers are being taught would improve their chances of being able to survive a deadly confrontation—which is seldom the case—most police departments do not give their officers enough time to master the basic shooting skills taught in the police academy or enough practice to maintain whatever skills they learned. After several years, most officers will not be able to shoot as well as they did when they graduated from the academy.

Reality-based training is a popular concept in law-enforcement circles, and most departments agree that officers should be given realistic training. If this is what they believe, it's hard to understand why national statistics and police reports show that most firearms training is not realistic. This book cannot explain why firearms training is not realistic, but it can recommend ways to fix the problem.

TARGET SHOOTING VS. TACTICAL SHOOTING

Target shooting that has the following characteristics cannot be expected to prepare someone for a gunfight:

- Targets are stationary, visible, frontal, and familiar.
- All targets are placed at predictable locations and distances.
- Shooting positions are stationary, and cover is not required.
- Feet, lower body, and upper body are parallel to the target.
- Most shooting is done with two hands and a front-sight focus.
- Specialized guns or holsters are used instead of standard equipment.
- Some targets are placed at distances between 75 feet and 150 feet.
- Success is based on numerical scores instead of a pass-or-fail system.
- Shooters use the isosceles stance and close one eye when they aim.

Since most gunfights are sudden, unexpected, unpredictable, and erratic, the targets for tactical training need to be:

- Stationary or moving.
- Visible or partially visible.
- Familiar or unfamiliar.
- Frontal or rotated to other angles.
- Placed at unexpected places.
- Located at unknown distances.

••

People who cannot be combat effective when using a target focus and shooting with one hand at less than 21 feet do not have the handgun skills needed to be competent tactical shooters.

••

One-handed shooting is used almost as much as two-handed shooting because the support hand might be needed to do other things, such as hold a flashlight, or your support hand might not have enough time to connect with your dominant hand. If the winner in a gunfight was determined by who gets the most points, a police officer who scores three center-of-mass hits would get a higher score than the subject who returns fire and kills the officer with one head shot. Gunfights are won by causing incapacitation, not by scoring points.

All the legendary tactical shooters have stated that target shooting does not prepare you for tactical shooting and tactical shooting does not prepare you for target shooting. Some of these legendary experts include:

- General Julian S. Hatcher
- Captain William E. Fairbairn
- Captain E.A. Sykes
- Colonel Rex Applegate
- Colonel Jeff Cooper
- Colonel Charles Askins
- Border Patrol Agent Bill Jordan
- NYPD Officer Jim Cirillo

Although some of these men were exceptional target shooters, they clearly recognized that a gunfight is much more than a shooting match. Colonel Rex Applegate insisted that you cannot adapt the sport of target shooting to the realities of combat, and some legendary competition shooters have openly admitted that competition combat shooting is a sport. It's not easy to understand why some people believe or say they believe a gunfight is a shooting match, but some of the experts listed above have suggested a lack of combat experience, political correctness, a personal or financial interest in target shooting, or poor judgment might be involved.

Reality-based training might be a popular concept in law enforcement, but it's used in first-aid training more than firearms training. If police departments applied concepts such as goal analysis, instructional objectives, performance analysis, and measurable objectives to firearms training, they would not have police officers standing out in the open shooting stationary paper targets, using the center of mass as their only aim point, or qualifying only once a year.

DRY-FIRE PRACTICE AND LASER PRACTICE

Dry-fire practice is the process of aiming, pulling the trigger, and watching the sights or the top of the gun when the gun is empty in order to improve trigger control. Being able to pull the trigger quickly without disrupting the alignment of the gun indicates good trigger control. Because you are not using live ammunition, dry-fire practice reduces training cost, and it's very safe if you take precautions to make certain any gun being used for dry-fire practice is empty. Dry-fire practice is a very effective way to improve both motor skills and mental skills, and you can use it when shooting double action or single action, with one or both hands.

When you are using a target focus instead of a front-sight focus, guns that activate a laser beam to indicate where the gun is pointed when the trigger is pulled are even more effective than dry-fire practice. Whereas dry-fire practice is normally used in conjunction with visual sight alignment, laser-practice can be done with or without the sights, and the laser dot will give immediate feedback about whether you hit the target.

Laser practice is more expensive than dry-fire practice because you need a laser device that attaches to your gun and emits a laser beam when you pull the trigger or you need a laser training gun that shoots nothing but a laser beam. The laser devices you insert into the barrel of the gun you are practicing with are usually less expensive than the laser training guns that are used exclusively for laser practice. Laser practice is safer and less expensive than live-fire practice.

Most lasers come with a warning that you should not shoot someone in the eye with a laser beam, but some of the companies that produce these devices do not consider this a danger. If you have any concerns about safety after you read the instructions that come with a laser device, you should contact the manufacturer. Most of the early laser-training devices used a red laser beam, but some of the newer ones also offer a green laser beam, which is usually more visible during the day than is a red one.

A competent tactical shooter can put three laser hits in a 4-inch circle at 21 feet when using a target focus. Aligning the top of the gun with your line of sight tends to produce the best accuracy, but your target will be less visible, and most tactical shooters are combat effective when the gun is slightly below their line of sight. Shooting from the hip is the least accurate kind of tactical shooting.

If you are a tactical shooter, you should be able to hit a 4-inch target at 21 feet that's barely visible because of poor lighting when your sights are covered. Unlike target shooters, who need enough light to focus on the front sight, a tactical shooter needs just enough light to see the target. Because you can see where a laser beam hits, the first shot is usually harder to make than follow-up shots. You can buy laser targets, but red reflectors make excellent targets for red lasers.

Laser Pistol Course

Practicing with a laser pistol is both convenient and economical because you do not need to go to a gun range or buy live ammunition. You can use a standard pistol with a laser device inserted into the barrel for laser practice, but using a pistol that cannot fire live ammunition, such as the SIRT laser training pistol, eliminates the possibility that someone might be accidentally injured or killed by a bullet. If you are using a barrel insert for laser practice and you are not shooting double action, you may need to cock the hammer or rack the slide before each shot.

The tactical laser course described below is designed to be economical because the materials are inexpensive and the course can be set up in most squad rooms or living rooms. Since most tactical shooting is done at less than 21 feet, your maximum distance will be 21 feet. If you master the use of a laser pistol at 21 feet, the next distance you would normally use is about 45 or 50 feet.

All the laser practice shooting will be done using a target focus, which is the kind of focus you would normally use for a tactical situation less than 21 feet away. As Colonel Applegate pointed out in *Kill or Get Killed*: "*In close combat work, the sights will not ordinarily be used*, due to lack of time, darkness or poor light conditions, enemy fire, or other considerations." Colonel Applegate stated that the maximum distance for using a handgun without the aid of sights is about 50 feet.

In *Fighting Handguns*, Jeff Cooper noted that circumstances arise when "the need for speed is so great, and the range so short, that you must hit by pointing alone, without seeing your gun." Cooper considered point shooting (target-focused shooting) easier to learn than sighting (front-sight-focused shooting), and he based this belief on observations he made when training the average infantryman to shoot silhouettes at 30 feet.

Since a laser training pistol has no recoil and laser beams travel in a straight line, a competent tactical shooter should be able to place most shots within a 4-inch circle during practice sessions. Even though you could use a front-sight focus at 0 to 20 feet, as Colonels Applegate and Cooper clearly indicate, using a front-sight focus at close range will usually decrease your chances of winning a gunfight. If you have a problem learning to shoot without focusing on your front sight, covering the front sight with tape may help you overcome this problem.

If you have already mastered basic marksmanship and are ready to make the transition from target shooting to tactical shooting, using a laser training pistol will make the transition easier. Rather than starting with a 6-inch target and working your way down to a 4-inch target, accept the fact that you may not hit the target every time you shoot, learn from your mistakes, and persevere until most of the time you can hit a target no larger than 4 inches. Start slowly and do not try to increase your speed until you have acceptable levels of accuracy at slow speeds.

To the extent possible, when using a laser training pistol you should use the same techniques you would practice with when shooting live ammunition. Many of the techniques used in the Porter method can be applied to a laser training pistol, such as stance, grip, or trigger pull. However, some techniques—such as handling recoil, clearing malfunctions, or doing a tactical reload—can be practiced only with live ammunition. Laser practice is a supplement, but it is not a substitute for live fire.

The magazines that SIRT pistols use do not hold ammunition but are functional to the extent that you can practice loading and unloading them. The trigger on a SIRT pistol has a trigger pull that is similar to that on a semiautomatic pistol, such as a Glock, but the laser beam continues to stay on for as long as you pull back on the trigger. To make a laser beam function more like a bullet than a steady beam of light, pull and release the trigger the same way you would normally pull and release the trigger on a semi-automatic pistol.

Being able to shoot a 4-inch group with a SIRT pistol is no guarantee that you can shoot a 4-inch group with a handgun that has significant recoil. But even if the group you get when shooting live ammunition is larger than the group you get when shooting a laser pistol, it will still usually be smaller than it would be if you didn't practice with a laser pistol. If you can get a 4-inch group when shooting twice with a laser pistol and a 5-inch group when shooting twice with live ammunition, at least one of the two bullets will usually be combat effective if you are trying to make a head or heart shot.

Good training and frequent practice are required to develop tactical shooting skills, but you need much less time and money than it takes to become a champion target shooter. Being a skilled tactical shooter and being a skilled target shooter are not mutually exclusive, but as Jeff Cooper pointed out in *Fighting Handguns*: "It's quite possible for a man to be an excellent shot and a very poor gunfighter, but it's nearly impossible for a man to be a good gunfighter without being at least an acceptable marksman." If you have already mastered basic marksmanship and would like to become a tactical shooter, using a SIRT pistol is one of the most practical, convenient, and cost-effective ways to practice.

How you design a laser practice course will depend on your ingenuity and resources. Reflectors make good targets for a red laser beam, and putting two circular reflectors on a board with at least 6 inches of separation can be used to represent the aim points for head and heart shots.

Most of the targets you shoot at during a gunfight will be moving, and bouncing a rubber ball off a wall and then shooting at it while it's still moving is a good way to practice shooting at a moving target with a laser pistol. If police officers have never been trained to shoot moving targets, you cannot blame them for not hitting someone who is moving and shooting at them at the same time or blame them for injuring bystanders or hostages when the officers shoot at a moving target.

Here are some of the basic elements, principles, and techniques you need to consider when designing your own laser pistol course:

- Use high and low ready positions with the arms retracted or extended.
- Practice shooting with your strong hand, weak hand, and both hands.
- Practice shoot-and-move, move-and-shoot, and shoot while moving.
- Alternate between firing one shot and two or more shots at each target.
- Focus on head shots and heart shots but also practice pelvic shots.
- A good sequence is two heart shots followed immediately by two head shots.
- Use multiple targets to represent multiple adversaries.
- As soon as you see a target, try to shoot what you are looking at.
- Even if there are no additional targets, scan the area after you stop shooting.
- Always think of your targets as imminent deadly threats.

Most tactical shooters do not have the resources needed to shoot thousands of rounds per year, but they do have the resources to shoot a laser pistol thousands of times per year. Not only can training with a laser pistol improve your chances of being the first one to shoot or the first one to get a hit, but it can also help you achieve the most important goal: be the first one to get a hit that causes immediate or timely incapacitation.

Laser pistols are excellent for practicing at night because the laser beam will tell you if you hit what you were aiming at and there is no risk of bullet damage if you miss your target.

Three things are extremely important if you want to get the most benefit from practicing with a laser pistol: realism, frequency, and the elimination of bad habits.

Realism

You need to view every target as a deadly threat and behave accordingly. Tactical shooting is about being able to incapacitate a deadly threat as quickly as possible, and any shots that do not contribute to this goal are useless. A 2-inch group might win more target shooting competitions than a 4-inch group, but a head shot made with a 2-inch group has equal value to one made with a 4-inch group if they both cause immediate incapacitation. Many of the skills that are valued by target shooters, such as hitting targets at 150 feet or being able to reload with incredible speed, are unlikely to make much difference during a gunfight.

Frequency

Shooting is a degradable skill because the motor skills that make you a competent tactical shooter will decrease over time if not practiced frequently. Because of its convenience and cost-effectiveness, practicing at least once or twice a week for at least 15 minutes per session with a laser training pistol should not be difficult. Because of the instant gratification you get when you hit the targets at which you are aiming, many tactical shooters will find that developing shooting skills can be challenging and enjoyable.

Elimination of Bad Habits

Traditional police firearms training is notorious for being a source of bad habits, such as stacking your brass in a neat pile so it's easier to pick up after you finish shooting or carefully placing your empty magazines in a back pocket rather than dropping them on the ground. It's bad enough that most police officers are not required to use cover when they reload, but letting them finish shooting a target and then holster their gun without reloading an empty gun or scanning the immediate area for potential threats can have fatal consequences.

After you finish shooting a target, you should reload if necessary, hold your gun in a ready position, and scan the area for more potential targets before you holster your gun. If you get in the habit of not reloading or not scanning the area before holstering your gun, you might repeat this habit in the real world and get killed because your gun was empty or holstered when a second target appeared.

The belief that doing what you were trained to do will save your life is not reasonable if it increases your risk of getting killed. As a rule, never do things during a training session that will increase your risk of getting killed in the real world, such as relaxing too soon after you shoot a target.

One thing that is hard to create when you are shooting at stationary paper targets that do not shoot back is the element of surprise, which would not be a problem if deadly criminals who are armed with a gun would always stand still and let you take the first several shots before they returned fire. One way to create the element of surprise when practicing with a laser training pistol is to throw several tennis balls into a room in such a way that you cannot see where they land and then see how long it takes you to locate and shoot all of them.

Shoot as many of the balls as you can before you enter the room and try not to put yourself in a position where shooting one ball would make you an easy target for any of the other balls—if the balls were capable of shooting you. If you are working with a partner, he can position the tennis balls before you enter the room. To make searching for the balls more challenging, throw them into a dark room and use the flash-and-shoot technique to neutralize them.

The SIRT laser pistol has a rail that makes it easy to mount a light under the barrel, and some lights, such as the M3 Tactical Illuminator made by Insight, make it easy to switch the light on and off without changing your grip on the gun. When using the M3 with a two-handed grip, you can use your support-hand thumb to manipulate the on-off switch without reducing the pressure you have on the grip.

SIRT pistols resemble a Glock, but a large number of tactical pistols also resemble a Glock. If you use a Glock or Glock-like pistol that has a rail under the barrel for mounting a light, the flash-and-shoot skills that you develop when using a SIRT pistol and gun-mounted light can easily be used when you are firing live ammunition from a Glock or similar pistol and using the same kind of light.

NONLETHAL HANDGUNS

Most of the Airsoft spring-powered pistols are suitable for practicing at close range, and these replica pistols are inexpensive and realistic. Airsoft handguns are considered nonlethal (about 300 fps), but this does not mean they are incapable of causing serious injuries. Any bad habits you develop because of incorrectly using a nonlethal handgun might be repeated when using a lethal handgun.

Force-on-force training is purposely shooting a nonlethal gun at a person to improve your handgun or tactical skills. Any time you are doing force-on-force training with a nonlethal handgun, wear appropriate safety equipment and verify that anyone you are practicing with is also wearing required safety equipment.

Paintball guns are potentially more dangerous than Airsoft guns, but they are generally safe to use if players wear appropriate safety equipment and follow the safety procedures that apply to paintball guns, which are also called *markers*. Barrel plugs that prevent paintballs from exiting the barrel should not be removed until everyone is wearing eye protection and other required safety equipment. Before you start force-on-force training, the muzzle velocity of a marker should be tested with a chronograph to make certain the velocity of the paintballs is not more than 300 fps. Never remove eye protection until the practice exercise is over. Head, face, and neck protection (neck guard) should be required.

If you are doing force-on-force training, do not give shooters more paintballs than they would normally have when they carry a handgun for self-defense. To the extent possible, a hit that completely misses standard aim points should not be counted as a hit. Since a bullet that hits a leg will not stop someone from returning fire and killing you, a paintball that hits the leg should not be counted. Any shot that hits the head should be counted as a hit even if it misses the exact aim point. If you count poorly placed shots during force-on-force training, you are not training people to use correct shot placement during a deadly confrontation.

A break is the paint mark a paintball leaves on the body upon impact. Marks less than the size of a quarter might not be from a direct hit, and they should not be counted. Paintball force-on-force practice can be one-on-one, team-against-team, or one or two players against a team. For paintball practice to be useful, the settings and scenarios should be realistic and not designed for entertainment.

Replica air pistols that shoot pellets or BBs are realistic, inexpensive to shoot, and accurate, but they should not be considered nonlethal weapons. They should be treated the same way as a handgun that shoots regular bullets. The pellets or BBs from an air gun normally have less range and penetration than bullets propelled by gunpowder, but they may cause serious injuries, such as blindness, or even death. The maximum velocity for an air pistol is usually about 1,000 fps, but the velocity for most air pistols is in the range of 300 to 600 fps.

RICOCHET

A ricochet is the rebound that occurs when a bullet bounces off a surface. Some of the factors that affect ricochets are the shape or velocity of the bullet, the composition of the target, and the angle of incidence, which is the angle between the bullet's path and the surface of the target. Bullets are more likely to ricochet off hard targets, such as reactive metal targets that move when shot, than soft targets, such as plastic bottles or polymer-based, self-healing reactive targets.

Ricochets have limited tactical value because it's hard to predict where a bullet will go after a ricochet. If you use the wrong angle of incidence, the ricochet angle may be too high or too low, and if the surface you hit is uneven, the bullet may move laterally. Hitting a hard (unyielding) surface tends to give you a lower ricochet angle than hitting a soft (yielding) surface.

Some studies indicate you can shoot a bullet along a hard, smooth wall at an angle less than 45 degrees, and the bullet may flatten and travel between 1 and 8 inches off the wall. This may not give you reliable accuracy, but it does give you a reason for standing at least a foot away from walls. Ricochets from a shotgun will give you a better chance of being combat effective than those from a handgun.

Ricochets are dangerous when shooting metal targets. The deflection angle after a bullet hits a reactive metal target is usually about 12 degrees, but predicting where the bullet will land is almost impossible. Most people hit by ricochets are not seriously injured, but a few people have been killed. Never use reactive metal targets at less than the safe minimum distance recommended by the manufacturer.

At close range, bullets that hit rubber or wooden targets are less likely to ricochet than those that hit targets with a hard metal surface that prevents penetration. Aluminum cans have a hard surface, but bullets are more likely to penetrate the thin metal than ricochet off the surface. Pellets or BBs that do not penetrate the surface of a can may dent the can and then fall to the ground.

Paper targets are not likely to cause a ricochet, but the metal frames that are used to hold them may cause one. You can avoid this problem by using wooden or plastic frames to mount paper targets, or you can mount paper targets on a cardboard box. Paper pie plates or balloons stapled on a wooden stick are good targets for practicing tactical shooting at close range, and a balloon filled with helium and tied to a string can give you practice shooting at a moving target. Plastic or rubber toys that hang on a string can also be used as moving targets.

Some companies make frangible bullets that are considered safe when using reactive metal targets at close range because they disintegrate upon impact, but not all frangible bullets are made for this purpose. Companies that make metal targets should be able to give you the minimum safe distance for using the target. A target that cannot be used at 45 feet or less is not suitable for most tactical training.

MENTAL PRACTICE

Mental practice is very effective because the changes that occur in the brain afterward are similar to the ones that occur after physical practice. Scientific studies have shown some athletes benefit as much from mental practice as from physical practice. Both practices can improve motor skills, and mental practice does not limit the kind of training scenarios you can create.

Creating a what-if scenario that ends with correct shot placement is a good way to use mental practice. Some studies have found that mental practice is most effective when used with physical practice. If you are a tactical shooter and you are mentally creating imaginary targets, keep both eyes open when you shoot.

For mental practice to be effective, you should be relaxed, the mental images should be sharp and clear, and you must understand what the goals are and what needs to be done to achieve them. In addition to tactical skills, mental practice should include attitudes, emotions, and vocalizations because adding extra details will make your mental practice more realistic.

Many people do not understand that your brain is your most important weapon and there is much more to a gunfight than just a shooting match because using your brain can give you the tactical advantages you need to win a gunfight. Mental practice gives you the ability to practice gunfights in your mind and learn from your mistakes without having to suffer the fatal consequences that might have occurred if you made similar mistakes in a real gunfight. To paraphrase an old Samurai maxim: tomorrow's fights are won during today's mental practice.

Most scenarios are created by using what-if situations, but you can make mental practice more interesting by using one basic scenario, such as a building search, and changing the characteristics, number, or location of the adversaries you are facing. This forces you to be more flexible so you can adapt and overcome.

Even Brian Enos, a legendary competition shooter who was shooting about 25,000 rounds per year, used mental practice to improve his shooting skills. Most of his visualizations and mental rehearsals probably involved interactions with targets more than with human adversaries, but the fact that someone with his shooting skills used mental practice is a strong indication that he believed mental practice can improve marksmanship.

If you get very good at using mental practice, you may be able to stay calm but feel your respiration or pulse rate increase when you enter a stressful part of a scenario. The first time you try mental practice, go straight through a new scenario without stopping to correct mistakes. After you become more familiar with a new scenario, you can stop and repeat the parts that cause you problems. Using mental practice is a good way to build speed and self-confidence. Rather than repeat scenarios you have already mastered, create new ones.

SELF-DEFENSE IS NOT A SPORT

Competition shooting does not make you a good tactical shooter any more than being an Indy 500 racecar driver makes you a good New York City taxicab driver. Being a top competition shooter or a top racecar driver takes years of practice, and the fine motor skills you need to win a shooting competition or an Indy 500 race are not the same motor skills you need to win a gunfight or survive in New York City traffic. Not only are the skill sets different, but competition shooters and racecar drivers use customized equipment that most tactical shooters or cab drivers would not use. Unlike competition shooters, who can spend years perfecting their skills, most police shooters do not get more than a week of firearms training before they are on the street, and then they qualify once a year.

In the real world, most tactical shooters do not have the time or re-sources needed to become top competition shooters any more than most cab drivers have the time and resources needed to become Indy 500 drivers. It might be nice if tactical shooters and cab drivers had unlimited time and resources, but that kind of wishful thinking is not realistic.

It's hard to argue with champion target shooter and excellent tactical shooter Colonel Charles Askins, who wrote in *Colonel Askins on Pistols & Revolvers* that keeping your eye focused on the front sight makes it difficult to hit a living target that's moving. According to some written accounts, Colonel Askins averaged about 33,000 practice rounds per year for 10 years and killed more than two dozen men.

TACTICAL TRAINING IN THE REAL WORLD

Target shooters, such as Brian Enos, can probably mount a gun, get a perfect sight picture, and hit a target faster than most tactical shooters, but that's after many years of high-quality practice and shooting close to 25,000 rounds per year. Tactical shooters need to learn their tactical shooting skills in a few days, and most police officers do not shoot more than 50 rounds per year. Because of limited time and resources, the training for most tactical shooters needs to be realistic, effective, and economical, and it must focus on essential skills.

Some of the skills target shooters learn are useful, such as using a front-sight when shooting at 75 feet, but most deadly confrontations occur at less than 21 feet. A front-sight focus is very effective at close range if you get extra points for scoring the tightest group, but in a gunfight, a 4-inch group might be more combat effective than a 2-inch group and none of the aim points are less than 4 inches. As Jeff Cooper pointed out, unless you are talking about recreational marksmanship, the ability to hit a 2-inch circle is no better than the ability to hit a 4-inch circle.

A realistic training course will focus more on shooting at distances of less than 21 feet than on distances of 21 feet or more, and on one-handed shooting almost as much as two-handed shooting. You will fail the course for being too slow, but you will not fail the course for having a 4-inch group instead of a 2-inch group. Most shooting will be done with both eyes open, and shooters will be required to use cover when shooting and change locations after they shoot. As in gunfighting, you might not be allowed to continue if you miss a critical target.

A good tactical course should have a wide variety of targets. Some of them will be unexpected, moving, or placed at unusual angles; others will force you to make a shoot-or-don't-shoot decision. The lighting for the targets will range from good to very poor, and the stances you need to use will range from stable to unstable. Since most deadly confrontations are unpredictable, tactical training should force students to improvise, adapt, and overcome when normal tactics fail.

Unlike most annual qualifications where police officers show up, shoot, and leave, tactical and shooting skills should be taught during the same training session. If tactical skills are used correctly, you might be able to avoid the need for deadly force by not giving people who pose a deadly threat any reason to believe they can win if they fail to comply with your commands or warnings.

Using cover, concealment, or flashlights, and being able to reload quickly or fix malfunctions are skills you may need during a gunfight, and realistic training will force people to learn these skills or fail the course. Training should be based on what a tactical shooter needs to survive, and useless or unnecessary training should be eliminated. The best way to prove tactical training is realistic is to show a direct correlation between performance during training and survival on the street.

HANDLING STRESS

The best way to counteract panic is to give people realistic training that will improve their chances of surviving a deadly confrontation. It's easy to understand why people who normally rely on their front sight suddenly panic when someone is shooting at them while they are standing out in the open and trying to find the front sight. Even a flash-sight picture can be hard to get if a target is moving, you have very poor lighting, and you have less than 1 second to aim and shoot.

Some people believe panic is normal and you should adjust your shooting so you can work around disruptive psychological reactions by doing things such as convulsively gripping your gun or pulling the trigger by squeezing the grips with all four fingers at the same time. It's doubtful the people who recommend or teach these techniques would use them themselves during a gunfight, because using them will have an adverse effect on your speed and accuracy.

If using these techniques helps you avoid panic and the loss of speed and accuracy does not get you killed, these techniques might have some value. On the other hand, people who are properly trained can often remain calm and functional when facing danger without using techniques that decrease combat effectiveness.

Anyone who has ever worked with a group of well-trained tactical shooters knows that all of them are not equally brave and most of them have no desire to be heroes, but when the chips are down, all of them will do what it takes to get the job done. Despite the fear, sweating, or signs of stress, they will do what they were trained to do and remain functional as long as what they were trained to do seems to be working. But you might see some of them panic if they discover their training or equipment is useless and they have no idea what to do next.

The same people who recommend extreme muscle tension as a remedy for panic are often the same people who tell tactical shooters they should almost always use a front-sight focus. If you are in a state of panic that forces you to maintain a death grip on your gun and make a tight fist to pull the trigger, you are not likely to have the fine motor skills needed to use a front-sight focus because the excessive muscle tension will make it hard to keep your gun steady.

If your training is good and you have confidence in it, you are less likely to have extreme psychological reactions, such as paralyzing fear or panic, when facing a deadly threat. Even under extreme stress, most people will do what they were trained to do *if they were properly trained*. If you want to help people avoid panic, give them good training, have them practice enough to make the essential skills almost automatic, and teach them to stay focused on the threat. People who blame bad performance on panic seem to ignore the fact that if your training is bad, your performance will usually be just as bad with or without panic. Police officers who panic endanger themselves, other officers, and bystanders.

REALISTIC TARGETS

One of the disconnects between reality and the way police departments run firearms training is having the officers stand in a straight line and shoot stationary, front-facing targets. In the real world, criminals do not stand quietly facing police officers and wait to be shot. Unlike the paper targets, criminals can be sideways, diagonal, sitting, squatting, prone, supine, or standing with their backs facing you, and they can move erratically across a level surface, climb to a higher level, or duck into a hole. Almost nothing is predictable about human movement.

Since targets that are standing upright and facing you do not represent the different postures you are likely to encounter on the street, at least a few practice targets should represent people who are standing sideways or lying on the ground. Reactive targets placed at different distances or angles would be more realistic and more challenging to shoot than stationary targets that are always placed at known distances and always facing you. Targets that appear for a brief time and then disappear would improve accuracy, speed, and confidence. If you want to make targets realistic, you need to make them just as unpredictable as those you might encounter in a gunfight.

Another major problem with most of the paper targets being used by police departments is a poor correlation between the areas of a target you need to hit to score points and the areas of the body you need to hit to cause immediate or timely incapacitation. Hitting center of mass is less likely to cause immediate or timely incapacitation than it is to cause death hours after a shooting.

Making targets unpredictable is usually more important than making them smaller. Using unpredictable targets that surprise people and force them to shoot quickly and with combat-effective accuracy is better preparation for a gunfight than using small targets that encourage people to use a front-sight focus at close range because 2-inch groups get higher scores than 4-inch groups.

To help people avoid accidental shootings and lawsuits, everyone should be required to complete shoot-or-don't-shoot scenarios. Targets that always look the same might improve your shooting skills, but they will not do much to improve your discrimination skills because most deadly criminals do not look like a blue human silhouette or have an X-ring in the center of their torso. In order to have shoot-or-don't-shoot scenarios, some of the targets need to have distinguishing characteristics that automatically make them discrimination targets.

One thing that will make tactical shooters more combat effective is using targets with realistic aim points. Center-of-mass targets encourage poor shot placement, and many of the X-rings used on center-of-mass targets won't cause immediate or timely incapacitation because there are very few critical tissues below the X-ring. If you want to improve shot placement, give people incentives for hitting aim points that are more likely to cause incapacitation.

REALISTIC PRACTICE

In the real world, you normally have your gun in your hand or you are drawing your gun before you settle into a stance. Since the ground you are standing on is not always level and it might be slippery, you shoot from any stance you can use under the circumstances. One way to teach people how to use a tactical stance is to have them randomly walk in a small, marked-off area at a steady pace until a target pops up and then have them draw their gun, settle into a tactical stance, and shoot.

Shooting while moving is harder to learn than shoot-and-move or move-and-shoot. On the other hand, being able to shoot while moving can be a valuable skill, especially when facing multiple adversaries. To shoot while walking, shoot after you step forward and most of your body weight is on your front foot. Since you can shoot with either the hand opposite your front foot or the hand on the same side, you can shoot each time you step forward.

A tactical shooter also needs reality-based environments. Essential skills include learning how to move along walls without getting close enough to be hit by a ricochet, how to enter rooms or turn blind corners, and how to use cover or concealment. These skills can be safely taught using laser pistols or paintball guns, and you can create inexpensive environments using movable walls and used furniture. Advanced tactical shooters should also have frequent force-on-force training where tactical shooters can test their skills against each other. Laser pistols and replica paintball guns are safe and inexpensive for this kind of training, but paintball guns make it easier to separate winners from losers.

TARGETS FOR SHOT PLACEMENT

Practicing shot placement will be easier if you use three-dimensional targets that resemble the human body, and the scoring areas should be about the same size as the aim points. Despite anatomical differences between a head, heart, and pelvic shot, a 4-inch circle is a good shape and size when practicing all three aim points. Hits should be counted regardless of how tightly the shots are grouped.

Since a 2-inch group is not more combat effective than a 4-inch group, all shots that hit the same aim point are counted the same regardless of how tight the group is. Besides having targets that resemble a body, some of the targets should have postures other than standing, and some of the targets should not face forward.

Reactive targets are good for teaching people to hit aim points because they can give you immediate visual or audible feedback. Reactive targets can be used as moving targets or surprise targets. For advanced tactical shooters, reactive targets are normally the same size as aim points, although larger reactive targets might be used when practicing speed drills or working beginners. It is seldom useful to make reactive tactical targets larger than 6 inches in any direction.

You can make reactive targets even more useful by adding a characteristic that allows you to change the status of the target back and forth from shoot to don't-shoot, such as putting a green label on shoot targets and a red label on don't-shoot targets. To make target discrimination more challenging, you can use pop-up or rotating targets that are marked as shoot or don't shoot, or you can mark a target as a shoot target by shining a red laser beam on it.

Targets that can change their status from shoot to don't-shoot or from don't-shoot to shoot can help people improve target discrimination. To pass a shoot-or-don't-shoot course, you need to hit all the shoot targets and none of the don't-shoot targets. Target shooters can make up for a bad start by shooting well at the end, but tactical shooters cannot make up for shooting one innocent person by shooting two criminals. Improving target discrimination also builds confidence.

In the real world, moving targets can travel along a horizontal, vertical, or curved line, and they can approach or move away from you. These kinds of movements are not easy to duplicate, and using live ammunition increases the risk of damaging the mechanism that produces the movement. Using a laser training pistol is a good way to practice shooting moving targets without damaging the target or the mechanism that moves the target.

To be combat effective, when your gun is already in your hand, you must be able to hit a 4-inch circle at a distance of 21 feet in 1.5 seconds or less when using a target focus and holding the gun in one or both hands. Since a person attacking you with a knife can cover about 21 feet in 1.5 seconds, taking more than 1.5 seconds to shoot may put you at risk. In other words, you can be quick or dead.

LOW-LIGHT AND NO-LIGHT PRACTICE

A large percentage of all deadly confrontations takes place in a low-light or no-light environment, which is why tactical shooters must be able to shoot with speed and accuracy when the sights are not visible and the target is barely visible. Since a competent tactical shooter should be combat effective when shooting with one hand, holding a flashlight in one hand and shooting with the other should not be a problem. When shooting with two hands, tactical shooters who have a gun-mounted light can use flash-and-shoot, which is easy to learn and use.

Standing behind your light will make it easy for people to see where you are and score a heart shot by shooting in the direction of your light. If your target is holding a flashlight in the right hand and close to the head, a quick burst of three shots about 12 inches under the brightest part of the beam and slightly to the right will increase your probability of making a heart shot. If the flashlight is in the left hand, place the shots about 12 inches under the light and slightly to the left. If the light is almost in front of the face, place the shots about 12 inches below the light. Because of the direct or reflected light from a flashlight, you can usually tell which hand a flashlight is in and where the person is holding it. People who hold their handgun in front of their face, hold the flashlight in the other hand with the knuckles facing upward, and rest the wrist of the shooting hand across the back of the wrist of the support hand make excellent targets. If you are shooting at targets that do not shoot back, having the light in front of your head does not create a physical risk, and competition shooters often get very good scores when holding their gun and flashlight in front of their head just below eye level.

The FBI method is not popular with target shooters, but shooting with one hand and holding the flashlight in the other with the arm out to the side and angled upward about 45 degrees makes you harder to shoot. Flashing the light on and off to check an area and then moving can also help you avoid getting shot.

When using a high-intensity, gun-mounted light, flash-and-shoot is the most effective technique, especially if you can hold the gun in both hands and activate the light with the thumb of your support hand. If both thumbs are pointed forward, the thumb of the support hand can often be used to activate the light by pressing the switch and turn it off by releasing the switch. Activating the light for a fraction of a second so you can verify your target, shoot, and then move to a new location will improve your chances of not getting hit by return fire. To make follow-up shots, use flash-and-shoot after you move to a new location.

You can practice flash-and-shoot by putting a gun-mounted light on a laser training pistol or gun that has a laser-training device inserted in the barrel. If you are using a red laser and red reflectors as targets, the reflector will flash when it's hit by the gun-mounted light and flash again if you hit it with a laser beam.

Some people use a laser sight that is attached or integrated into a handgun when trying to locate targets in dim light, but a competent tactical shooter will usually be faster and more accurate using a gun-mounted light and target-focused shooting. For a shooter with limited training or a tactical shooter who is shooting from the hip or from a position that makes it impossible to see the gun, a laser sight may improve your combat effectiveness if you have enough ambient light to verify the target without using a flashlight or some other light source.

You can buy a gun-mounted light that produces both white light and a laser beam, but these devices are usually more effective on a carbine or shotgun than on a handgun. Beginners seem to like laser sights more than experienced tactical shooters do, but tactical shooters who become accurate when aiming with a laser beam often find that learning to use a laser sight was harder than they expected.

If you have a laser sight on a handgun, it should be used to supplement but not replace target-focused or front-sight focused shooting. A laser beam might not be visible when you have very bright light or heavy smoke, rain, or fog, and the batteries in a laser sight can lose power. Green lasers are brighter and more effective than red lasers during the day. Using a laser sight at night can reveal your location; a laser beam will not illuminate areas the way flashlights, spotlights, or headlights will; and some people may shoot back when hit by a laser beam.

Laser sights, which are also called *laser aimers*, can have a psychological impact on aggressors who believe you can hit any spot that is touched by the laser beam. In reality, the movement of a laser beam creates a wobble zone that makes pinpoint accuracy very difficult, and it takes extremely good motor skills to make a precision shot with laser sights unless you are using a rest. It should also be remembered that laser beams travel in a straight line, whereas bullets travel along an arc. From a sniper's perspective, a night-vision scope is usually a better choice than a laser sight when making long-range precision shots during the day or night.

Night sights are not essential, but they can be useful to a tactical shooter who wants to use a front-sight focus and has enough light to verify the target. Good-quality night sights are expensive, and police officers are more likely to have night sights on their duty weapons than on a backup gun or a gun they carry off duty. Some people have a hard time using night sights because they tend to focus on the rear sights or try to focus on the front and rear sights at the same time.

When practicing tactical shooting in low-light or no-light environments, a good drill is to have one person act as a spotter and locate targets with a flashlight and to have another person shoot the targets the instant they become visible. The spotter has the ability to control how long a target remains visible, and the targets should be placed at various distances and picked by the spotter at random. If this technique is used during a gunfight, the person using the light should be behind cover and may be able to illuminate rooms by bouncing the light off the ceiling.

VIDEO GAMES

You can learn more about using speed, accuracy, shot placement, and cover from playing most of the first-person-shooter video games than you can from shooting at a center-of-mass bull's-eye on a stationary paper target. Most of the combat video games were designed to be realistic—some people believe they are too realistic—but video designers frequently do a better job creating realistic deadly confrontations than the people who design the shooting ranges for police officers. Video designers use realistic elements in their games—such as close-quarter combat, poor lighting, and multiple adversaries—to make the games realistic, and playing these games will improve your mental, visual, and motor skills.

To be successful playing a video game, such as Tom Clancy's *Splinter Cell*, you need to have situational awareness and tactical skills and be able to react quickly, or face getting killed. You need to learn how to ambush your enemies and avoid being ambushed by them. The handgun stances used by the protagonist in *Splinter Cell* are similar to those used in the Porter method.

The main failing most video games have is that the motor skills you develop are useful for operating a video controller, but they will not improve the shooting skills that are needed when using a handgun for self-defense, such as grip, trigger pull, and gun alignment. Some of the video games can be used with a light pistol, but most of these pistols feel more like toys than functional handguns. Using a good replica handgun when you play a video game would increase the realism.

Most video games have more shoot scenarios than don't-shoot scenarios, which reduces realism. In the real world, you have more don't-shoot scenarios than shoot scenarios. Some video games require target discrimination, and this adds realism without detracting from the excitement.

The best video games do not provide unlimited ammunition, and they force you to reload when your gun is empty. According to the 5-5-5 rule, most gunfights take place at 5 feet or less, they are over in 5 seconds or less, and no more than 5 shots are fired. Video gunfights often occur at close range and you need to be fast and accurate, but the number of times you shoot is often closer to 50 than 5.

One skill you can develop from playing video games is learning to scan, interpret, and react quickly when a target appears. This skill is not required when shooting stationary targets that do not shoot back. People who learn to shoot targets that move or appear and disappear quickly develop the visual and motor skills that improve their chances of hitting a fast-moving adversary.

Video games help you develop the right attitude for a gunfight because the targets shoot back. When shooting targets that do not shoot back, tactical shooters should visualize that every target they are shooting at is trying to shoot back. This will make practice more realistic and help them develop a survival mindset.

CRITIQUE POLICE DRAMAS AND YOUTUBE VIDEOS

The police dramas you see on television and or in the movies can be very realistic in some respects, especially if the director is using competent technical advisors, but whether a person lives or dies in a gunfight is determined by the people who write the script and not by the tactical capabilities of the actors.

If you watch a show where the good guys are standing out in the open with handguns and the bad guys are shooting at the good guys from behind cover with rifles or shotguns and losing, you are looking at a scenario that is unlikely to happen in the real world. Individuals standing out in the open will have a very hard time defeating people who are protected by cover, and handguns are something you use only when you don't have access to a rifle or shotgun.

A handgun might be better than a rifle or shotgun when doing a building search if the length of the barrel makes weapon retention difficult, but in most cases, you should leave your handgun holstered if you have access to a rifle or shotgun. Comparing a handgun to a high-velocity assault rifle or a shotgun is a lot like trying to decide who stands a better chance of survival after a motorcycle accident: the person driving the truck or the person driving the motorcycle.

Police dramas are one of the few places where you can see a police officer look in one direction, shoot in a different direction, and knock the bad guy halfway across the room with one shot from a handgun. In real life, even if you hit the person you are not looking at, handgun bullets will not knock someone over.

In defense of police dramas, some of them are more technically correct than the videos you see on YouTube that were taken by cameras mounted on police vehicles. A large number of these videos show serious tactical mistakes, such as not watching the hands of a suspect, holding a flashlight in the hand you normally use to shoot with, not watching what the passengers in a car you stopped are doing, not conducting a pat-down search for weapons, or not calling for backup.

Many of the newer police dramas show the officers using more of a tactical stance than the kind most police officers use when they qualify. Now that the special-response teams and the officers in police dramas are using tactical handgun skills and the special-response units in most police departments are using tactical handgun skills, it seems that the only people who are not using them are the police detectives and uniformed officers in most departments.

After reading this book, you should be able to critique the police shootings you see on YouTube videos. If you believe fatal mistakes were made, identify them and try to avoid them. You may also notice that luck will sometimes compensate for a lack of skill, action is usually faster than reaction, and hesitation can get you killed. What's most disturbing when watching YouTube videos is that some criminals seem to be better trained than the police officers who are trying to arrest them.

USING A SHOTGUN AS A SECOND WEAPON

Because of their size and weight, tactical shotguns are harder to conceal or maneuver than handguns, which is why most tactical shooters carry a handgun when using a shotgun. All the examples in this chapter are based on how you would use a pump shotgun, such as the Mossberg 590A1 or the Remington 870. Pump shotguns are usually safer to use than semiautomatics, and they are almost 100-percent reliable if you use a full stroke when you rack the slide instead of a partial stroke (short stroke). The U.S. military used the Mossberg 590A1 until it was replaced by the M26 (a single weapon that combines an M4 carbine with a shotgun), and most police departments are still using the Remington 870.

If you are familiar with the way a semiautomatic shotgun operates, most of the topics discussed in this chapter, such as safety, ballistics, aim points, and shooting techniques, can be applied to a semiautomatic. Pump shotguns are less likely to malfunction because of dirt or shooting low-powered shotgun shells, but semiautomatics may have less recoil, you might be able to shoot more rounds per minute, and they are easier to shoot with one hand or when you are prone.

Semiautomatic shotguns tend to have less *felt* recoil than pump shotguns, especially the semiautomatics that are operated by gas instead of recoil, but most tactical shooters can learn to manage the recoil from a 12-gauge pump shotgun. When you are making follow-up shots, it is easier to stay aligned with your target when using a semiautomatic, but people who use the recoil from a pump shotgun to help them pull the fore-end back and then push the fore-end forward to help them realign the barrel on a target might not notice much difference. It is also easier to mount lights on semiautomatic shotguns than pump shotguns.

After you shoot a pump shotgun, it will not automatically reload the way a semiautomatic shotgun does, which gives you the option of keeping the chamber empty if you do not have another target. If a shotgun is not drop-safe, which means dropping the shotgun may cause an accidental discharge when the safety is on, having an empty chamber with the safety switched *off* is safer than having a round in the chamber when the safety is *on*. Even if you believe the shotgun you are using is drop-safe because it meets military specifications, you should verify this belief by contacting the company that manufactures the shotgun. If a shotgun is truly drop-safe, switching the safety on will do more than just block the trigger.

Unlike semiautomatics, pump shotguns almost never malfunction when firing low-powered birdshot, which means you can use it for a lot of your practice. Compared to buckshot or slugs, birdshot is relatively inexpensive, and it has much less recoil. In addition to good tactical training, being able to run a shotgun correctly requires periodic practice using realistic targets.

Shotguns are devastating weapons—when used correctly at close range, they have about the same destructive force as a high-powered rifle. If you are facing a home-invasion robbery, a shotgun can be less effective than a handgun in some situations and more effective in others. When you are searching a room, a handgun is easier to maneuver and retain than a shotgun, but a shotgun combined with good cover or concealment and patience is better than a handgun when defending a doorway or narrow hallway or when you are setting an ambush for dangerous criminals who have illegally entered your home.

At close range (0–20 feet), a 12-gauge shotgun with a barrel that's between 18 and 20 inches can be very effective when facing multiple adversaries or people who use a flanking maneuver to circumvent your cover because one shot from a shotgun will usually cause much more tissue damage at this range than one from a handgun. Even when making a near-contact wound, the diameter of the entry wound will usually be greater than 0.729 inch, which is the bore diameter of a 12-gauge shotgun and more than twice the diameter of a .357 Magnum.

Since most tactical shotguns have a barrel that's 18–20 inches and a diameter that's 0.72 inch (improved cylinder) to 0.73 inch (cylinder bore), the distance at which 00 buckshot starts to spread beyond a 4-inch circle is about 5–10 feet, but this distance can be affected by the kind of ammunition you are using. If buckshot is fired at close range and the pellets are bunched when they hit the cranium, you may see a limited amount of spreading if the first pellets that hit the cranium slow down and the pellets behind them veer off to the side (billiard ball ricochet effect).

If the aim point and the length of the permanent cavity are the same, increasing the diameter of the entry wound will usually increase the size of the permanent cavity and increase tissue damage. Shotguns are extremely destructive at close-range because tightly-packed groups of pellets or shotgun slugs produce a much larger permanent cavity than a handgun bullet. At close-range, a shotgun wound to the chest is more likely to cause timely incapacitation than a handgun wound to the chest, but even a shotgun might not cause immediate incapacitation.

Even though pelvic shots made with a handgun at close range seldom cause extensive tissue damage or pelvic instability, a pelvic shot made with a shotgun at close range can be devastating. According to Paul Dougherty, who edited a book titled *Gunshot Wounds*: "Generally, gunshot fractures of the pelvis tend to be discrete injuries and do not disrupt the pelvic ring stability. . . . The exception to this rule is gunshot wounds."

A shotgun blast can fracture the hip joint (acetabulum or proximal femur) and bone fragments along with shotgun pellets, fragments from a shotgun slug, or shotgun-shell wadding may be present.

A head shot with a handgun is capable of causing immediate incapacitation, but a close-range head shot made with a handgun is less likely to cause immediate incapacitation than a close-range head shot made with a shotgun. Because of pressure from gas rapidly exiting the barrel, almost any contact shotgun wound that hits the cranium will cause immediate incapacitation.

Since Hollywood has grossly exaggerated the effectiveness of shotguns in the same way it has that of handguns, anyone planning to use a shotgun for self-defense needs to understand the difference between fact and fantasy. A rifle is a better weapon for dealing with a sniper or a hostage situation than a shotgun, but a shotgun is a better weapon than a rifle if someone is attacking you with a knife. Even military units that carry submachine guns have reported that a shotgun can be more effective than a submachine gun during close-quarter combat because of the shotgun's close-range lethality.

During World War I, U.S. soldiers fighting in trenches quickly discovered the value of having both a handgun and shotgun (trench gun) available when facing enemy soldiers in dark, narrow trenches at close range. Most trench guns had a small bead at the end of the barrel, but it's doubtful the small bead would have been visible in a dark trench. Although some trench guns had lugs for mounting a bayonet, many of the soldiers preferred using a sharpened spade, which was easier to maneuver and less likely to stick in the enemy than a bayonet.

During a conflict in the Philippines that started around the late 1800s, the U.S. military discovered that the Islamic Moro natives who lived in the southern Philippines were extremely fierce warriors and very good at waging suicide attacks when armed with nothing but a short, wavy sword called a *kris*. Contrary to popular belief, it was not the .45-caliber Colt revolver but the 12-gauge Winchester Model 1897 shotgun that proved to be the best weapon for stopping a charging Moro. (Model 1911 .45 ACP pistols were not used in this conflict.)

The military used 12-gauge shotguns during the Philippine conflict because it was easier to stop someone at close range with nine tightly packed 00 buckshot pellets than with a single .45-caliber revolver bullet. At a distance between 5 and 15 feet, it might take slightly less time to aim a shotgun than to aim a handgun because the pellets will have started to spread, and just one 00 buckshot pellet might cause almost as much tissue damage as one .45-caliber bullet.

Shotguns have a long history of being used successfully in warfare, and their effectiveness in close quarter combat is undeniable, but submachine guns with short barrels and suppressors are more likely to be used by today's military units than shotguns. You can load a submachine gun faster than you can load a shotgun that has a tube magazine, and the rounds for a shotgun are much heavier than the rounds for a submachine gun.

The shotgun is equal or superior to a submachine gun when used at close range, but law enforcement officers and private citizens are more likely to be involved in close-quarter confrontations than modern soldiers. If soldiers need a shotgun, they can use the M26, which combines a carbine on the top with a shotgun on the bottom, and the shotgun is a straight-pull bolt action that uses a charging handle to extract, eject, and load shotgun shells from a box magazine.

Almost any shotgun can be used for self-defense, but tactical shotguns have features that make them better for self-defense than hunting or sporting shotguns, such as short barrels, high-capacity tube or box magazines, and synthetic stocks. Shotguns that have a limited capacity, such as single- or double-barrel shotguns, or shotguns that have a long barrel are not appropriate for self-defense. Synthetic stocks are not essential, but they seldom break if the shotgun is dropped or used as a club. Most tactical shotguns are black and have a nonreflective surface, which make them less likely to reflect light and expose your position at night.

The maximum combat-effective range for 00 buckshot is about 75 feet, and even if you aim correctly, half of the pellets will usually miss if you are trying to make a head shot. The most reliable combat-effective distance for 00 buckshot is about 20 feet, and a competent tactical shooter should be able to use a target focus and put some of the pellets in a 4-inch circle at this distance.

If the shotgun you are using for self-defense will not shoot a group smaller than 5 inches at 10 feet and changing the ammunition will not correct this problem, try using a different shotgun. A tactical shotgun that groups the majority of pellets near the center of a pattern tends to be more combat effective than one that hollows out the center and increases the density of pellets near the edge.

Even if you have a small, tight group, one or more pellets may be separated from the group by several inches. Erratic pellets that are visibly separated from an otherwise tight group are called *flyers,* and they can decrease combat effectiveness. A shotgun or ammunition that consistently produces flyers at 10 feet might be a danger to bystanders, especially at longer distances, and should be avoided.

To find out what kind of pattern a shotgun produces, you can shoot some test patterns at 10, 20, 45, and 75 feet. Changing the brand of ammunition or the size of the buckshot can change the size, density, or configuration of your patterns. Since changing from one kind of ammunition to another can change the pattern your shotgun produces, you should always shoot new test patterns whenever you change to a new shotgun or new ammunition.

Most of the law enforcement officers who have access to a shotgun have never fired test patterns at different distances with the kind of shotguns or the kind of ammunition they use. Even if the pictures are correct for the shotgun and the ammunition being used, just showing officers pictures of shotgun patterns does not mean they will be able to hit what they are aiming at. Having the officers shoot the patterns themselves will help them understand the capabilities of a shotgun and why they need loading and shooting skills to be effective with a shotgun.

At 0 to 20 feet, buckshot does not drop enough to make trajectory a major concern and most of your adversaries will not be moving fast enough to make leading your targets necessary. The first reason people miss when they are aiming a shotgun at a close-range target is the belief that buckshot will spread out and compensate for poor marksmanship, and the second reason is using a front-sight focus. At close range, tactical shooters should follow the same advice given to pheasant hunters: keep your eye on the bird and not the barrel or the bead.

Using a front-sight focus might be realistic if your target is stationary and you are trying to make a precise shot with shotgun slugs, but most close-range shooting is done with a target focus. Except for hunters who are using shotgun slugs, most hunters use a target focus when hunting with a shotgun. They look at the target they want to shoot and shoot what they are looking at.

Even if a shotgun is chambered for 3 1/2-inch Magnums, a 2 3/4-inch standard load is usually sufficient for tactical shooting, and using a shorter round may allow you to load more rounds into a tubular magazine. The main advantage of having a shotgun that chambers 3 1/2-inch Magnums is being able to share ammunition with someone who is using the same kind if you run out of ammunition.

The average number of rounds fired during a deadly confrontation is three to five rounds, and most tactical pump shotguns carry at least six rounds. If you want to carry extra rounds or a different kind of round than you have in your shotgun, you can add a sidesaddle shell holder to the left side of the receiver that carries six extra rounds, use a stock that carries four extra rounds, or put a butt cuff on the right side of the stock that carries six extra rounds. If you are facing a deadly threat and your shotgun is empty, your best option is to transition from the shotgun to a handgun. Competition shooters may carry 40 rounds and use arm, belt, or chest carriers.

In the United States, the slugs used in most smooth-bore shotguns are either 1-ounce Foster slugs or 1-ounce Brenneke slugs. The performance of a shotgun slug can vary depending on the brand, the kind of slug being used, and the kind of shotgun or choke being used. Many people believe that Federal's Truball slugs or Brenneke's K.O. slugs are more accurate and give you deeper penetration than standard Foster slugs. Sabot slugs are the best slugs for accuracy, but they are more likely to exit a human body than a Foster or Brenneke slug. Sabot slugs are used in a rifled barrel instead of a smooth bore, but rifled barrels decrease the effectiveness of buckshot because they spin the buckshot and decrease the density of buckshot near the center of the pattern (hollowed-out pattern).

You cannot achieve or maintain shotgun proficiency without learning and practicing the same kind of things you would learn or practice when trying to develop handgun proficiency, such as grip, stance, trigger pull, alignment with a target, speed loading, and how to handle malfunctions. When using a shotgun, the correct grip and stance can help reduce recoil, and using correct loading procedures can help you avoid facing someone with an empty gun. You should also consider what to do with a shotgun if you need to use both hands because you cannot holster a shotgun the way you can a handgun if you need to have both hands free.

When using a shotgun that has a tube magazine, correct loading procedures are essential because you need to load shotgun shells one at a time, and you need to keep your magazine as full as possible by reloading whenever possible. Being able to hold two or three shotgun shells in your hand at the same time when you reload can make reloading faster, but holding one round in your hand at a time when you reload reduces the risk of dropping a round if you are moving and reloading or reloading under pressure. Competition shooters often reload with their shooting hand, but tactical shooters should normally try to load with their support hand and keep their shooting hand on the grips unless the support hand is injured.

Dropping a round directly into the ejection port may be useful in some cases, such as when you know your gun is empty and the ejection port is open, but in most cases pushing a round into your tube magazine will be safer and just as fast. If you find out your shotgun is empty because you hear a click when you pull the trigger, rather than open the action, drop a round into the ejection port, and close the action. You can simply push a round into the loading port and rack the slide. If you want to be effective and fast, look for the most effective ways to do things—which are often the simplest way to do things—and then repeatedly do them the same way until doing so becomes almost automatic.

If you have buckshot in the chamber and you want to load a shotgun slug, you could pull the slide back to eject the round of buckshot in the chamber, remove any round that's in the ejection port because the shell carrier was activated when you pulled the slide back, and drop a shotgun slug in the ejection port. If you have space in your tube magazine for a shotgun slug, push a shotgun slug into your tube magazine and rack the slide. This will eject the buckshot and load the shotgun slug. You could also shoot the buckshot at your target before you load the slug.

If your tube magazine was full when you racked a round into the chamber, your magazine will have space for one more round even if you didn't start with one empty space. Some tactical shooters like to start with an empty chamber and one empty space in their tube magazine. If your magazine is loaded with buckshot, this makes it easy to load one shotgun slug into the magazine and make the first round in the chamber a shotgun slug. In other situations, you might want to rack one round of buckshot into the chamber and load two shotgun slugs into the magazine.

A competition shotgun shooter and a tactical shotgun shooter have different needs: competition shooting is about winning matches whereas tactical shooting is about staying alive. Competition shooters do not lose points for looking at their shotgun when loading rounds into a magazine or ejection port, but tactical shooters should be able to load a shotgun without looking at it because their eyes need to scan the surrounding areas for potential threats and the barrel of the shotgun should be pointing where the eyes are looking.

Most competition shotgun shooters do not lose points by taking their hand off the grips, rotating the gun so the loading port is facing upward, reloading with their shooting hand, or not using cover or concealment when they reload, but doing these things might get a tactical shooter killed. In tactical shooting, you cannot score enough points to compensate for getting seriously injured or killed.

Competition shooters often load rounds into the ejection port by reaching over the top of the receiver. Reaching over the top may be faster if you have a shotgun shell holder on the right side of your gun, but it may also block your field of view if the top of your barrel is in your line of vision. To simplify reloading a tube magazine or your ejection port, always reach under the receiver.

If you are using a buttstock or sidesaddle shell holder, keeping the brass facing down makes it easier to reload by reaching under the receiver, thereby making it easier to activate the slide if you are using a pump shotgun because your hand is closer to the bottom of the slide than it would be if you reached over the receiver. If you are in a prone position and you rack the slide and reload with your shooting hand because it's easier to use your shooting hand than to use your support hand, you can still reach under the receiver to reload.

If you reach over the receiver to load a round into the ejection port, you may be able to rack the slide by reaching over the top of the barrel to grab the fore-end, but this technique might not work very well if the barrel is hot or you have a hand guard on top of the barrel. What makes this technique even less practical is that you would still need to shift your hand to the bottom of the fore-end if you want to use a high-ready position and you needed to use the hand to support your shotgun.

When training a tactical shooter, you need to make the training realistic, make the movements as simple as possible, and eliminate unnecessary movements. If you carry extra ammunition, keep it in the same places and keep it somewhere that makes loading with your support hand both quick and easy. It's very impressive to watch competition shooters pull shells from five or six different places, but competition shooters are not worried about being shot and they often use techniques that would be impractical or dangerous during a gunfight.

Practice time and the number of shotgun rounds fired per year are two other factors that need to be considered. Most police officers do not shoot more than five rounds per year, but most competition shooters practice between matches and shoot thousands of rounds per year. The only way you can make police officers more effective is to teach basics and not waste time on nonessential movements.

According to Hicks law, adding nonessential movements, such as rotating a shotgun so the loading port faces up when you reload, will increase total response time. For competition shooters, using cover or concealment or kneeling down when you reload is almost never important, but for tactical shooters, these things are almost always important—especially if you want to avoid getting shot.

Since a tactical shooter seldom shoots more than about three to five rounds during a deadly confrontation, if you carry five or more rounds in a tube magazine and six extra rounds in a sidesaddle shell holder on the left side of the receiver, you should have enough rounds. Furthermore, most tactical shooters who are using a shotgun will also have a handgun plus extra ammunition for the handgun.

You should not carry shotgun shells in your front or back pants pockets. A few police officers who have done this have mistakenly loaded small, plastic cigarette lighters or lifesavers into their shotgun instead of shotgun shells. It can also be hard to remove shells from a pocket if the pocket is tight against the body or you are using a kneeling or prone position.

If someone is shooting at you from behind cover, buckshot might not penetrate the cover, but it might buy you enough time to load a shotgun slug that will penetrate the cover. If someone is shooting at you from 75 feet away, you may hit the person with some of your pellets, but shotgun slugs are usually more accurate and more combat effective at this distance.

When using a smooth-bore 12-gauge shotgun with a front-barrel bead but no sights, a realistic combat-effective distance for slugs is about 75 feet. You might be combat effective at a longer distance with just a bead, but using a ghost ring, rifle sight, or optical sight will make it easier to shoot at distances beyond 75 feet. Even with optical sights, a smooth-bore shotgun is a poor substitute for a tactical rifle when shooting at 100 yards or more. When using slugs, a smooth-bore shotgun should be zeroed in at 150 feet and then tested at 10, 20, 45, and 75 feet.

Buckshot is usually a better choice than a shotgun slug when shooting a moving target at 45 feet or closer because the buckshot will spread and cover a slightly larger area than a slug. If your target is behind a car door, a slug is usually better because even if 00 buckshot penetrates the side windshield or weaker parts of a door, it may not have enough kinetic energy to cause incapacitation.

If you have time and you have room in your tube magazine for one more round, you can push a slug into the tube, use the buckshot in your chamber for suppression fire, and then load the slug and use it as a follow shot. In most situations, it makes more sense to shoot the buckshot and then rack the slide to load a slug than to let the buckshot round fall on the ground and then load the slug.

Shotgun safety follows most of the same rules as handgun safety follows, plus a few additional procedures. First, if a shotgun is not drop-safe, the safety on the shotgun will not give you the same protection from unintentional discharges that a handgun safety would normally provide. Second, unloading a handgun to make it safe is often easier and safer than unloading a shotgun that has a tube magazine.

An unloading method that works with some pump shotguns is as follows:

1. Activate the safety and keep your fingers off the trigger.
2. Remove any rounds in the chamber or ejection port and close the action.
3. Position the shotgun so the loading port faces upward and the barrel is pointing in a safe direction.
4. Release the detent (shell latch) that is holding rounds in the tube magazine.
5. Empty the magazine by removing one shell at a time.

It is safer to remove rounds from a tube magazine after the chamber and the ejection port are empty and the action is closed than to rely on using the safety and keeping your finger off the trigger to prevent an unintentional discharge while you rack the slide to eject all the rounds in the shotgun. Never use any method for unloading a shotgun that's not specifically approved by the manufacturer, and try to practice loading and unloading a shotgun with dummy rounds instead of live rounds whenever possible.

It is not uncommon to see police officers put the safety on, hold the slide release down, and rack the action of a pump shotgun until all the rounds in the shotgun have been ejected. Using this method can lead to unfortunate outcomes if your safety malfunctions or is accidently switched off and one of your fingers that is not pressing down on the slide release (action bar release) bumps the trigger.

Regardless of how you unload a shotgun, visually and physically check the chamber and the magazine to make certain the weapon is empty. After you have unloaded a shotgun, it's a good policy to leave the safety on and the chamber open when you are walking around with the shotgun. Any shotgun that has the action closed should be considered loaded until you have visually and physically checked the chamber and magazine yourself to verify they are empty.

You can modify shotguns with accessories that might be useful, such as a folding stock if a shotgun is used from inside a car or a sling. If you transition from a shotgun to a handgun, letting the shotgun hang from a tactical sling is usually a better option than holding it in your hand or dropping it on the ground. Some of the accessories or modifications used by target shooters, such as installing optical sights or porting a barrel to reduce recoil, can reduce combat effectiveness. Optical sights can be damaged if a shotgun is dropped, and the noise, blast, or flash from a ported barrel can deafen, blind, or burn people who are near the barrel.

It's easy to imagine what can happen if someone takes your shotgun away from you and tries to shoot you with it, and letting shotgun retention turn into a wrestling match instead of ending the situation quickly will increase your chances of getting shot. A shotgun is very effective at close range, but shotgun retention is harder than handgun retention, especially if you are navigating dark hallways or searching confined spaces. A shotgun with a barrel shorter than 18 inches might be easier to retain, but having a barrel shorter than 18 inches is usually illegal without approval from the Bureau of Alcohol, Tax, Firearms, and Explosives.

If someone illegally grabs the barrel of a loaded shotgun you are using for self-defense, it's hard to imagine the threat being considered anything less than deadly—and the nature of the threat should dictate your response. Other responses might be possible, but the first line of defense is usually pointing the shotgun at your adversary and pulling the trigger. Even a miss might be enough to make your adversary release your shotgun and retreat.

Your second line of defense is to keep the barrel of your shotgun pointed away from your body, draw your handgun, and fire as many times as needed to neutralize the threat. As previously discussed, a head shot will usually be more effective than a heart shot. If using your handgun is not an option and you have access to a knife, the arms, neck, or eyes are usually your best targets. Biting your attacker's arm or striking his eyes is also an option, but either is usually less effective than using your handgun or a knife.

It's essential that a competent tactical shooter be able to shoot a handgun with either hand, but a right-handed shotgun shooter can shift the shotgun to the left shoulder and use the left eye when shooting around the left side of a barricade. This works better for most shotgun shooters than switching to a weak-hand grip.

Depending on your strength, you may be able to reload a shotgun while it's pressed against your shoulder and your cheek is pressed against the side of the stock (cheek weld), but many people cannot hold a heavy shotgun in this position. If you cannot hold your shotgun steady, you may drop some of the shells you are trying to load. Another option is to put the stock under the upper part of your shooting arm and press your arm inward to hold it in place while you reload. Either way, you should maintain a firm shooting grip on your shotgun and keep the barrel pointed in the direction of potential targets.

If you need to reload, always try to find cover or concealment, or make yourself a smaller target by kneeling down. A tactical shooter should be able to reload and shoot while moving, which makes him a harder target and might help him move to a better position, such as a flanking position or higher ground. Shooting while moving away from your adversary might be beneficial in some cases, but moving too far away can make your shotgun less combat effective. A prone position will make you a smaller target, but it will also reduce your mobility.

If a pump shotgun is empty and you want to be able to load the chamber by racking the slide, you can open the action, recheck to verify that the chamber is empty, close the action, pull the trigger, and then load the tube magazine. If you do not pull the trigger, you will need to activate the slide release, which is usually located in front of or behind the trigger guard, before you can rack the slide.

Even if you have a way to prevent unauthorized use, such as locking a vehicle shotgun mount, transporting a shotgun with a live round in the chamber is more dangerous than transporting the gun with an empty chamber. Even if you remember to activate the safety, which is not always the case, bumping the safety may switch it to fire and result in an accidental discharge when the gun is removed.

Some people believe you should not rack a slide until you are ready to shoot because the sound will give you a psychological advantage or cause your adversary to flee or surrender. If you want to stay concealed and racking the slide may expose your position, you can do the following:

1. Rack the slide when you will not expose your position.
2. Do a press check—verify you have a round in the chamber by opening the action just far enough to see the brass and then close it.
3. Activate the safety.
4. Keep the safety on and your finger off the trigger until you verify a target.

Many of the techniques that are used with a handgun can also be used with a shotgun. If you keep your finger off the trigger until you decide to shoot, not only will it take you longer to shoot and possibly reduce your accuracy, but you should be trained to use this technique and required to use it when you qualify at a range.

Police officers in the field and on the range often forget to switch the safety to off before they pull the trigger, and some safeties are hard to use because they are small or they stick, which explains why switching the safety on or off can be a problem for poorly trained shooters. You should be able to tell if the safety on your shotgun is on or off and move it from off to on when blindfolded and moving.

The basic tactical positions for a shotgun are high ready, low ready, retention, and carry. When you use the *high-ready position*, the butt is seated in your shoulder pocket, and your cheek is pressed against the stock. This position tends to be the most accurate because the top of the shotgun is aligned with your line of sight. Focusing on the bead at the end of your barrel might be appropriate for competition shooting, but most tactical shooters use a target focus instead more than a front-sight focus unless they are shooting slugs.

If a target is stationary and you want to verify the alignment of your barrel, you can briefly focus on the front sight and then shift back to a target focus. Since buckshot gives you a larger margin of error than slugs, there is less need to verify barrel alignment when using buckshot. By eliminating unnecessary movements, such as verifying your barrel alignment, you can reduce your response time.

Some people recommend using a front-sight focus when shooting a shotgun at any target that is more than a few feet away. When you are target shooting, using a front-sight focus at close range is relatively harmless because the worst that can happen is you might lose a match. On the other hand, incorrectly using a front-sight focus at close range during a deadly confrontation can get you killed.

The *low-ready position* is similar to the high-ready position, but the top of your shotgun is below your line of vision. This position is often used when scanning a room for targets because the shotgun obstructs less of your field of view than when it's level with your line of sight. If you need to shoot quickly and the target is relatively close, you can shoot from a low-ready position.

When using the *retention position*, the stock is under your shooting arm, which brings the end of the barrel closer to your body and makes it harder for someone to grab the barrel. When using the *carry position*, the shotgun is parallel to your chest and pointed toward the ground and away from your body or the body of anyone you do not want to shoot. A shotgun can be carried with one hand on the grip and the other on the fore-end or supported by a two-point tactical sling.

One way to practice using a target focus with an empty shotgun is to hold the shotgun in a low-ready position, pick a target, close your eyes, mount the gun by shifting into a high-ready position, align the barrel with your target while your eyes are closed (pulling the trigger is optional), and then open your eyes and check the alignment. The goal is being able to verify the alignment with your sights after you open your eyes. If a trained archer can hit a 4-inch circle at 20 feet without using sights, a tactical shooter should be able to hit the same target without sights.

A second way to practice using a target focus at 20 feet is to use a shotgun that has the sights covered or removed. If you consistently get a good pattern at 20 feet with the sights covered or removed, you should be able to use a target focus during a deadly confrontation if the target is no more than 20 feet away. Even if you do most of your practicing with birdshot, you should verify your ability to use a target focus at this distance with the kind of buckshot or slugs you plan to use.

For a tactical shotgun shooter, being able to use a target focus at close range is important, but you still need to hit the correct aim points, and the pellets or slugs need to penetrate deeply enough to damage critical tissue if you want to cause timely or immediate incapacitation. If you make a heart shot at 20 feet with 00 buckshot and you stop the heart immediately, be aware that your adversary may continue to function for 10 to 15 seconds after the heart stops.

If you make a heart shot with 00 buckshot at 45 feet, some of the pellets may miss the heart, but if you are getting good patterns with your shotgun, the number of pellets that penetrate or perforate the heart might be sufficient to cause cardiac arrest. If you attempt a heart shot with 00 buckshot at 75 feet, some of the pellets may hit the heart, but others may miss the entire body. If your adversary is standing sideways and you hit the correct aim point for the heart, some of the pellets may hit the body but not penetrate far enough to reach the heart or the large vessels above it. It's also possible for a pellet to penetrate the heart and have no visible effect on a person's functionality until hemorrhaging causes death.

If you make a head shot with 00 buckshot at 20 feet or less, the probability is very high that you will cause immediate incapacitation because of tissue damage to the brain stem or the upper cervical spinal cord. If the distance is 45 feet, your chances of causing immediate incapacitation will decrease, but you may still hit the brain stem or the upper cervical spinal cord. If the distance is 75 feet, it's possible that none of the pellets will penetrate the cranium unless they enter through an eye socket, but you cannot rule out the possibility that one or more of the pellets will penetrate the cranium and hit the brain stem or the upper cervical spinal cord. At 75 feet you are more likely to penetrate the upper cervical vertebrae and hit the upper cervical spinal cord if you are aiming at the neck.

Even if a 00 buckshot pellet (54 grains) and a 9mm bullet (115 grains) have a similar muzzle velocity (about 1,150 fps), nearly the same diameter (.34 inch for 00 buckshot and .36 inch for the 9mm), and about 12 inches of penetration when fired into ballistic gelatin at close range, as the distance from the muzzle increases, the velocity and penetration for the 00 buckshot will decrease at a faster rate than the velocity and penetration for the 9mm bullet. This is because the bullet is heavier than the buckshot and a bullet-shaped projectile is aerodynamically more efficient and has less air resistance (drag) than a spherical projectile. As a rule, increasing the velocity or weight of a projectile tends to increase penetration.

If buckshot and a 9mm have about the same penetration at close range and the diameter of the wound channel created by the buckshot is larger, the buckshot will cause more tissue damage. Even though multiple hits to the head at 75 feet with 00 buckshot might give you some advantage, buckshot loses about 50 percent of its velocity and penetration at 75 feet, and you can reduce any advantage you might get from the multiple hits by firing more than one 9mm round at the head.

If you hit the correct aim point, a head shot made at 75 feet with a shotgun slug stand a better chance of causing immediate incapacitation than a head shot made at the same distance with 00 buckshot because the slug should have better penetration than the buckshot. The diameter of a Foster or Brenneke shotgun slug is about .73 inch, which is about twice the diameter of 00 buckshot (.34 inch).

If you have a shotgun, try to resolve a deadly conflict while your adversary is still within the combat-effective range for your shotgun. The maximum realistic distance for buckshot is 75 feet, and the maximum realistic distance for a shotgun slug is 150 feet. You might be able to make body hits with a shotgun slug at 100 yards, but rifles are more combat effective at this distance than shotguns.

Being combat effective and being a danger to innocent bystanders are two different issues because 00 buckshot can pierce the skin at 400 yards and a shotgun slug can be lethal at 300 yards. Being hit by a shotgun slug from 300 yards away is more likely to be the result of an accidental shooting than an aimed shot.

Buckshot is frequently ineffective against someone behind a car door, but switching from buckshot to a shotgun slug may give you slightly better penetration, depending on what part of the door a slug hits. Some slugs are only slightly more effective against a car than buckshot because they can fragment after hitting metal or fail to penetrate windshields unless you hit them at close to a 90-degree angle. Shotgun slugs are more likely to penetrate side windshields or the bottom of a front or rear windshield than the middle or upper part of a front or rear windshield.

A JHP 9mm may give you better penetration through a car door than 00 buckshot, but switching from a JHP 9mm to an FMJ 9mm may increase your chances of penetrating a car door. Buckshot is often most effective when aimed in such a way that the pellets ricochet under the car and into the legs or bodies of people who are using the car for cover.

In law enforcement, being able to use a target focus can be useful when dealing with a suspect who is running for cover and might be armed. If you are close to the suspect, follow him with the barrel of your shotgun, watch his hands, but do not get close enough for him to grab your shotgun. If the suspect stops, maintain a safe distance but keep your shotgun pointed at him. If you want to verify your alignment while he is stationary and you have a bead but no front sight, you can use your eye as the rear sight if your gun is properly mounted against your shoulder and you have a solid cheek weld.

Although some people seem to believe that almost any blast from a shotgun will have one-shot stopping power, it's possible that you will miss, someone you hit in the chest might be wearing a bullet-resistant vest, or you hit the body but fail to damage enough critical tissue to cause incapacitation. If you are facing an imminent deadly threat, two shots are more likely to neutralize the threat than one shot, and a good sequence is upper chest first and head second. Even if a shotgun blast to the head does not reach the brain stem or upper cervical spinal cord, you may damage the eyes and cause blindness that incapacitates your adversary.

The lights on a shotgun are used incorrectly more often than those on a handgun because they are usually larger and brighter and they can be hard to turn on and off unless they have a remote pressure switch. If your shotgun has a gun-mounted light, you can use flash-and-shoot: flash the light on and off to check the area and shoot as the light goes off if you have a verified target. Gun-mounted lights are easier to use on semiautomatic shotguns than on pump shotguns.

As stated, tactical shooting is not target shooting, and you do not need to have a sight picture. Illuminated night-sights might be useful if you need to make a precision shot, you have enough light to verify your target, and you are not under pressure to shoot immediately—which might be the case if you are facing an armed suspect who does not know your location or has a gun pointed at someone else.

People who recommend using a shotgun to neutralize hostage takers usually ignore tactical anatomy. If you miss the hostage but fail to hit the suspect's upper cervical spinal cord or brain stem, the suspect may have enough time to shoot you and the hostage. Estimating what kind of pattern a shotgun will shoot so you can hit a hostage taker but not the hostage (scalloping) is almost an act of desperation.

If you decide to shoot a hostage taker with a smooth-bore shotgun, the maximum distance should be 20 feet for buckshot and 75 feet for slugs. Even if the hostage is not injured by pellets or slugs, he might be injured by other projectiles from a shotgun shell, such as a plastic wad. Handgun bullets are usually more accurate than buckshot or shotgun slugs.

If you hear a click when you pull the trigger because your shotgun is empty and you have a loaded handgun, switching to the handgun is usually faster than reloading the shotgun. If you do not have a loaded handgun, drop a round into the tube magazine and rack the slide. If racking the slide does not feed a round into the chamber, you may be able to correct the malfunction by pulling the slide back, removing any rounds that are in or sticking out of the ejection port (stove pipe), dropping a fresh round into the ejection port, and then closing the action.

If one hand is disabled, you can shoot a shotgun with the other hand, but switching to a handgun and shooting it with one hand would be easier. One way to load or rack a shotgun with one hand is to kneel down, put the butt on the ground, and use inward pressure from your knees or thighs to hold the shotgun upright.

If you have a right-handed grip on a shotgun and you need to shoot around the left side of a barricade, you can move the butt to your left shoulder and shoot with your right hand (shoulder bump)—which can be very painful if the butt is not pressed against your left shoulder pocket—or you can switch to a left-handed grip.

It makes sense not to move forward until you know that the areas you will be passing are clear, but circumstances often make it impossible to thoroughly search every area before you advance. Even if an area is clear when you go by, this does not prevent someone from getting behind you after you have passed. If you are doing a building search and you have a two-point tactical sling that wraps around your neck, searching the building might be safer if you carried the shotgun on the sling and used your handgun. If someone suddenly appears behind you, it's faster and easier to swing a handgun 180 degrees to the rear than a shotgun.

If the butt of your shotgun is not already pressed against your shoulder and you unexpectedly identify a target to your right or left side, mount the shotgun and rotate your body at the same time. Making the movements that mount your shotgun and turn your body simultaneously will decrease your total response time. When a shotgun is properly mounted, almost the entire butt will press against your shoulder pocket, your cheek will press firmly against the top side of the stock, and your head will be upright or tilted slightly forward and outward.

Competition shooters often swing their shotguns by pivoting from the hips, but tactical shooters may find that moving one or both feet is more effective than pivoting from the hips. Tactical shooters are more likely to use the best possible stance under the circumstances than a stance that has been rehearsed and perfected.

You do not need to lead people who are moving directly at or away from you or lead people who are not more than 45 feet away. If a target is moving in a lateral direction and within 45 feet, keep both eyes open to improve depth perception, align your barrel on the target, swing the barrel to stay aligned on the target, and continue swinging the barrel until after you pull the trigger.

To reduce the recoil you feel when you shoot a shotgun:

1. Use a recoil pad and let the force from the recoil spread over most of the surface.
2. Keep the butt pressed against your shoulder and do not let it touch your upper arm.
3. Relax your body, lean slightly forward, and roll with the recoil the same way a boxer rolls with a punch. You can also use a stock that's designed to reduce recoil.

One way to reduce flinching is to have someone load your shotgun with an unknown combination of birdshot and dummy rounds. Dummy rounds may look and feel like live rounds and they may contain lead shot, but they do not have a primer or propellant. If you flinch when you pull the trigger on a dummy round, you need to continue this drill until you stop flinching. After you stop flinching, you can repeat the process using an unknown combination of buckshot and birdshot and continue the drill until neither round makes you flinch.

Even if you are using dummy rounds to practice loading and unloading a shotgun or you are using them for dry-fire practice, treat the shotgun the way you would if you were using live rounds and keep the barrel pointed in a safe direction. If you are practicing with birdshot instead of buckshot, remember that even though buckshot has greater penetration at 45 feet, birdshot can be lethal at close range.

Sometimes you are better off following gut instincts than trying to follow a set of rules, such as "always move away from danger if someone is armed with a gun." This rule is based on the premise that you are a better shot than your adversary and increasing the distance between the two of you will decrease your adversary's accuracy more than it decreases yours. On the contrary, if you are facing an imminent deadly threat from a gun, shooting from where you are standing or moving closer so you can make a head shot might be more effective than trying to move away. If you have a shotgun and your adversary has a rifle, moving away may increase your adversary's combat effectiveness and decrease yours.

You should also be careful about making the assumption that you will be a better shot than most criminals. Since the national hit rate for police officers is about 20 percent, most police officers do not shoot more than five shotgun rounds per year when they qualify, and some departments do not require officers to qualify with a shotgun, a criminal with hunting experience might be much more competent with a shotgun than most police officers. The Miami-Dade Police Department had a case where one man armed with a double-barrel shotgun killed three of its detectives.

In addition to demonstrating their shooting skills during annual qualifications, law enforcement officers should also be required to demonstrate their ability to load and unload a shotgun and to manipulate the safety without looking at the gun—which is exactly what you may need to do if you are running with a shotgun at night. If you are required to keep your finger off the trigger until you decide to shoot, you should be required to use this method every time you qualify.

Shotgun training should include targets that move forward, backward, and sideways. If tactical shotgun training is rated on a 1-to-10 scale with 1 the worst and 10 the best, shooting a stationary target would be a 1, shooting a reactionary stationary would be a 3, shooting a target that moves at a known speed along a known path would be a 5, and shooting a target that moves along an unexpected path at unexpected speeds would be a 10.

To say that handguns are not good for anything but fighting your way to a shotgun is unrealistic. During the 1986 FBI shootout in Miami with two men suspected of armed robbery, agent Ed Mireles fired four rounds of 12-gauge buckshot at both suspects, but the gunfight was not over until the agent walked over to their car and shot them with his .357 Magnum revolver. One suspect was stopped by a head shot that entered through the right eye socket and severed the spinal cord, and the other suspect was stopped by a chest shot that bruised the spinal cord.

On the following pages are photographs depicting various tactical shotgun carry and retention positions, loading options, and shooting techniques for special circumstances.

Tactical Shotgun Techniques

High ready position.   Low ready position.

Field of view: You cannot focus on your shotgun and look for adversaries at the same time. With the possible exception of when you are forced to load with one hand because your other hand is disabled and you need to glance at your shotgun, you should not look at the loading port or the ejecting port when loading a shotgun. What you should do is keep your eyes moving and scan for potential targets.

Retention position.

Carry position.

High loading.

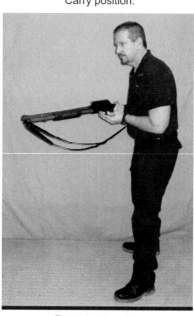

Retention loading.

Ejection port loading.   One-hand loading.

Left barricade: If you are using a right-handed grip on the stock and you need to shoot from the left side of a barricade, switching to a left-handed grip is usually a better option than shifting the stock to your left shoulder (shoulder bump).

Shotgun retention: If someone grabs the barrel of your shotgun, you can try to aim the shotgun at him and shoot, or you can transition to your handgun and shoot. The best aim point for a shotgun will usually be a pelvic shot, and the best aim point for a handgun is usually a head or heart shot.

One-hand shooting.

Left barricade.

Retention—shotgun.

Retention—handgun.

BIBLIOGRAPHY

Anderson, James E. *Grant's Atlas of Anatomy*, 8th ed. Baltimore: Williams & Wilkins, 1983.

Anderson, W. French. *Forensic Analysis of the April 11, 1986, FBI Firefight*. Boulder, CO: Paladin Press, 2006.

Applegate, Rex. *Kill or Get Killed*. Boulder, CO: Paladin Press, 1976.

Applegate, Rex, and Michael D. Janich. *Bullseyes Don't Shoot Back*. Boulder, CO: Paladin Press, 1998.

Askins, Charles. *The Art of Handgun Shooting*. New York: A.S. Barnes & Company, 1941.

————. *Askins on Pistols & Revolvers*. Washington, D.C.: National Rifle Association, 1980.

————. *The Gunfighters*. Boulder, CO: Paladin Press, 2007.

Backhouse, Kenneth M., and Ralph T. Hutchings. *Color Atlas of Surface Anatomy*. Baltimore: Williams & Wilkins, 1986.

Blum, Lawrence. *Force under Pressure*. New York: Lantern Books, 2000.

Bogduk, Nikolai, and Lance T. Twomey. *Clinical Anatomy of the Lumbar Spine*, 2nd ed. Melbourne, Australia: Churchill Livingstone, 1991.

Cassidy, William L. *Quick or Dead*. Boulder, CO: Paladin Press, 1993.

Churchill, Robert. *How to Shoot*. London: Geoffrey Bles, 1925.
———. *Churchill's Shotgun Book*. New York: Alfred A. Knopf, 1955.

Cialdini, Robert B. *Influence: The Psychology of Persuasion*. New York: William Morrow and Company, Inc., 1993.

Clemente, Carmine D. *Anatomy*, 2nd ed. Baltimore: Urban & Schwarzenberg, 1981.

Coates, James Boyd, Jr., and James C. Beyer, eds. *Wound Ballistics*. Washington D.C.: Office of Surgeon General, Department of Army, 1962.

Cooper, Jeff. *The Complete Book of Modern Handgunning*. New York: Bramhall House, 1961.

———. *Cooper on Handguns*. Los Angeles: Petersen Publishing Co., 1974.

———. *Fighting Handguns*. Boulder, CO: Paladin Press, 2008. First published by Trend Books, 1958.

Cunningham, Eugene. *Triggernometry: A Gallery of Gunfighters*. Norman: University of Oklahoma Press, 1996.

Davies, Ken. *The Better Shot*. Shropshire, England: Quiller Press, 1992.

Di Maio, Vincent J.M. *Gunshot Wounds*, 2nd ed. Boca Raton: CRC Press, 1999.

Dougherty, Paul J., ed. *Gunshot Wounds*. Rosemont, IL: American Academy of Orthopaedic Surgeons, 2011.

Dressler, Joshua. *Criminal Law*. St Paul, MN: Thomson Reuters, 2010.

Enos, Brian. *Practical Shooting: Beyond Fundamentals*. Clifton, CO: Zediker Publishing, 1990.

Fairbairn, W.E., and E.A. Sykes. *Shooting to Live*. Boulder, CO: Paladin Press, 2008 (reprint).

Farnam, John S. *The Farnam Method of Defensive Shotgun and Rifle Shooting*. Austin: DTI Publications, 1997.

Fattah, Abdullah. *Medicolegal Investigation of Gunshot Wounds*. Philadelphia, PA: J.B. Lippincott Company, 1976.

FitzGerald, Henry J. *Shooting*. Boulder, CO: Paladin Press, 2007. Originally published in 1930 by J. Henry FitzGerald.

Geller, William A., and Michael S. Scott. *Deadly Force*. Washington, D.C.: Police Executive Research Forum, 1992.

Haag, Michael G., and Lucien C. Haag. *Shooting Incident Reconstruction*, 2nd ed. San Diego: Academic Press (Elsevier Inc.), 2011.

Hatcher, Julian. *Textbook of Pistols and Revolvers*. Fairfax, VA: National Rifle Association, 1995.

Heard, Brian J. *Handbook of Firearms and Ballistics*. 2nd ed. Hoboken, NJ: John Wiley & Sons Ltd., 2008.

Hendrix, Robert C. *Investigation of Violent and Sudden Death*. Springfield, IL: Charles C. Thomas Publisher, 1972.

Jordan, Bill. *No Second Place Winner*. Concord, NH: Police Bookshelf, 1965.

Kandel, Eric R., and James H. Schwartz. *Principles of Neural Science*, 2nd ed. New York: Elsevier, 1985.

Kirchner, Paul. *Dueling with the Sword and Pistol*. Boulder, CO: Paladin Press, 2004.

Lawrence, Eric, and Mike Pannone. *Tactical Pistol Shooting*, 2nd ed. Iola, WI: Krause Publications, 2009.

Leflet, David H. *HEMME Approach to Lumbopelvic Disorders*. Bonifay, FL: HEMME Approach Publications, 2005.

Levangie, Pamela K., and Cynthia C. Norkin. *Joint Structure and Function*, 4th ed. Philadelphia: F.A. Davis Company, 2005.

Lumley, John. S. *Surface Anatomy*, 4th ed. Edinburgh: Churchill Livingston, 2008.

MacPherson, Duncan. *Bullet Penetration*. El Segundo, CA: Ballistic Publications, 2005.

Magill, Richard A. *Motor Learning and Motor Control*, 7th ed. Boston: McGraw Hill, 2004.

Mann, Don. *The Modern Day Gunslinger*. New York: Skyhorse Publishing, 2010.

McGivern, Ed. *Fast and Fancy Revolver Shooting and Police Training*. Springfield, MA: King-Richardson Co., 1938.

McSwain, Norman E., Jr., and Morris D. Kerstein, eds. *Evaluation and Management of Trauma*. Norwalk, CT: Appleton-Century-Crofts, 1987.

Morrison, Gregory Boyce. *The Modern Technique of the Pistol*. Paulden, AZ: Gunsite Press, 1991.

Murray, Kenneth R. *Training at the Speed of Life*. Gotha, FL: Armiger Publications, Inc., 2006.

Pinizzotto, Anthony J., Edward F. Davis, and Charles E. Miller III. *Violent Encounters*. Clarksburg, WV: U.S. Department of Justice, Federal Bureau of Investigation, 2006.

Plaster, John L. *The Ultimate Sniper*. Boulder, CO: Paladin Press, 2006.

Plaxco, J. Michael. *Shooting from Within*. Clifton, CO: Zediker Publishing, 1991.

Remsberg, Charles. *Blood Lessons*. San Francisco, CA: Calibre Press, LLC, 2008.

Rosa, Joseph G. *The Gunfighter: Man or Myth?* Norman: University of Oklahoma Press, 1969.

Rutledge, Devallis. *The Officer Survival Manual*. Placerville, CA: Custom Publishing Company, 1988.

Samaha, Joel. *Criminal Law*, 9th ed. Belmont, CA: Thomas Learning, Inc., 2008.

Saurez, Gabriel. *The Tactical Shotgun*. Boulder, CO: Paladin Press, 1996.

Snyder, LeMoyne. *Homicide Investigation*, 2nd ed. Springfield, IL: Charles C. Thomas Publisher, Ltd., 1967.

Spitz, Werner U., and Daniel J. Spitz, eds. *Spitz and Fisher's Medico-legal Investigation of Death*, 4th ed. Springfield, IL: Charles. C. Thomas Publisher, Ltd., 2006.

Swan, Kenneth G., and Roy C. Swan. *Gunshot Wounds Pathophysiology and Management*, 2nd ed. Chicago: Year Book Medical Publishers, Inc., 1989.

Taubert, Robert K. *Rattenkrieg!* North Reading, MA: Saber Press, 2012.

Taylor, Chuck. *The Combat Shotgun and Submachine Gun*. Boulder, CO: Paladin Press, 1985.

Taylor, John. *Shotshells & Ballistics*. Long Beach, CA: Safari Press, Inc., 2003.

Trachtman, Paul. *The Gunfighters.* Alexandria, VA: Time-Life Books, 1974.

Vilos, Mitch, and Evan Vilos. *Self-Defense Laws of All 50 States*. Centerville, UT: Guns West Publishing, Inc., 2010.

Warlow, Tom. *Firearms, the Law, and Forensic Ballistics*, 3rd ed. Boca Raton, FL: CRC Press, 2012.

Wiener, Stanley L., and John Barrett. *Trauma Management for Civilian and Military Physicians*. Philadelphia: W.B. Saunders Company, 1986.

Williams, James S. *Tactical Anatomy Instructor Manual*. Big Lake, TX: Tactical Anatomy LLC, 2006.

Williams, Peter L., and Roger Warwick. *Gray's Anatomy*, 36th ed. Philadelphia: W.B. Saunders Company, 1980.

ESSAY DATED 1875 (NEW YORK)

Author unknown. *The Pistol as a Weapon of Defense in the House and on the Road.* Reprinted as a book by Paladin Press, 2004.

DVDs

Applegate, Rex. *Point Shooting.* Boulder, CO: Paladin Press, 1995.

Cirillo, Jim. 1996. *Modern-Day Gunfighter.* Boulder, CO: Paladin Press, 2006.

Fackler, Martin, and Jason Alexander. *Deadly Effects.* Boulder, CO: Paladin Press, 1987.

Grover, Jim. *Combative Pistol.* Boulder, CO: Paladin Press, 2002.

Jordan, Bill. *Fast and Fancy Shooting.* Boulder, CO: Paladin Press, 1989.

Munden, Bob. *Outrageous Shooting.* Chaska, MN: Stony-Wolf Productions, Inc., 2011.

E-BOOK

Crews, Jim. *Advanced Urban Shotgun.* Stevensville, MT: Gunology, 2012.

ABOUT
THE
AUTHORS

David H. Leflet holds a master of science degree from Michigan State University, where he majored in security and criminal investigation. After graduation, he joined the Dade County Public Safety Department, now called the Miami-Dade Police Department. With the MDPD, Leflet was a member of the Hostage Release Team (sniper) and the Special Response Team (team leader). Leflet was a state-certified defensive tactics instructor most of his career, holds advanced black belts in karate and juai jung karbo, and shot distinguished expert with revolvers and Colt .45 ACP semiautomatic pistols.

Before he retired from Dade County, Leflet executed several hundred break orders, which authorized a forcible entry if necessary, and participated in dozens of deadly confrontations involving knives or guns, including several cases where he did empty-handed knife or gun disarms. The courses he created and taught included personal injury reduction training, emergency first aid, and counterterrorism. He spent the last few years of his Dade County career in the Training Bureau, during which time he developed computer-based training programs for law enforcement.

Curtis L. Porter served in the United States Marine Corps and saw combat action during the Gulf War. During his tour of duty in Kuwait, he was a platoon sergeant in charge of a Marine combat unit, and he received medals and commendations for devotion to duty, courage under fire, and uncommon valor during combat operations.

It was during the Gulf War that Curtis started developing the handgun techniques that later evolved into the Porter method. These techniques are the direct result of using a handgun as his primary weapon when conducting numerous building searches in Kuwait, and he carefully organized and refined these techniques when serving as a Marine small-arms instructor.

After leaving the Corps, Porter worked as a police officer and continued to refine the Porter method. Unlike the firearms training offered by most police departments, the Porter method uses tactical-shooting techniques instead of target-shooting techniques when facing a deadly threat. It is designed to help police officers and civilians survive a deadly confrontation.